Welfare and Charity in the Antebellum South
New Perspectives on the History of the South

Florida A&M University, Tallahassee
Florida Atlantic University, Boca Raton
Florida Gulf Coast University, Ft. Myers
Florida International University, Miami
Florida State University, Tallahassee
New College of Florida, Sarasota
University of Central Florida, Orlando
University of Florida, Gainesville
University of North Florida, Jacksonville
University of South Florida, Tampa
University of West Florida, Pensacola

Timothy James Lockley

WELFARE

and

CHARITY

in the Antebellum South

UNIVERSITY PRESS OF FLORIDA

Gainesville · Tallahassee · Tampa · Boca Raton

Pensacola · Orlando · Miami · Jacksonville · Ft. Myers · Sarasota

12 11 10 09 08 07   6 5 4 3 2 1

Library of Congress Cataloging-in-Publication Data
Lockley, Timothy James, 1971–
Welfare and charity in the antebellum South / Timothy James Lockley.
p. cm. — (New perspectives on the history of the South)
Includes bibliographical references and index.
ISBN 978-0-8130-3173-6 (alk. paper)
1. Charities—Southern States—History. 2. Social service—
Southern States—History. 3. Poor—Services for—Southern States—
History. 4. Southern States—Social conditions. I. Title.
HV98.S9L63 2007
361.709755'09034—dc22   2007027533

The University Press of Florida is the scholarly publishing
agency for the State University System of Florida, comprising
Florida A&M University, Florida Atlantic University, Florida
Gulf Coast University, Florida International University, Florida
State University, New College of Florida, University of Central
Florida, University of Florida, University of North Florida,
University of South Florida, and University of West Florida.

University Press of Florida
15 Northwest 15th Street
Gainesville, FL 32611-2079
http://www.upf.com

New Perspectives on the History of the South

EDITED BY JOHN DAVID SMITH
Charles S. Stone Distinguished Professor of American History
at the University of North Carolina at Charlotte

"In the Country of the Enemy": The Civil War Reports of a Massachusetts Corporal,
edited by William C. Harris (1999)

The Wild East: A Biography of the Great Smoky Mountains, by Margaret L. Brown
(2000; first paperback edition, 2001)

*Crime, Sexual Violence, and Clemency: Florida's Pardon Board and Penal System
in the Progressive Era,* by Vivien M. L. Miller (2000)

*The New South's New Frontier: A Social History of Economic Development in
Southwestern North Carolina,* by Stephen Wallace Taylor (2001)

Redefining the Color Line: Black Activism in Little Rock, Arkansas, 1940–1970,
by John A. Kirk (2002)

The Southern Dream of a Caribbean Empire, 1854–1861, by Robert E. May (2002)

*Forging a Common Bond: Labor and Environmental Activism during the BASF
Lockout,* by Timothy J. Minchin (2003)

*Dixie's Daughters: The United Daughters of the Confederacy and the Preservation
of Confederate Culture,* by Karen L. Cox (2003)

*The Other War of 1812: The Patriot War and the American Invasion of Spanish East
Florida,* by James G. Cusick (2003)

*"Lives Full of Struggle and Triumph": Southern Women, Their Institutions and
Their Communities,* edited by Bruce L. Clayton and John A. Salmond (2003)

German-Speaking Officers in the United States Colored Troops, 1863–1867,
by Martin W. Öfele (2004)

Southern Struggles: The Southern Labor Movement and the Civil Rights Struggle,
by John A. Salmond (2004)

Radio and the Struggle for Civil Rights in the South, by Brian Ward
(2004, first paperback edition, 2006)

Luther P. Jackson and a Life for Civil Rights, by Michael Dennis (2004)

*Southern Ladies, New Women: Race, Region, and Clubwomen in South Carolina,
1890–1930*, by Joan Marie Johnson (2004)

Fighting Against the Odds: A History of Southern Labor since World War II,
by Timothy J. Minchin (2005, first paperback edition, 2006)

*"Don't Sleep with Stevens!": The J. P. Stevens Campaign and the Struggle to
Organize the South, 1963–80*, by Timothy J. Minchin (2005)

*"The Ticket to Freedom:" The NAACP and the Struggle for Black Political
Integration*, by Manfred Berg (2005)

"War Governor of the South": North Carolina's Zeb Vance in the Confederacy,
by Joe A. Mobley (2005)

Planters' Progress: Modernizing Confederate Georgia, by Chad Morgan (2005)

The Officers of the CSS Shenandoah, by Angus Curry (2006)

The Rosenwald Schools of the American South, by Mary S. Hoffschwelle (2006)

*Honor in Command: The Civil War Memoir of Lt. Freeman Sparks Bowley,
30th United States Colored Infantry*, edited by Keith P. Wilson (2006)

*A Black Congressman in the Age of Jim Crow: South Carolina's George
Washington Murray*, by John F. Marszalek (2006)

The Spirit and the Shotgun: Armed Resistance and the Struggle for Civil Rights,
by Simon Wendt (2007)

Making a New South: Race, Leadership, and Community after the Civil War,
edited by Paul A. Cimbala and Barton C. Shaw (2007)

*From Rights to Economics: The Ongoing Struggle for Black Equality in the
U.S. South*, by Timothy J. Minchin (2007)

*Slavery on Trial: Race, Class, and Criminal Justice in Antebellum
Richmond, Virginia*, by James M. Campbell (2008)

Welfare and Charity in the Antebellum South, by Timothy James Lockley (2008)

For Jo, Alice, and Edward

Contents

Figures

Acknowledgments

DURING THE FIVE YEARS that I have been researching and writing this book, I have made more than a dozen transatlantic trips to libraries and archives throughout the South. The staff at each archive, and especially those which I had not visited before in Alabama, Virginia, and North Carolina, were always helpful in guiding my research, continually pulling additional manuscripts, and answering my questions. Several people helped me obtain permission to use images in this book including Marilyn Culpepper at the Historic Mobile Preservation Society and Grace Cordial at the Beaufort County Library. I was fortunate to be able to stay with friends during some of my visits and I would particularly like to thank Connie Schulz, Norman Owens, Christine Cramer, Michele Gillespie, and Genie Jensen for their hospitality and saving me, for at least part of the time, from the faceless anonymity of hotels.

I have benefited from scholarly conversations with many colleagues, particularly Chris Clark, Gad Heuman, Sarah Richardson, Roger Fagge, Steve Hindle, Betty Wood, David Brown, Jonathan Wells, Nancy Zey, John Murray, and Michael Byrd. All forced me to re-think parts of this book and undoubtedly have made it better than it would otherwise have been. I am also grateful for the encouragement of John David Smith who first suggested that this book become part of the New Perspectives on the American South series at the University Press of Florida.

For two years I had the invaluable help of Andy Roadnight as a research assistant. Andy did a great deal of the groundwork to get this project going: contacting archives, searching library catalogues, and trawling through endless reels of microfilm. In particular Andy constructed an important database of materials relating to the citizens of Asheville, North Carolina, which is heavily used in chapter 4. We talked through, and refined, many of the arguments presented here, and without Andy's help this book would have taken many more years to complete.

The Arts and Humanities Research Council provided substantial funding for the early part of this project, including paying Andy's salary, and toward the end provided me with an extra three months of sabbatical leave. Archival visits in 2003 and 2004 were aided by generous visiting fellowships from the North Caroliniana Society and the Virginia Historical Society. The Department of History at the University of Warwick provided me with travel money and the sabbatical to enable me to complete this book.

Most important, I would like to thank my wife, Joanne, who has worked tirelessly at vitally important tasks, like supplying caffeine at regular intervals, distracting the children at crucial times, and removing them when they decided to set up camp in my office. Together with Alice and Edward, she has also provided the well-needed breaks from writing that I think all academics need to stay sane.

Welfare and Charity in the Antebellum South

Introduction

ON JULY 25, 1824, the Reverend John Stark Ravenscroft, Bishop of North Carolina, stood before the citizens of Raleigh expounding on his theme that "as children of the same universal Parent, and members of the great human family, we owe compassion and help, to every suffering individual." Relief of the poor would not only benefit the needy; it also had wider social implications: "Poverty, that is, real privation of the necessaries of life, is the fertile seed-bed of vice and crime; and these mutually act, and react, in the production of each other. In so far, therefore, as the peace and comfort of society are concerned, it is the duty of all, inasmuch as it is in their interest, to counteract this moral disease, by striking at its root." If assistance was carefully targeted at "the humble, thankful and industrious poor, . . . [they] do not long continue poor. Industry and exertion, produce competence; economy soon obtains a surplus, and honest independence, with all its grateful inducements, comes within reach." With a more harmonious, pious, and prosperous society as the prize, "shall a ring, or a trinket, or a selfish indulgence or appetite, enter into competition with the claims of Christ, and of society? . . . at how cheap a price can we do good, lasting heaven-enduring good, and be rewarded for it besides. My brethren and hearers, let us think; let us calculate; let us buy of this stock, which yields usurious interest, both now and forever!"[1] A retiring collection was taken for the Raleigh Female Benevolent Society which, according to the Raleigh *Register*, "was, the times considered, liberal."[2]

Ravenscroft's address was not a one-time affair. The clerics of Raleigh preached on behalf of charitable institutions every year as did their counterparts in Savannah, Charleston, New Orleans, Richmond, Norfolk, Nashville, and Mobile. The fact that active and organized benevolence existed in nearly every antebellum southern community of any size should not be surprising to us, yet students of the antebellum United States could be forgiven for thinking that charity was a purely northern phenomenon. The sheer weight of scholarship that has studied, in depth, the charitable and reform movements of New England, New York, and Pennsylvania has not been counter-balanced by comparable work on the South. Aside from Barbara Bellows's excellent study of philanthropy in antebellum Charleston, the historiography of southern benevolence consists mainly of article-length case studies or initial chapters in larger works on benevolence.[3] In some respects this bias is understandable; most of the largest antebellum cities were in the North and they were often home to numerous benevolent societies. Moreover, northern benevolent societies were not only greater in number, but their records have also tended to survive to the present day in better condition than those of their southern counterparts. As moths to a flame, historians have naturally been attracted to relatively complete records concentrated in just a few locations. Yet, as this book will demonstrate, northern towns and cities did not have a monopoly on benevolence in the antebellum United States.

It is perhaps worth clarifying exactly how the terms "charity," "welfare," "philanthropy," and "benevolence" are used in this book. I broadly conceive of these terms as relating to the relief of want, suffering, and sickness. Charity comes in several different guises but this book is concerned with assistance freely offered to those without the means to help themselves. This assistance might come in the tangible form of food, clothing, medicines, furniture, fuel, and cash, or it might be found in the provision of services otherwise unaffordable—for example, medical care, lodging, or education. Some studies of antebellum benevolence have included Bible, tract, missionary, and temperance societies that aimed to convert, reform, and morally improve individuals under the rubric of "charity" as they shared many aims, ideals, and indeed personnel with other benevolent societies. However, such organizations were not exclusively devoted to the poor—plenty of wealthy people were intemperate and irreligious—and therefore moral and religious reform societies have been excluded from this study apart from instances when they also undertook more general relief of suffering.

Charity comes in two forms, either public (funded from taxation and administered by officials) or private (funded and managed by organizations or by individuals). Public charity was present in every southern community, but for this study to provide a national perspective on antebellum benevolence it was necessary to establish just how many charitable societies there were in the antebellum South. After countless hours spent digging through the catalogues of archives, reading newspapers, and sifting through legislative papers, and with the aid of a couple of helpful bibliographies, I was able to document more than six hundred antebellum benevolent societies in the slaveholding states. With such a large number of organizations—and this figure does not count hospitals or poorhouses organized by state or local authorities—it is evident that benevolence flourished in the antebellum South in proportions roughly similar to its presence in the North, taking into account the smaller white population in the South. Why then has southern benevolence languished in relative obscurity? In part this can be explained by the poor survival rate of the records of southern charitable organizations: humidity, hurricanes, tornados, fires, and the Civil War as well as losses caused by forgetfulness and house clearances have left about 90 percent of southern charitable societies with no antebellum records at all. The limited nature of the primary materials posed a significant challenge. The existence of many societies can be proved only through newspaper references to their activities or from an act of incorporation preserved in legislative files. These clippings can be very useful but are no replacement for comprehensive minutes and accounts. However, there are cities—Charleston and Savannah, for instance—where comprehensive records survive from several different societies and a more complete picture of the activities of charitable organizations emerges. They also provide a broad framework into which more isolated sets of records from places like Norfolk, Mobile, and Columbia can be placed.

This book is meant to restore southern benevolence to its proper national context and to demonstrate, partly, that the charitable activities occurring south of Mason and Dixon's line were in many respects similar to those farther north. Perhaps more interesting, though, is the distinctiveness of southern benevolence. North and South differed greatly in the sizes of their populations, the orientations of their economies, their degree of urbanization, the amount of foreign immigration they experienced, and their attitudes toward free and slave labor. It would indeed be surprising if antebellum benevolence were identical in both regions given their different contexts. By examining, in turn, the initiative taken by southern women at the start of the nineteenth century, the increased interest and involvement of southern men from about 1840 onward, and the role of private (or unorganized) giving, I hope to show that there was an identifiable southern mode of benevolence. These central chapters are framed by two showing that assistance to the poor was not merely a private business. States, counties, parishes, and towns all had a role in providing a safety net of aid to the most disadvantaged people. This was particularly important in rural areas where private charitable organizations were few and far between. The funding and management of common school systems that were free at the point of use was also the responsibility of elected officials. When taken together, it becomes clear that there were noticeable changes in southern benevolence as the antebellum era progressed, as well as increasingly important differences between southern and northern benevolence.

Antebellum southern benevolence did not emerge from a vacuum and it is worth spending a little time mapping out the heritage of public and private help that had existed before 1800. The southern colonies drew heavily on their British, and specifically English, heritage when devising strategies for assisting the poor. In England local parish vestries were permitted to raise a local tax to support those unable to support themselves, and most operated a complex system trying to ensure that they supported only their own residents—not transients—while all the time trying to minimize the amounts spent.[4] Only Catholic Maryland, of all the southern colonies, failed to give Anglican parish vestries a similar central role in the assessment and distribution of local taxes for the relief of the aged, infirm, sick, and orphaned. Yet even in Maryland it was to Anglican parish vestries that the colonial assembly turned for the administration of legacies left for the poor.[5] In Virginia and North Carolina, Anglican vestries shared their duty to provide for the poor with county courts, which alone had authority to indenture orphan children; but in South Carolina and Georgia there were no alternative tiers of local government, so the Anglican parish vestry monopolized public poor relief.[6] The men elected annually as vestrymen, together with the two churchwardens in each parish, were invariably drawn from the upper echelons of society and alone determined who was a fit recipient for aid.[7]

The surviving records of Anglican parish vestries give us some glimpses of how public poor relief operated in the southern colonies. Admittedly the records are scattered, and despite being more numerous for Virginia and South Carolina, they are by no means comprehensive for any colony. The general impression gained from these records is that the number of people receiving parish relief, and the cost, was increasing in the last decades of the colonial era. In part this was because the population of the southern colonies was growing, but there is some sense that economic hardships caused by the numerous Anglo-French wars were also a factor.

Several different studies of poor relief have agreed that relief policies in the colonial South tended to be far more generous than those farther north. While settlement laws restricting eligibility for relief existed on southern statute books they seem to have been rarely enforced. Equally, those dispensing aid did so at a level that afforded the recipients a reasonable standard of living rather than merely subsistence. Alan Watson has argued, with respect to North Carolina, that the "determining factor in defining the poor was need" rather than economics, while Virginia Bernard has cleverly suggested that since Virginian vestrymen owned books that promoted the relief of the poor "as a matter of course, not as a singular virtue," they therefore subscribed to a form of patrician benevolence normally associated with the English aristocracy.[8] One of those books was Richard Allestree's *Whole Duty of Man*, originally published in the mid-seventeenth century but republished in Williamsburg in 1746. Allestree informed his readers that the poor had "a better right to our superfluities than we ourselves have" and that "he that is in poverty and need, must be relieved by him that is in plenty; and he is bound to it not only in charity, but even in justice."[9]

Allestree was not the only one encouraging wealthy southerners to be generous toward the poor. Marylanders were told by the Reverend Thomas Bacon that "true Christian charity consists in that constant, steady, universal love and benevolence towards all mankind . . . in its nature it is pure and disinterested, remote from all hopes of views of worldly return, or recompense from the persons we relieve . . . in its extent it is unlimited and universal."[10] The Reverend Henley told his congregation in Williamsburg in 1771 that "riches . . . are intrusted to our care, to alleviate by a skilful application, the sufferings of mankind." While naturally "the industrious, the honest and the peaceable, have a better title to favour than the mischievous or negligent," in general, "in proportion to the exigence should be the relief." Furthermore, it was not only the poor who benefited from a generous system of charity since "there arises from deeds, and even, dispositions of humanity, an honest glow of pure delight. The pleasure also which flows from the gratitude of a beneficiary, more than repays the benefactors expence."[11]

My own research on poor relief in the rural parishes of colonial South Carolina emphasized the particularly generous level of support afforded the white poor. This generosity, I suggested, was not simply because those administering the system were some of the wealthiest individuals in British North America who could afford to be liberal, but was intended to draw an obvious distinction between the white poor and the enslaved Africans who formed the majority of the colony's population. In this sense South Carolina's vestrymen used their position to demonstrate to poor whites that there were some privileges to which they were entitled merely because of their race.[12]

The situation in the two largest settlements in the colonial South was a little different, as both Charleston and Baltimore chose the route of institutionalization for their paupers, with Charleston's poorhouse opening its doors as early as 1738. While a few rural parishes in colonial Virginia had experimented with poorhouses, with mixed results, the concentration of paupers in the two port cities of Charleston and Baltimore meant that strategies for dealing with the poor more closely resembled those of Boston and New York than elsewhere in the South.[13] Vestrymen at St. Philip's in Charleston, for instance, increasingly made a distinction between paupers who were victims of circumstances and those who had led idle and dissolute lives. In their petition to the South Carolina Assembly seeking funds for the construction of a workhouse, the vestrymen of St. Philip's blamed the increase in pauperism on the "Number [of] Idle, Vagrant and vitiously Inclined People, either brought in by Shipping, or on Various Pretences, resorting hither from divers Parts of the Provinces And by Drinking and other Sorts of Debauchery Speedily reducing themselves to Poverty and Diseases."[14] Even so, poor relief taxes rose in Charleston from £625 in 1732 to £14,000 in 1775; however, the numbers actually refused aid or sent back to their home parish were actually very small, and outdoor relief was consistently more generous than in northern cities.[15]

The situation in colonial New England could not have been more different from that prevailing in the South. Ruth Herndon's recent study of poverty in eighteenth-century Rhode Island has vividly demonstrated that the warning-out of potential paupers was a common occurrence as town officials tried their hardest to reduce the tax burden on locals. Far from being principally concerned with the sufferings of the individuals before them, New Englanders interpreted poverty mainly as an economic problem. As Herndon comments, even "those who were entitled found poor relief a severe charity."[16] J. Richard Olivas has highlighted the role played by Puritan ministers, in complete contrast to Anglican ministers in the South, in articulating a welfare policy that was extremely restrictive for the able-bodied poor. The Reverend Charles Chauncey told his congregation, for example, that it was God's wish that paupers "shall not be maintained at the charge of others" unless sick or infirm. In cities like Boston, which had problems with cyclical unemployment, such views left large numbers of people in dire straits with no prospect of relief. In Philadelphia, out-relief (assisting paupers in their own homes) was ended by the colonial legislature in the 1760s and all paupers were required to receive indoor relief in one of several institutions designed to get sick paupers better and all in receipt of help back into work. Few were supported for a lengthy period of time, and far more women were helped than men.[17] Some officials farther South might have agreed with these policies; however, the actions of parish officials speak louder than words. There were no strict policies on institutionalization in either Charleston or Baltimore, with out-relief continuing alongside indoor relief; outside the major towns men were as likely to receive relief as women, with some chronically ill or disabled paupers receiving relief for decades at the public expense. Welfare policies in the colonial South were therefore generally focused on the relief of want and suffering among poor whites rather than with reducing expenses, and therefore taxes.

In addition to having a relatively generous system of public poor relief, colonial southerners also organized private benevolent societies. The St. Andrew's Society of Charleston was founded in 1729 and was swiftly followed by the St. George's Society (1733), the South Carolina Society (1737), the French Benevolent Society (1760), the Fellowship Society (1762), and the German Friendly Society (1766). Although concentrated in Charleston, private benevolent societies also appeared in Savannah (the Union Society founded in 1750 and the St. Andrew's Society founded in 1764) and in Williamsburg (the Society for the Relief of Clergymen's Widows and Orphans founded in 1754). The memberships of these institutions could be considered exclusive since they were normally based on nativity or ethnic origin. Those who organized the St. Andrew's Society in Savannah, for instance, were publicly rebuked by "A Commoner" for issuing an invitation to other "gentlemen" to join them while leaving "no room for commoners."[18] Yet the disbursements offered by these earliest societies were normally given to all white individuals who required assistance regardless of ethnic origin. The St. Andrew's Society in Charleston declared that "the principal design of this club is to assist all people in distress, of whatsoever nation or profession he may be"; the South Carolina Society desired "to relieve our fellow-creatures in distress, and to promote their welfare"; and the members of the Fellowship Society sought nothing more than "to promote the good of mankind."[19] These societies raised most of their income from members, with a joining fee and additional subscriptions payable at each meeting of the society, but they also welcomed donations and legacies. The charitable funds of the South Carolina Society grew from nothing in 1737 to more than £50,000 by 1770, achieved by the funds' managers through such means as lending out a proportion of their capital to local merchants at a set rate of interest. There were also benefits for members, as they were guaranteed paid funeral expenses and pensions for widows and children. The South Carolina Society spent at least twice as much on pensions for members' families as it did on other benevolent purposes between 1750 and 1770. Yet in 1770 the Society also spent more than £1,000 on the education of twenty indigent children who would otherwise have gone without any schooling. The Fellowship Society directed most of its funds into its hospital, having observed "the distress of such distempered poor, as from time to time come to Charles Town, for advice and assistance, and how difficult it is for them to procure suitable lodgings, and of conveniences, proper for their respective cases, for want thereof many must suffer greatly, and some probably perish, that might otherways be restored to health and comfort, and become useful to themselves, their families, and the public for many years after."[20] The Fellowship Society was also prepared to assist those in distress whom they deemed to be worthy individuals. In 1778 Mrs. Mary Cripp wrote seeking help after her house had been destroyed in a fire. Accepting that she was "very infirm from the breaking one knee and dislocating both, so as to render her incapable of acquiring a maintenance by honest industry as she would not cheerfully endeavour to do," the society agreed to rebuild her home on her now vacant lot. Six years later the widow of a former member,

Mary Ann Donovan, informed the society that she was "greatly distressed owing to the embarrassed situation of her late husband's affairs." The committee appointed to investigate her situation reported that her only income was what she received from hiring out three slaves, who might at any time be seized for the repayment of debts. Although Donovan asked only for her rent to be paid, the committee recommended an annual pension of £40.[21]

Private benevolence was not limited to outdoor relief. The most famous of the colonial charitable enterprises, George Whitefield's orphanage at Bethesda in Georgia, offered institutional care for young children. Prior to Whitefield's arrival in Georgia orphans were normally placed with local men of standing such as Henry Parker, First Bailiff of Savannah, and planters Patrick Houstoun and Michael Burghalter.[22] But as soon as he arrived in Georgia in 1737 Whitefield became interested in founding an orphan house that would provide a permanent settled home for disadvantaged children.[23] Although he was no doubt genuinely concerned about helping orphan children, Whitefield also desired to impose his own religious idealism and enthusiasm on young minds. To this end he deliberately decided to establish his orphan house on a five-hundred-acre site several miles from Savannah "because the children will be more free from bad examples, and can more conveniently go up on the land to work."[24] Moreover, a residential home, rather than a binding-out system, would alleviate the problem of children who "forgot at home what they learned at school."[25] The daily routine for the children at Bethesda consisted of religious services, school lessons, and vocational training, "but no time is allowed for idleness or play, which are Satan's darling hours to tempt children to all manner of wickedness as lying, cursing, swearing, uncleanness etc."[26]

The high-handed manner in which Whitefield went about trying to ensure that all orphans ended up at Bethesda caused numerous headaches for the president of the colony, William Stephens.[27] Henry Parker, for example, complained that Peter Tondee was taken from him just "now he is grown capable of doing him some service." Whitefield brushed aside such objections with the comment that Peter should be "employed for the benefit of the other orphans."[28] Similarly the Milledge children, who were being cared for by their older brother, John, after the death of their parents, were taken to Bethesda forcing John to make representations to William Stephens to have them returned. Stephens and James Oglethorpe agreed that although Whitefield had been granted a monopoly of the care of orphans by the Georgia Trustees who were ultimate authority for the colony in London, this did not allow him to take those children who had someone to care for them and who would not otherwise have come under the auspices of the colonial government. However, when John Milledge arrived at Bethesda to claim back his brother and sister, he was informed by Whitefield that they "were at their proper house already" and was sent away. Only when Whitefield left Georgia was John Milledge able to get his siblings back.[29] After this incident the Trustees sent new regulations to the colony ordering that orphans could be placed at Bethesda by the magistrates only if they were "destitute of friends, or means for their subsistence or support."[30]

The institutional vision offered by Whitefield was not shared by all involved with the colony. The Earl of Egmont thought that the regime at Bethesda was "too strict [as] not a moment of innocent recreation, tho' necessary, is allow'd in the whole day," and Christopher Orton reported that the orphans suffered because of their "hard usage."[31] Deaf to these concerns, Whitefield boasted that "it is a constant in my house, he that will not labor neither shall he eat."[32] While Whitefield's critics shared his understanding that charity was "a virtue of the highest rank" and that it was vitally important to teach children while young, before they became "beset with innumerable temptations," they did not think that the Bethesda regime was appropriate. Orphans, they argued, should be given practical training that they would be able to use in later life instead of being taught academic subjects or encouraged to "give themselves up entirely to prayer and meditation."[33]

Despite Whitefield's desire to take in "all the orphans I could find in the colony," the number of children helped at Bethesda was actually quite small and dwindled rather than grew as Georgia transformed itself from a colonial experiment into a clone of South Carolina.[34] A fire in 1773 left the site in ruins and the Bethesda estate was eventually divided up in the early nineteenth century.[35] Fortunately Bethesda was not the only source of help for orphan children in colonial Georgia. The Union Society was formed by working men in 1750 "to support and educate orphan boys" though until the founding of the Female Asylum in 1801 the Union Society also helped girls.[36] It is surely significant that two of the founding members of the society were carpenters Richard Milledge and Peter Tondee, both of whom had resided at Bethesda, though it seems likely that the society was established not to emulate Bethesda but to offer an alternative to it. In a marked departure from the Bethesda model, the Union Society reaffirmed faith in the binding-out system. The youngest children on the bounty of the society were generally housed with local families while the older children were apprenticed to learn a trade. For these children, moral regeneration and improvement would come through industry and sobriety instead of prayer and religious study.[37]

In both South Carolina and Georgia other attempts were made to provide a modicum of free education to poor children. In 1769 Savannah's St. Andrew's society "having taken under consideration the great advantages that arise to the poor and indigent from charitable societies" determined to finance "the education of ten children, the indigence of whose parents would otherwise deprive them of that valuable blessing."[38] The gentlemen of Georgetown, South Carolina, formed the Winyah Indigo Society in 1755 specifically to fund a free school, "which undertaking, they hope will in time, if duly encouraged and properly established, be of great advantage to the religious as well as the civil concerns of this province."[39] Several parish vestries in South Carolina established free schools for local children, and during the 1770s and 1780s no less than ten free school societies were formed in South Carolina stretching from the coast to the more remote Cheraw and Ninety-Six Districts. Other charity schools were formed in the colonial South and were normally administered by Anglican parish vestries.[40] The Charity Working School in Talbot County, Maryland, was intended "to rescue a number of poor children from ignorance, idleness, vice, immorality, and infidelity, and enable them to be more useful to themselves, and the community they belong to." Of particular concern to supporters of this school was that "many poor white children [were] as ignorant as the children of the poor benighted Negroes." The education they received would spread "piety and useful knowledge and industry among the children of the poor, who again will communicate [that] to their children."[41]

It would be wrong, therefore, to believe that both state welfare and private benevolence were post-Revolutionary creations in the South. The public and private charitable activities discussed throughout the rest of this book were built on foundations that shaped and in some respects determined the direction of antebellum benevolence. Colonial benevolence in the South, whether state or private, was more likely to be open-handed and relatively generous than inward-looking or parsimonious. With occasional exceptions, colonial southerners preferred out-relief to institutionalization, and while concerned with morality, provincial authorities understood their principal role to be alleviating suffering, not reforming society. Successive chapters, starting with state-funded provision for the poor, will explore how far these colonial trends were reestablished after the American Revolution and how they evolved during the antebellum era.

1

The Safety Net

By May 1826, Henry Hoover Jr. had clearly reached the end of his tether. For several years he had been caring for his elderly father at home. The "feeble" old man was "unable to walk without assistance" and had gradually become so incapacitated that he had "to have some person present to feed him" and was "not able to do his private occasions without assistance from some of the family." Henry Hoover had taken in his father partly to keep him from "going on the poor list" but found the extra burden increasingly difficult to bear. Not only was there an extra mouth to feed, but the time spent caring for the old man was time not dedicated to managing the family farm. In good economic conditions Hoover could manage, but "times has [*sic*] altered since" and Henry admitted that he was now financially "embarrassed" and was struggling "to support his own family." The only recourse open to Hoover was to apply to the county Wardens of the Poor for assistance. The case evidently elicited sympathy from the Wardens of the Poor as they granted Henry Hoover $40 per year toward the cost of his father's care.[1]

The case of Henry Hoover was by no means unique in the antebellum South. Thousands of the poorest individuals took advantage of the publicly funded safety net that was intended to provide food, clothing, and lodging for those who were no longer able to care for themselves. The disestablishment of the Anglican church after the American Revolution had eventually deprived parish vestries of their role in providing for the poor, though in South Carolina some Anglican vestries were still administering poor relief as late as 1800.[2]

Sometimes states needed to be prompted to reestablish formal regulations for the relief of the poor. In October 1787, five years after the departure of British troops, the Grand Jury of Chatham County, Georgia, complained "that the poor of this county remain unprovided for, and that the burthen of supporting them rests on a few benevolent individuals."[3] Another three years would pass before the state legislature acted. In most southern states a new system of county government was instituted with geographical boundaries that often mirrored the old Anglican parishes. Within these new jurisdictions county courts were established that had the power to tax local people in order to provide for the sick, the infirm, and the elderly, and to indenture orphan children. Although these systems were new, their mode of operation differed little from the old parish system. The Revolution might have swept away British power but the poor, orphaned, sick, and elderly remained, and it was often easier to reestablish the old systems of relief under a new name than actually institute a new regime. Most counties established subsidiary bodies known variously as the Wardens, Overseers, or Commissioners of the Poor to administer the system of relief. This group of men, normally consisting of five or six local luminaries, had the job of investigating and proving the veracity of claims made by those seeking relief and deciding what an appropriate level of help would be. Their function was almost identical to the pre-Revolutionary Overseers of the Poor, and indeed differed little from their counterparts in England. The North Carolina Poor law, enacted in 1777, stated precisely this fact: "the Overseers of the Poor . . . shall have the same powers and authorities as vestries heretofore had in their parishes in every respect."[4] In southern urban centers, however, the Overseers of the Poor often found themselves overwhelmed by the sheer numbers seeking relief. Different strategies had to be adopted to deal with the urban poor; this chapter will explain the reasons behind those differences and try to gauge their success.

New southern states west of the Appalachians adopted the county system of government as the norm during their evolution from territories into states but did not always create bodies such as the Wardens of the Poor. In Mississippi, for instance, the County Board of Police had responsibility for the poor, while in Missouri and Tennessee it was the County Court of Common Pleas. In Georgia, which as a colony had operated the vestry system of relief, Inferior Courts were given the power "to inquire into the circumstances of the poor, bind out orphans, and appoint guardians . . . and appoint Overseers of the Poor."[5] The power to appoint Overseers of the

Poor was not always used, however. The justices of the Inferior Courts of Chatham and Effingham counties in Georgia dealt with relief applications themselves, without an additional tier of bureaucracy, and it took the authorities in Buncombe County, North Carolina, eleven years to appoint their first Wardens of the Poor.[6] Considering the confused nature of southern public poor relief, with responsibility for the poor varying not only between states but also within them, it is hardly surprising that comparatively little is known about how state-funded southern poor relief worked and why it operated as it did. Where records exist they are often scattered and disjointed, or subsumed within a vast array of other records. Yet only by working with these disparate sources can a clearer picture of the nature of public poor relief in the southern states emerge.

Where they existed, the Overseers of the Poor in rural areas normally met quarterly to transact business. In Virginia the Overseers were supposed to report "a distinct state of the number, names and situation of the poor, and an account of their expenditures in their respective districts" and once a year "settle the amount of the poor rate" that would be raised by taxes on the local population the following year.[7] In Alabama it was the responsibility of the county court to levy the poor rate, but then to keep it separate before it was paid to the Overseers of Poor who, at the end of the year, had to render a full account of the money expended on relief to the judge of the county court.[8] Some boards of overseers decided on who should receive help only at their regular meetings, whereas others delegated discretionary powers to individual overseers so that they were able to provide relief at any time, only seeking confirmation of their decisions at later meetings. When the Commissioners of the Poor of Lancaster District, South Carolina, received a "petition of sundry citizens in favor of Steven Chase being placed on the Poor list. Saml Robinson our chrm was authorized to examine into his case and do whatever he thought best for this case and report at our next meeting."[9] Whether overseers assessed eligibility alone or collectively is, ultimately, a slightly semantic point since all those who desired help from the public purse had to have their worthiness measured in some manner. The legislature in the new state of Tennessee in 1797 specifically ordered that counties be "required and empowered to take cognizance of all the poor persons in the county, whom the justices or a majority of them might adjudge proper to be supported at the charge and expense thereof."[10] Consequently, understanding the criteria used by overseers when they decided who would receive help and who would not is crucial to the interpretation of the welfare levels provided by the average antebellum southern state.

In all states where a modicum of relief was provided to the poor, the amount spent and the number helped was very small. James Silk Buckingham, visiting Georgia in the 1840s, commented that "the poor are so few that no returns are ever made of their numbers or the cost of their subsistence." A sample of Virginia counties between 1840 and 1860 reveals that, on average, less than 1 percent of the free population was in receipt of relief at any one time. Roughly similar figures can be obtained from counties in North Carolina, South Carolina, and Georgia.[11] The fact that very few individuals were in receipt of state charity suggests that relief was provided only to the truly incapable, namely, those who would most likely have died without support. Those who came into the category of truly incapable included the blind, the insane, the severely physically disabled, the very sick, and abandoned or orphaned infants. The Overseers of the Poor of Pittsylvania County, Virginia, described their county paupers in 1849 as an "awful looking crew, some Blind, some Cripled, some Idiots, some has fits and almost every disease amongst them." Information from poorhouses confirms this rather crude description of the poor. Residents of the Shenandoah County, Virginia, poorhouse in 1823 can be divided fairly equally among the handicapped, the insane, the elderly, and the severely ill. In 1830 the Wardens of the Poor of Pasquotank County, North Carolina, were supporting seven healthy children under the age of six; four elderly people over the age of sixty-five; four sick children who were blind, palsied, and lame; and six adults aged between sixteen and forty who were classified variously as an "idiot," "lame," "pains in hands," and in "delicate health."[12] Of the fourteen residents of the Bedford County, Tennessee, poorhouse in 1850, six were over sixty years old, six were "insane," and two were blind. Sickness and infirmity almost inevitably went hand in hand with age, and state welfare was often principally about care for the elderly. Half the residents of the York District, South Carolina, poorhouse in 1860 for instance were over sixty years old, and some were over ninety. Exactly the same story can be told of many other southern poorhouses because throughout the South it was generally accepted that "no person shall be entitled to the benefits of the provision for the poor who is able to maintain himself or herself by labor, or if not, has sufficient means."[13]

In order to get some relief from the Wardens of the Poor paupers first had to bring their case to the attention of the relevant people. In some districts the wardens would travel about the community and find deserving cases by themselves or were sent to investigate possible claims. In Lancaster District, South Carolina, one of the Commissioners of the Poor was ordered to visit William Thompson and his wife and provide relief only "if he is satisfied that they are fit persons for a portion of the poor fund."[14] Elsewhere cases were represented to the wardens either by paupers themselves or by their proxies. In Georgia the law directed that "application to be provided for as a pauper may be made at any time to the Commissioner of the Poor, a justice of the Inferior Court or a clerk of such court, upon which a hearing must be had, [with] the least possible delay, by the justices, and the person to whom such application is made, is authorised to provide for such applicant as other county poor until the hearing is had."[15] Letters written to the wardens about specific cases are rare, but where they exist they reveal a great deal about the language used to elicit sympathy, and who was considered a deserving case and who was not. Isaac Hughes wrote a letter on behalf of William Thomas to the Wardens of the Poor of Craven County, North Carolina, in 1843 requesting "some small sum so as to enable him to live, he has a wife & three children." Hughes noted that Thomas has "been sick for a year or more" and represented him as "a very correct man and one particularly suited to excite the sympathy and good feelings of those who know him." The wardens granted him $4 per quarter.[16] The importance of local support for applications for help was such that paupers often went out of their way to collect signatures of local residents on their applications. Joseph Wellman obtained eleven of them to append to his application to the Wardens of the Poor of Rowan County, North Carolina, in 1826, reminding the wardens that "by accident nine year since I lost my left leg" and that "I only git my little subsistence by spinning toe and flax which at the common or present price puts it out of my power to earn a sufficiency to support myself with a small family." He was granted $16 per year.[17] By securing the support of other people in the vicinity, especially the wealthier or more notable inhabitants, paupers were increasing their chances of convincing the Overseers of the Poor that their case was genuine and should be supported. Overseers of the Poor themselves were normally drawn from the wealthiest section of society and it is not unreasonable to assume that they would take the word of those whom they might have known socially or commercially at face value. Indeed, the Commissioners of the Poor in Williamsburg District, South Carolina, even resolved that they would only consider applications from those who "shall bring certification from two or three respectable men in their vicinity that they are objects of charity."[18]

For some paupers, the small amounts distributed by the Wardens of the Poor was sufficient to allow them to remain in their own homes, with their families, and continue to work as well as they could. In such instances poor relief was effectively "topping-up" the income of the household and might not even have provided the principal source of funds. The Overseers of the Poor of Dinwiddie County, Virginia, reported in 1834 that since their poorhouse was not "sufficiently large to accommodate all who are objects of charity, the board have been for several years in the habit of giving some aid to them, which with their own exertions, enable them to live at a less expense than if they were in the poorhouse." The Overseers of the Poor in Shenandoah County, Virginia, admitted in 1843 that "the sum for supporting the outdoor paupers is not deemed adequate for their support but is paid to keep them from being supported wholly by the Overseers of the Poor."[19] Of course, many paupers were not able to contribute toward their own support, and when paupers were no longer able to care for themselves, family members could approach the Wardens of the Poor seeking financial help from the county toward their maintenance. Andrew Eller petitioned on behalf of a blind young woman Magdelin Eller who was already receiving $50 per year for her support stating that

> she has lately multiplied and brought forth to mail [two male] bastard children, which she has on her oath charged me with being the father of them and in fact [I] have no reasons to doubt the charge. But so it is that your memorialist is a poore young man, without land or property and unable to support his unfortunate blind woman and her two children, without your charitable ade, he respectfully proposes to your worships, that if you will continue this unhappy blind woman on your pension list, and allow her such sums as will inable me to hire a servant to ade her in life, I agree to marry her and support and take charge of her children.

Perhaps because refusing the application would have resulted in supporting the mother and the two children anyway, the wardens agreed to his proposal.[20] This case suggests that paupers were not simply passive recipients of aid but could be active agents able, to some degree, to negotiate and bargain over their care. It also suggests that officials did not view or treat all paupers in the same manner.

Those controlling the local poor fund had several options when deciding how to support the poor. They sometimes paid cash directly to paupers, but more often they paid money to a third party to be spent on the pauper's behalf. The Overseers of the Poor of Middlesex County, Virginia, stated that their preference was to "make contracts with the friends of those unable to procure their living, on the best terms they can, some they agree to pay 25¢ to aid in the support, others they authorize to buy corn, bacon, & groceries, and their accounts are brought in to the board supported by the order of the Overseer or Overseers who gave them and sometimes the Overseers buy articles in person of merchants & the merchants bring in their accounts at the annual meeting."[21] Where services were provided to paupers by third parties—for example, food, medicine, clothing and fuel bills, as well as burial fees—overseers commonly settled those accounts directly. Most overseers were not wedded to a particular form of relief and would dispense charity in a variety of forms to meet individual needs. The Overseers of the Poor of Spotsylvania County, Virginia, for instance, at the same meeting gave cash directly to George Arnold "a blind man" and George Granville "a poor man," paid numerous third parties to support paupers in their own homes, and paid Elizabeth Bradwell, Alex Atkins and Ben Strutton to house paupers on behalf of the county.[22] The Wardens of the Poor in Ashe County in western North Carolina preferred to give money to local worthies who then paid the bills of the poor rather than giving money directly to paupers themselves. John Hawthorn, a farmer with property valued at more than $1,000 in 1850, was entrusted with $35 to pay the bills of Richard Tribitt and his wife Margaret, who were both over eighty years old. Ashe County Wardens also paid medical bills and funeral expenses for those who were, or had been, in receipt of help from the county.[23] Local officials therefore administered a very flexible and responsive system that changed constantly to meet specific individual circumstances. The needs and requirements of most paupers were assessed, and the relief offered was intended to supply that want. Moreover, relief was rarely given just once to avoid starvation. The records from Gwinnett County, Georgia, between 1826 and 1837 show that the average time spent on relief was four years before death, migration, or a change in circumstances removed a pauper from the relief rolls.[24]

When paupers were incapable of their own care, overseers commonly paid for them to be boarded with a local person who would care for them. Taking in county paupers was a major responsibility but also potentially lucrative. The Commissioners of the Poor in Williamsburg District, South Carolina, paid between $15 and $35 to those who boarded a pauper and for some, this could make the difference between solvency and seeking relief themselves. George P. Burrows, for instance, received $15 for himself in 1860 from the Williamsburg District Poor Commissioners, and a further $55 for two other paupers who were boarded at his house. In Madison County, North Carolina, single mother Mary Brown received $10 toward the board of sixty-nine-year-old James Guthery. For individuals such as Burrows and Brown, boarding paupers provided them with a much-needed income and, depending on the health of the pauper, free labor that might increase the productivity of the household.[25]

The vast majority of the written records relating to county poor relief in the South relate to those who successfully obtained help, so uncovering information about those who applied for help but were refused is not easy. Refusing help to those who applied was one way that Wardens were able to keep the poor rates down and limit relief to those who were truly desperate and needy. A typical method of limiting relief throughout antebellum America was to apply the settlement laws inherited from the old English poor law. Those who were recent arrivals in the county within the past year could be denied relief if they applied for it and removed back to their "home" county. The Commissioners of the Poor of Cumberland County, North Carolina, sent James and Matthew Runnels, together with their wives and children, back to nearby Columbus County where they had a legal settlement because they were "poor persons . . . likely to become chargeable to the said county of Cumberland." Even though this transportation cost them nearly $40, the Commissioners of the Poor evidently believed that it would be a longer-term saving, and—just so there was no misunderstanding—they obtained the signature of one of their counterparts in Columbus County to acknowledge receipt of the paupers.[26] Similarly the Wardens of the Poor of Granville County, North Carolina, instructed their constable to remove Betsey Lawrence back across the state line to Mecklenberg County, Virginia, together with "her little plunder" since she was "likely to become chargeable to this parish."[27] Those who could not be removed because of illness received appropriate emergency treatment until they had recovered or died, with counties claiming the costs expended on them from the paupers' home counties.[28] Some counties were even willing to provide poor individuals with money to migrate westward and thereby cease being a burden on the county. Pasquotank County, in coastal North Carolina, gave one pauper $100 to remove herself and her family westward, an amount only marginally above what they had been paying every year to support her.[29] Residency requirements were most stringently applied in the eastern states, especially Virginia and North Carolina. Elsewhere, Kentucky had no residency requirement, and in Mississippi the requirement was only six months instead of a year. It should be noted, however, that the removal of paupers back to their home county was not as common an occurrence in the South as it was farther north.[30]

Even if some individuals could be turned away in this manner, those who had obtained a legal settlement were not so easily denied: other reasons had to be found. The Commissioners of the Poor of Anderson County, South Carolina, were able to refuse help to Malinda Caldwell in 1850 after receiving letters from local people complaining that she was "exceedingly quarrelsome and bad tempered" that she had "a bad moral character" and above all that she was "being not more than 25 or 30 years of age, able bodied and healthy and fully competent mentally and physically to make a living for herself."[31] The example of Malinda Caldwell might have been occurring in hundreds of other southern counties but unfortunately the extant evidence is normally silent on refusals. Very occasionally minutes of the Overseers of the Poor might note when an individual like Polly Eller of Rowan County, North Carolina, was "stricken from the poor list" but the explanation was merely noted as being for "reasons appearing to the board." Carteret County, North Carolina, had supported Joseph Weeks for sixteen years before abruptly declaring that he would "not be allowed anything more hereafter," though the reason for their decision also remained unrecorded.[32] One individual applied to the Inferior Court of Chatham County, Georgia, "for relief for an infirm daughter" but again for unspecified reasons "the court declined to act thereon for the present."[33] Other counties tried to keep costs down by asking the families of paupers to contribute toward their care or by preventing retrospective claims for relief from a person who took in a pauper or provided one with food and clothing and then submitted a bill to the Wardens requesting payment. Orange County, North Carolina, wardens even took out an advertisement in the *Hillsboro Recorder and North Carolina Democrat* stating "that this court will make no allowance for the nursing & maintenance of paupers out of the poorhouse where the charge is brought without the knowledge or consent of this board."[34]

While it is possible that the small number of refusals noted in the official records of the Wardens of the Poor is simply because few were refused assistance, it is equally likely that the official minutes of the Wardens of the Poor were not the place that such refusals would be noted. Official minutes mainly dealt with financial records, noting who received what amount for which function, and establishing correct procedures for elections to the board. Petitions from paupers seeking relief were not written down in the minutes but were instead filed separately as loose papers. Compared to the bound volumes of minutes, which themselves are few and far between, extremely few of these loose papers have survived the ravages of time. In North Carolina only twenty-four out of a hundred antebellum counties have any extant records of the Wardens of the Poor, and just three of those have any loose records that might also include petitions from paupers. And North Carolina is actually one of the better documented states for those interested in public welfare; records for many other states are far less comprehensive. Even where paupers' petitions survive, it is possible that only those that were granted were kept, and those that were denied were just thrown away. Therefore, while it is possible to state accurately that there are only a few scattered examples of poor relief being denied, it does not necessarily follow that this was because most people who asked relief received it.

The documents that survive are generally the end product of the process of applying for relief. Paupers might have had to approach a local planter or merchant in the first instance to ask them to make representations on their behalf to a Warden of the Poor. John Fitzgerald, for instance, wrote to Colonel Joseph Cathy, one of the Wardens of the Poor of Haywood County, North Carolina, on behalf of "old man Parks" who had "laid his case before me again and again begging for assistance, making allegations, if half of which were true, no person of any humanity would turn a deaf ear to his entreaty." Fitzgerald suggested that the wardens let it be known in the community that they "would pay any person who might take care of him, a stipulated sum, per week or month" and in the meantime he personally vouched to pay anyone who took Parks in.[35] If Fitzgerald's letter was to have any effect, and unfortunately the outcome of this particular case is not known, then the warden himself would have to make a judgment on the suitability of the applicant. This might have involved a personal visit to the pauper's home and possibly conversations with neighbors as to the moral standing of the individual. If the warden was not impressed with what he saw or what he discovered from neighbors, then the application would have gone no further. Wardens were normally empowered with the discretion to help those whom they found worthy, and there was no mechanism for those who were not "found worthy" to appeal to the other wardens. Moreover, because contacts between the poor and wardens were formed at the local neighborhood level, it is possible that those seeking relief would not have known who served as a Warden of the Poor in other parts of the county, and probable that they would have lacked the means to travel out of their own neighborhood anyway.

Wardens faced with applicants with valid claims upon their aid, who met the residency requirements, and who were suitably ancient, sick, or disabled to merit relief, still often tried to keep the public tax burden down to the lowest level. Many counties operated a policy of putting paupers up for "auction" whereby the contract for looking after them was awarded "to the lowest bidder . . . at a certain sum per month."[36] Paupers who were in effect hired out in this manner might well have been expected to work if they were physically able; indeed, the Wardens of the Poor in Sampson County, North Carolina, auctioned off only their able-bodied paupers, providing fixed allowances for others. The free labor that paupers offered made them an attractive proposition, and so it is not surprising that several of those who hired paupers did so repeatedly.[37] When counties had too few paupers to merit an auction, individuals were sometimes instructed "to contract with any person who will find him sufficient victuals, washing & lodging & clothing suitable to a person in his situation."[38]

The system whereby paupers were hired out, or were boarded out, did not mean that the Wardens of the Poor washed their hands of the pauper for an entire year. They were still legally and morally responsible for the paupers, and in at least some specific cases wardens tried to ensure that paupers were placed in suitable homes. While to some extent the wishes of the paupers were relevant, sometimes Wardens of the Poor had to deal with those who found that caring for paupers was not the easy way to secure additional income that they had hoped. One suspects that Polly Eller, a pauper in Rowan County, North Carolina, was a difficult person to look after since she went through three different placements between 1827 and 1829 and was eventually ordered to enter the poorhouse.[39]

Authorities were naturally keen to keep expenses down to the lowest level, and to ensure that only the sick, elderly, and infirm received help, but they also raised tax rates and increased allowances when they believed that it was necessary. The justices of the Inferior Court of Gwinnett County, Georgia, raised the allowances of a number of their long-term paupers during the 1830s, in some cases doubling the amounts that they had previously received. In no southern county did all paupers receive the same amount per year; in fact, it was normal for some individuals to receive up to twice as much as other paupers at the same meeting of the body responsible for distributing relief. While the reasons for these discrepancies were generally not recorded, it is most likely that, as noted above, some paupers were capable of small amounts of work, or had a smallholding that might provide eggs, chickens, milk, vegetables, and pork, thereby reducing the need to purchase food. The provision of small cash sums by the Overseers of the Poor permitted some individuals to remain in their own homes and with their families, and to retain a modicum of personal dignity.

The surviving data on poor relief rates is far from systematic but in general those on out-relief received between $10 and $30 per year, with a rough average of $20. This was hardly a vast sum, especially when working men could earn $2 to $3 per day as mechanics and carpenters, but equally a bushel of corn could be purchased for as little as 50¢ and beef for 10¢ a pound.[40] Relief amounts varied considerably within states; King William County, Virginia, spent nearly $50 on each of its paupers in 1840 while neighboring King and Queen County spent only $18 per head, and the day-to-day cost of living varied according to season and location. For these reasons it is impossible to state with authority just how generous antebellum southern poor relief actually was. Christopher Johnson's study of poor relief in antebellum Mississippi concluded that average relief amounts were about 50 percent higher than in New England and could amount to 85 percent of the average laborer's wage. Data from other states suggest that Mississippi was not typical of the South and that rural relief in most southern states was actually broadly similar to that in Massachusetts, Vermont, and New York.[41]

A sizable proportion of those helped by Overseers of the Poor were orphan children, and all southern communities had systems in place to deal with children without parents or guardians to look after them. Invariably, small infants were taken into care by an individual, with payments made for immediate care and sustenance. Orphans who owned property were normally assigned a guardian to manage the property until they reached adulthood, with income from crops or from the hire of slaves being offset against maintenance costs. In such circumstances the local county court normally required guardians to make an annual report of the profit of the estate and the legitimate expenses they had incurred.[42] Those who lacked an estate to support them were indentured, often at a very young age, to someone willing to relieve the state of the cost of maintaining them in return for free labor until the child reached the age of eighteen (for a girl) or twenty-one (for a boy). State assistance was not restricted solely to orphans; sometimes it also encompassed the children of single-parent households.[43] In Buncombe County, North Carolina, for instance, three-year-old Mary McEntire was offered for indenture by her mother after her father "absconded from his family" shortly after Mary's birth. The education and training offered by farmer Henry Wells, Mary's new guardian, was most likely far above anything Mary's mother, now a single parent, might have offered.[44] It wasn't just mothers who were unable to cope with all the pressures of parenthood. Andrew Randall "surrendered" his children, John and Jane, to be indentured to George Robison because he simply could not afford to care for them himself.[45]

On average, the rural county courts indentured about five children per year and there doesn't seem to have been a shortage of people willing accept the charge of these children.[46] Because girls were indentured until they were eighteen and boys until they were twenty-one, the free labor offered by the apprentices might have been a significant consideration, and undoubtedly children could make a vital contribution to the household economy.

Perhaps for this reason, Asheville resident Charles Slaigle accepted charge of Ephraim Ledbetter in 1838, only months after Elizabeth Goodwin, who had been with Slaigle for fifteen years, reached her majority.[47] While authorities accepted that guardians might gain a benefit from the labor of indentured children in return for the expense of caring for the child, they were not willing to allow abuse of that system. The state's interest in the children did not cease the moment they walked out of court;, indeed the children remained, officially at least, wards of court. Consequently, when they heard reports that the children were not receiving the care specified under the contract of indenture, the county court felt entitled to summon guardians to answer for their behavior. When John Travant complained to the Inferior Court of Camden County, Georgia, that his daughter Elizabeth "had been very illy treated by Mrs Judson," the wife of the man to whom she had been indentured, the court heard testimony from a number of witnesses that "sufficiently substantiated" the charges. Consequently the court "ordered that Joseph Judson shall deliver up to John Travant his said daughter with her indentures & clothing."[48]

County courts did not treat all orphans the same. After 1822, officials in Buncombe County, North Carolina, imposed certain obligations on guardians to provide schooling and training as well as normal sustenance for the children in their care, and many also had to provide goods and even cash payments to the children at the end of their indentures. About a fifth of orphan boys were offered the chance to learn a trade, and those who eventually became blacksmiths, masons, carpenters, and plasterers would have had good prospects for future economic security.[49] Girls who might perhaps have been offered the chance to learn seamstressing, millinery or mantua-making often had to make do with less specific training. Some girls were to be given a spinning wheel on turning eighteen, signifying some concern by the court for future employment needs, but these girls were certainly in the minority and no guardian was instructed to give a girl a spinning wheel after 1853.[50] The vast majority of those indentured after 1822 were to receive some form of education, the exceptions mainly being free black children, none of whom were to attend school.[51] In the 1820s and 1830s little difference can be discerned between the amount of education girls and boys were to receive, but as the antebellum period wore on, girls were increasingly discriminated against and by the 1850s boys were generally receiving more schooling than girls.[52] While literacy and numeracy were seen to be essential skills for both boys and girls, Buncombe County officials clearly believed that boys needed more education than girls to prepare them for their adult lives when they would be expected to maintain themselves and a family, and the officials acted accordingly.

The broad outline of orphan apprenticeship in Buncombe County holds true for much of the rest of the rural South, with a few minor adjustments. The Commissioners of the Poor in Williamsburg District, South Carolina, were happy to be able to remove Jesse Barker from the county poor list after James Ard offered "to feed cloathe & school said Jesse at his own expense." And while an 1830 South Carolina statute gave Commissioners of the Poor the right to apprentice chargeable children and to remove illegitimate children "from the vicious conduct and evil example of the mother" to prevent them being "brought up in vice and idleness," there are no surviving examples of this being implemented in rural counties. Those taking orphan children as apprentices in Georgia had to provide a bond guaranteeing their good behavior, while promising "to clothe and maintain said apprentice decently and shall school said until he be taught to read and write the usual rules of arithmetic." Furthermore, children aged fourteen were permitted to choose and register their legal guardian with the county authorities, giving the children a significant degree of control over their own lives.[53]

At the start of the nineteenth century rural counties in the South almost exclusively provided out-relief to paupers, either directly or indirectly, and in some areas this system did not change throughout the antebellum period. Increasingly, however, county authorities were swept along by the initially urban and later nationwide fashion for institutionalization of the poor in dedicated poorhouses or almshouses. Rural poorhouses were not the impressive stone or brick-built structures found in some cities; instead they were frequently rough timber-frame houses, often described as the "poor farm" or "county farm." In 1829 about half the counties in Virginia and North Carolina had poorhouses, a figure that had risen to about 80 percent by 1860. South Carolina and Mississippi also had poorhouses of sorts, though Georgia seems to have been immune from this trend with, so far as can be determined, no antebellum poorhouses even though the state legislature had authorized their construction in twenty-nine counties.[54] Counties came to see the utility of poorhouses at different times; Moore

County, North Carolina, opened a poorhouse in 1800, while nearby Cabarrus County opened one only in 1853. Overwhelmingly Wardens of the Poor justified the construction of a poorhouse on cost grounds. Officials in Patrick County, Virginia, thought a new poorhouse would reduce expenditure on poor relief by 50 percent; their counterparts in King and Queen County reported they had spent $1,500 supporting fifty-six paupers at the new poorhouse during 1850, but "before the poorhouse system went into operation the annual expense of the maintenance of the poor only for the last nine years was never less than $2,200 and some years as high as $3,100 and upwards."[55] The cost savings came from the economies of scale that resulted from the concentration of paupers in one location under the direction of a steward, and from some paupers removing themselves from the relief rolls because they were unwilling to enter the poorhouse. The Wardens of the Poor in Amelia County, Virginia, observed that the average number of paupers in the county fell from twenty-five to seven with opening of the poorhouse. In Essex County the reduction in pauper numbers was even more dramatic, with an average of one hundred persons disappearing from the relief rolls.[56]

In some counties the poorhouse operated also as a form of workhouse, with the paupers made to do some type of productive labor to help offset the operating costs of the institution. Paupers in Person County, North Carolina, were expected to undertake "moderate labor" while showing a "submissive spirit" to the Wardens. Isle of Wight County, Virginia, had "a plantation belonging to the parish, with suitable houses for the accommodation of the poor. The plantation or farm is cultivated, a steward is employed to superintend & labour on the farm, with such of the poor as are occasionally able to labour. A physician is employed to attend to the sick at the poorhouse—the more able white women wash, cook & attend to the infirm."[57] The 300-acre farm attached to the poorhouse in Duplin County, North Carolina, grew corn and supported "a small stock of hogs and cattle sufficient to afford milk & butter for the poor besides chickens, vegetables, fruit, &c." The farm not only reduced the running costs of the poorhouse but it was also believed to have a beneficial effect on the paupers themselves: "the health of many of the poor are improved by light employment [as] their minds are diverted from the causes of their trouble and are much happier by employment."[58]

1. Yadkin County Farm, North Carolina.

Reproduced by permission of the publisher from Roy M. Brown, *Public Poor Relief in North Carolina* (Chapel Hill: University of North Carolina Press, 1928), 26.

With the construction of a poorhouse Wardens were faced with just one remaining problem: trying to get paupers to go there. Officials in Goochland County, Virginia, believed some of their paupers would "actually suffer, rather than go to the poorhouse."[59] In 1820 the wardens of Lincoln County, North Carolina, informed their paupers that if any "refuse to go to the poorhouse or are detained by their friends, they shall receive no support from the board of Wardens." Early the following year seven paupers were struck off the poor list and as John Goins "personally informed them he would not go to the poorhouse," the wardens noted that he "consequently will from this date receive nothing."[60] Paupers were generally reluctant to go the poorhouse voluntarily; Governor Pleasents of Virginia stated that paupers would only enter the poorhouse "in the last extremity," and given the regimes that normally prevailed inside the institutions that is hardly surprising.[61] Paupers were not only required to work—the ninety paupers in the poorhouse of Halifax County, Virginia, in 1850 produced a monumental "77 barrels corn, 9 stacks black fodder, 5 stacks oats, 68 bushels wheat, 450 [lbs] tobacco, [a] parcel cotton and 939 yards cloth"—there were also restrictions placed on visitors, on movement, on timing and content of meals, on "spirituous liquors" and on sleep. The rules of one poorhouse stated simply that "all paupers in the poorhouse shall submit to the control of the superintendent and promptly discharge the duties required of them."[62]

Finding a suitable superintendent usually involved advertising for sealed bids and selecting the person who said he would do the job for the least amount of money rather than appointing someone based on his qualifications. In Cleveland County, North Carolina, John Roberts agreed "to keep the poor for the ensuing year and board, clothe, feed, shoe and hat them with good provision, clothes, shoes and hats, at four dollars per month except Robt Russ and for him he is to receive five dollars per month."[63] The agreement between the Wardens of the Poor of Woodford County, Kentucky, and the keeper of the poorhouse specified that in return for a salary of $120 "he is to work the poor-house farm for the support of the poor of said county, and of his own family, and to make any improvements which he can accomplish by his own labor that the committee of the poorhouse may direct, and any surplus of the produce of said farm shall be the property of the county."[64] Whether payment was per pauper or a set salary it is likely that for at least some individuals becoming steward or superintendent of a poorhouse was one way of avoiding pauperism themselves. A salary of $375 per year, like that paid by Halifax County, Virginia, was a substantial amount of money.[65] Since stewards had to move themselves and their families to the poorhouse it is unlikely that they owned substantial property elsewhere that required their attention. Those who owned their own land and could support themselves and their families would not have applied for a position that placed them under the direction, and sometimes close scrutiny, of the Wardens of the Poor and offered little job security. Wardens in Rowan County, North Carolina, required the steward of their poorhouse to "cut & hawl wood, and prepare it for the various fire places, and make fires for such of the paupers as are not able to make for themselves; he is to have their wearing apparel, together with their bed clothes regularly washed; to issue rations regularly and properly when necessary—to provide such articles of eating, wearing, mending &c as may be ordered by the board." While they expected the steward to exercise "due economy" they also reminded him that "the paupers are generally old, infirm and decrepid persons, that require more attention than persons in ordinary life, he is particularly required & requested to treat [them] with much humanity, and to make their situations as comfortable as possible. . . . Should the person engaged, not comply with these instructions, he shall be removed at their discretion."[66]

Sometimes stewards did not live up to the high expectations placed on them and overseers then had to deal with the situation. "Several tax payers" leveled nine separate charges against John Wilson, the steward of the Fluvanna County, Virginia, poorhouse in 1847. Most of the charges resolved around alleged broken promises that Wilson had made when elected to the post—for example, stating that his wife and son would help him care for the poor but in reality "his wife's health prevents her of being any use to the paupers" while his son had "commenced school and never has done, but little or no work on the farm." Moreover, he was accused of using the property of the poorhouse to enrich himself, such as using poorhouse tools to make himself a wagon. After considering the matter the overseers resolved "that the charges were not sufficient to expel or prevent said Wilson from being a candidate for re-election." It seems likely that Wilson was well connected with at least some of the Overseers of the Poor since at that same meeting they reelected him to be steward despite having an alternate and lower bid from someone else.[67]

The popular perception of nineteenth-century poorhouses, that they were fairly miserable places to be housed in, is supported by some of the contemporary evidence. Dorothea Dix, who spent a great deal of time visiting poorhouses throughout antebellum America, found that many were poorly maintained, with little comfort or care provided for the inhabitants. The Mercer County, Kentucky, poorhouse was described as "a forlorn and comfortless place" while the Cabarrus County, North Carolina, poorhouse was "very deficient in means for promoting the comfort of the infirm inmates. In a miserably dilapidated out-building, perhaps ten feet square, open on all sides to the ingress of the winds, rain and snow, I found a crazy man chained to the floor, filthy and disgusting." The poor of Davidson County, Tennessee, were housed in "ill-repaired out-houses and cold, cheerless cells," while in Rowan County, North Carolina, Dix commented that the poorhouse "requires so much to render it comfortable that it would be difficult to know how to enumerate its deficiencies."[68] Those responsible for building and maintaining poorhouses were also sometimes conscious of their faults. Wardens of the Poor in Lincoln County, North Carolina, reported that their paupers "seem as comfortable as the kindness of the keeper, and the miserable huts in which they live would admit," while counterparts in Nottoway County, Virginia, acknowledged that the poorhouse was not always the most suitable place for some paupers: "To the poor who have sufficient reason to make known their wants and their grievances and neglects, our poorhouses afford a tolerable refuge; but to the insane, they are most comfortless and pernicious places, in most cases aggravating slight aberrations of mind into confirmed lunacy."[69]

In general, however, most Wardens of the Poor were happy with how their institutions were managed, describing them as "in good order & the situation of the paupers comfortable." The wardens in Union County, South Carolina, thought that "the poor have been well attended to by our worthy Superintendents" and their counterparts in Anderson County, South Carolina, believed that "those unfortunate persons who are in our poorhouse are quite infirm from disease & old age, yet their misfortunes are well cared for & releaved as much as human power can do, through the sympathy of the Steward & Lady."[70] Those sent to inspect the Pittsylvania County, Virginia, poorhouse reported that "everything appeared to be [as] neat and clean as could be expected amongst so many sorts of people that are inmates of the place. The steward is a very worthy man and he aims to keep good order, and to have every thing carried on systematically. He has various domestic work carried on at the place, all that is able to work has to do what they can, in aid of the institution. In a word the paupers at the poorhouse live better than a great many that has to pay tax to support them."[71] Dorothea Dix also found several examples of well-managed southern poorhouses. She thought that the Fayette County, Kentucky, poorhouse "exhibited a comfortable appearance externally" while inside "the establishment seemed to be supplied with all the necessaries and many of the comforts of the table." The poorhouse in Iredell County, North Carolina, was described as "a model of neatness, comfort, and good order," something she attributed to "having a most efficient master and mistress, especially the latter, upon whose cares in these institutions by far the most is dependent." This particular institution, she declared, "would do credit to any state." Dix visited nearly thirty poorhouses in North Carolina alone, and commented on twenty-three of them: fourteen she found to be well managed, or with minor faults, and only nine did she consider to have major problems and to be failing in their duty of care to the poor.[72]

Though poorhouses were clearly to some degree fashionable in the antebellum South, they did not turn out to be the panacea that some had hoped. For one thing, poorhouses actually cost quite a bit of money to build and then maintain and sometimes were nothing more than expensive white elephants. Grand Jurors in Barnwell District, South Carolina, criticized the cost of supporting a poorhouse "at the public expense" on three grounds. First, they argued that paupers housed in the poorhouse lacked "any object in life" since all their wants were provided for and thus there were "no inducements to labor either for themselves or for the good of each other." Consequently the system acted as an encouragement to pauperism as it failed "to re-establish them from their fallen state to those traits of character essentially requisite to the attributes of free citizenship." Second, the "hearty handsome and promising children" in the poorhouse were surrounded by "drunkards, Negro traders, prostitutes, and misery." In such an environment Jurors fretted that the children "must continue to grow on in wicked and adulterous licentiousness" until they also became public charges in adulthood. Third, jurors recognized both the impracticality and the impact of having just one poorhouse for a district encompassing 2,500 square miles. Separating the elderly and sick from their "relatives and early associations" was, in their opinion, a "death blow" to many since it "destroys their identity and virtually consigns them to a living tomb." In recommending a resumption of out-relief the Grand Jury declared that "the country has long since been prepared to dispense with this institution."[73]

Although Barnwell District Grand Jurors did not explicitly make their argument against poorhouses on cost grounds many counties might have done. Seven of the poorhouses visited by Dorothea Dix in Kentucky and North Carolina were empty at the time of her visit, yet all of those institutions had cost money to build and continued to absorb funds in maintenance. If the poorhouse steward was paid an annual salary of several hundred dollars regardless of the number of paupers in residence, the faintly ludicrous situation arose of having a staffed poorhouse without any paupers. The taxpayers of Prince Edward County, Virginia, surely had a justifiable grievance against their Overseers of the Poor in 1850. That year they paid $1,198 to support no paupers at all.[74] Of course, some counties simply did not have that many indigent people, and so it was understandable that on occasion there would be no demands on the public purse, though that does not explain why a poorhouse was deemed necessary in the first place. Some poorhouses stood empty due to the attitudes of the poor toward institutionalization. Dorothea Dix, in her study of poorhouses in Kentucky, commented that "the poorhouse system throughout the state is exceedingly repugnant to the feelings of the poor, by whom it is considered often almost as disgraceful as to go to prison."[75] Even those who had accepted help in the poorhouse often subsequently wanted to leave. John Brown, an inmate in the Rowan County, North Carolina, poorhouse (described by Dix as "certainly not habitable"), petitioned the Overseers of the Poor to grant him a pension so that he could leave and "be amongst my friends." Although he phrased his request carefully: "I have no objection to the poorhouse, only that it deprives me of being amongst my relations," the overseers refused to grant his wish.[76]

As a result of criticisms about the cost of poorhouses, the policies of admission, and the pernicious effects they might have on the "worthy" poor, sometimes poorhouses actually closed. The one in Buncombe County, North Carolina, operated between the 1820s and the 1850s, but by 1858 the Wardens of the Poor had returned exclusively to a system of out-relief. Even where poorhouses remained open, which they mostly did, out-relief often continued to operate alongside indoor relief. Advice from the Auditor of Public Accounts in Virginia in 1830 stated that out-relief should be given "under particular circumstances [as] humanity itself might require."[77] Of sixty-nine Virginia counties reporting to the state on the disposition of their paupers in 1840, twenty-five exclusively used out-relief, fourteen exclusively used the poorhouse, but thirty used both systems.[78] The continuation of the out-relief system in parallel with indoor relief was partly due to cost. Overseers in Prince Edward County, Virginia, quickly realized that institutionalization was not always the best solution because "it excludes a number of worthy poor, who could with small aid from the public, make out very well from their own exertions on their little farms." Similarly in Buckingham County, Virginia, "there are some 42 persons provided for at places other than the poorhouse. This plan is adopted as a matter of economy the board being of opinion that in many cases it is better to make a small allowance to aid them than to admit them into the institution."[79] It was cheaper, in such cases, to top up incomes with $5 or $10 than spend $50 on full-time support in the poorhouse. Overseers in Frederick County, Virginia, made a very specific distinction between those who needed full-time care and those who needed only occasional support, reporting that "no poor are boarded out. Those who receive any aid from the board not in the poorhouse, receive only such aid as in the judgement of the overseer in whose district he or she may be, is necessary for their comfort. All who are so poor as to require to be wholly supported by the board are removed to the poorhouse." Overseers in New Kent County, Virginia, showed more of a humanitarian concern for the fate of local paupers when they "deemed it expedient and proper (in extreme cases) to furnish families and individuals from [i.e., outside of] the institution with necessaries of comfort and in order to carry this plan into effect, each trustee is authorized to expend the sum of $15 in their respective districts or neighbourhoods."[80]

Indeed the humanitarianism of individual overseers should not be overlooked. Despite having a poorhouse with twenty-three inmates, the Overseers of the Poor of Orange County, North Carolina, provided $10 to a fifty-year-old blind man, Nathaniel Creal, to help him support his two children, and $7.50 to three other parents with sickly children. Similarly officials in Pasquotank County granted Joseph Tuttle $15 "in consideration of his extreme poverty and his unwillingness to come to the poorhouse."[81] Overseers of the Poor in Ohio County, Virginia, objected in principle to the fashion for poorhouses stating that "the object of the law would not be obtained, which they apprehend was intended to afford relief to indejent sufferers, when it would not be obtained from other sources." In fact there are numerous examples of county authorities ending out-relief only for it to reappear slowly over the ensuing years. Overseers in Lincoln County, North Carolina, ended outdoor relief in 1820 because they suspected that they had been supporting those "whose friends are well able to support them, but finding they could impose on the Wardens have rec^d money for support of persons who they would not let go to the poorhouse and who they were unwilling to be separated from." The minutes of the board reveal, however, that out-relief continued. The conclusions of the Wardens of the Poor of Buckingham County, Virginia, in 1860 that out relief was simply "consistent with humanity" appear to have been widely accepted in the South. [82]

Because many Wardens of the Poor found themselves unable, or unwilling, to end out-relief, and aware that poorhouses were expensive and imposed significant demands on local taxpayers, they tried various other tactics to reduce expenditures. When paupers had assets, wardens sometimes seized them for sale, with any proceeds put toward the maintenance of the pauper. Grand Jurors in Georgetown, South Carolina, were quick to complain if they suspected that poor taxes were being "applied to the support of persons owning property." After the Wardens of the Poor in Craven County, North Carolina, were informed "that Ephraim Pearce is a lunatic, that he had no personal estate, and that the rent of his land is not sufficient to support the said Ephraim," they ordered "that the lands of the said Ephraim Pearce situate in Craven County, be sold by the Sheriff." The $225 subsequently received was used by the Wardens of the Poor for his support. Similarly the wardens of Pasquotank County, North Carolina, ordered "that Wm F. Banks be authorised and empowered to sell for cash, the hogs, cattle & any other property belonging to Tony Banks & his wife Chloe, now paupers and in this poorhouse, he first advertising the same for the space of ten days, and to make returns of the same to the next meeting of this board."[83] When the wardens of Beaufort County, North Carolina, heard that one of their paupers "Huldy Wilkinson, an idiot," had some property that had been retained by her previous guardian, they instructed one of their number to "apply for the guardianship of said Wilkinson & having obtained the same, to secure said estate either by law or otherwise." Their efforts eventually realized $119, enough for two years of maintenance for Huldy Wilkinson.[84]

This policy seems mainly to have been applied to those such as the mentally ill and permanently disabled, who entered the poorhouse for a long, possibly indefinite, period of time because they would never be able to care for themselves. Wardens of the Poor were not always so quick to dispose of the property of paupers who were likely to be institutionalized only temporarily. Taking away the meager possessions of those already destitute would have effectively reduced any possibility that they might eventually be able to leave the poorhouse and support themselves and their families. For example, David Perkins and his family entered the Orange County, North Carolina, poorhouse in April 1850, and the steward reported to the wardens that they had brought with them "2 hogs, 1 heifer, 2 beds & furniture, house furniture." When the family left the poorhouse in November of the same year the wardens directed that Perkins should "receive the same property which he brought with him to the poorhouse" and even granted him $2 a month for six months, presumably in the hope that he would then be able to maintain himself and his family.

Public poor relief throughout the South was meant to act as a safety net for all free people and was not restricted to whites alone. Free blacks and even some slaves received support from the Wardens of the Poor, though this was more likely in the upper South than in the deep South. In Talbot, Somerset, and Worcester Counties, Maryland, free blacks constituted just under 30 percent of the population but accounted for nearly half the poorhouse inmates. In Virginia where free blacks constituted 4 percent of the population they made up more than 6 percent of the paupers in the seventy-seven counties that made a formal report to the state in 1840. However, to put that figure into perspective, only about 60 percent of the population of Virginia was white but this portion constituted more than 93 percent of the recipients of relief.

North Carolina has several examples of free blacks being supported by the local authorities. The Wardens of the Poor of Granville County, for instance, informed the steward of their poorhouse, John Mallory that "Allen Charis, a free man of color lies very unwell at the house of William Tyler in Oxford, and is unable to provide the means of support. You will send your carryall and bring him to the poorhouse and administer to his comfort & relief in every way his situation may require." The 1850 federal census of the same county reported two mulattos, two blacks, and eleven whites resident in the poorhouse and similar mixed-race poorhouses were reported in Orange and Bertie Counties in the same year.[85] As in Maryland and Virginia, it seems that free blacks in North Carolina had access to public poor relief at a level that was at least proportionate to their numbers in a county, though ultimately whites received a vastly disproportionate share of available state welfare.

However, as one travels south and west, the extent of the available provision for free blacks becomes much harder to discern. Virginia required its counties to differentiate between white and black paupers in their annual returns to the Auditor of Public Accounts, but few other states asked for similar data, and some requested no data at all concerning public poor relief. In South Carolina, for instance, there is no evidence that free blacks ever received state help, though Grand Jurors in Georgetown in 1845 found it necessary to complain that relief was sometimes provided to "slaves, whose owners neglect to provide for their wants." In York District the twenty poorhouse residents in 1860 were all white, as were the twelve inmates of the Pickens County poorhouse in the same year. The comparatively comprehensive records of the Poor Commissioners of Lancaster and Williamsburg districts never once mention a payment to a free black person. Exactly the same can be said of numerous other counties in deep South states. A sample of fifteen counties from Alabama, Tennessee, and Mississippi that were listed in either the 1850 or the 1860 federal census as having a poorhouse reveals that, in stark contrast to poorhouses in the upper South, none had a free black inmate. To claim from this data that only the upper South states offered public support to free blacks would, however, be a step too far. It is possible that the absence of free blacks in the poorhouse records is mainly because the surviving records are scattered and fragmentary rather than systematic. Nobody required Commissioners of the Poor to collate data on the racial background of paupers, and so none were collected. Where more detailed information has survived regarding the day-to-day treatment of paupers it becomes clear that a small number of free blacks did receive assistance. Sumner County, Tennessee, for instance, supported a black woman who was "blind and left friendless" for more than a decade while Madison County, Mississippi, was also willing from time to time to support free blacks who needed help.[86] In states where free blacks constituted only a small fraction of the total population (less than 1 percent in Georgia, Alabama, Mississippi, and Tennessee) it is hardly surprising that few received poor relief; even so, public poor relief was overwhelmingly white in the deep South whereas it was slightly more racially varied in the upper South. Indeed, poor relief was whitest in those states with the highest proportion of enslaved persons. In 1860 slaves constituted more than 40 percent of the population in Georgia and Alabama, and more than 50 percent of the population of Mississippi and South Carolina. Poor whites, whose lives were deeply affected by living in a slave society even if they were not slaveholders themselves, were effectively receiving a privilege of race through their disproportionate access to state assistance. White paupers in rural counties always had the safety net of public relief beneath them, even if that safety net sometimes had holes in it.

While rural areas dealt with the problem of poverty in their midst by interweaving traditional out-relief with some fairly half-hearted experiments with poorhouses, the authorities in the South's major towns and cities took a much harder line. Much of the difference between rural and urban attitudes toward poor relief can be attributed to the size of the problem. It was unusual for a rural area to have more than fifty paupers at any one time, and most counties had ten or fewer, but in cities the numbers were much higher. Cities attracted migrants in search of work, and as many southern cities were also major ports they had to deal with a large number of transients and immigrants who were either sick or destitute on arrival. New Orleans had to cope with 15,000 to 20,000 immigrants each year in the 1840s and 1850s. A further 500 to 1,000 immigrants arrived in Charleston each year between the 1820s and the Civil War.[87] Immigration clearly affected urban poor relief systems: Charleston supported 107 city paupers in 1812 and a further 232 transients; seven years later numbers had risen to 157 city paupers and 348 transients; by 1856 more than 1,300 foreign-born paupers were housed in the city's poorhouse. In New Orleans the contrast was even greater: only 59 of the 8,867 patients treated at the Charity Hospital during 1835 were from the city, with the remainder split fairly evenly between those from elsewhere in the United States and those from abroad.[88]

In general, city authorities were far more prepared than rural counterparts to erect institutions to house their poor and to have more restrictive policies in place to ensure that the poor actually went there. Older east coast cities had adopted the institutional approach as far back as the eighteenth century, with Charleston opening its first poorhouse in 1738.[89] People admitted to poorhouses in southern cities were not that different from those admitted to rural poorhouses: the sick, elderly, and otherwise incapacitated predominated. Between 75 percent and 85 percent of those admitted to poorhouses in Charleston and Richmond, for instance, were sick, disabled, or injured.[90] Indeed, the poorhouses of many southern cities could just as easily be called "hospitals"; in some places the two terms were synonymous, and poorhouse and hospital were in fact conflated into one institution. The first southern hospital open to all was the New Orleans Charity Hospital, founded in 1737, and in other cities hospitals were sometimes among the first civic buildings to be constructed. The Natchez Hospital opened in 1805 "to give relief to all indigent boatmen" twelve years before Mississippi even became a state, and there were hospitals providing free medical care in Mobile by 1828, Memphis by 1829, Apalachicola by 1844, and Nashville by 1852. In general, the later antebellum period saw a proliferation of new institutions in southern cities to care for the rising numbers of paupers: in New Orleans, where the Charity Hospital had been the mainstay for the poor for more than a century, the city authorities opened new poorhouses in 1858 to cleanse the streets of "a class of population who are now a sore upon the body politic"; in Charleston the old poorhouse was complemented by the construction of Roper Hospital between 1850 and 1854 and a new almshouse in 1852 solely for reception of white paupers; in Baltimore both almshouse and public hospital were in place before 1800, but a second almshouse was needed in 1816 and two further hospitals before 1834.[91]

The popularity of institutions in southern cities mirrored what was happening further north. David Rothman first articulated the popularity of institutionalization for the poor post-1820.[92] In fact, poorhouses in the South were not suddenly popular after 1820; they were just more common than they had been before, and much of that increased popularity can be attributed to the rapid rise in the number of immigrants into the South in the antebellum era. City authorities, like many of their rural counterparts, believed that poorhouses were cheaper than the alternative of out-relief. In Charleston, city officials claimed "that the public charity can be dispensed to the Poor with more economy, by supporting them in the house, than by furnishing them with rations out of doors."[93]

Those charged with distributing poor relief often took a highly paternalistic approach toward their duties. Robert Greenhow, president of the Overseers of the Poor of Richmond, Virginia, told his fellow overseers in 1820 that "the trust imposed on us, is indeed an important one; we are the constituted almoners of the city; we are the nominated guardians, friends, and protectors of the destitute & forlorn, the widow & the orphan; & we are vested with the power of administering to their necessities as commensurate with the means afforded us & the applicants for relief, in our opinion deserve." Such a responsibility was not to be taken lightly since "As the cautious, prudent, industrious master, who has a large and for the most part helpless family to bring up, support & educate, will use his every effort to regulate his expenditures, and bring them within the verge of his circumscribed income, so are we in like manner, bound to act towards those consigned to our care." Greenhow was also conscious that not all applicants for relief were genuine, and he warned his colleagues: "Highly coloured deceptive tales of woe, painting in dolorous terms the wants and deprecations of the solicitor; your ears will be frequently assailed with, and every means to excite your sympathy will be practised. Fallacious too often these have been proved to be. You must turn a deaf ear to them; and proceed to investigate them."[94] Similar concerns regarding the differences between the worthy and the idle poor can be found in Charleston: "Inasmuch as it is a subject of general notoriety that permanent provision for persons in the uninterrupted possession of health has served but to the increase of pauperism; it is thence incumbent on the Commissioners of the Poor, when dispensing public charity to discriminate between . . . all whose dependence arises from sickness decrepitude or unavoidable calamity . . . [and] all whose indigence is induced, if not from profligacy and intemperance, from an aversion to habits of industry and economy."[95]

Only passing thought was given by those in charge of poorhouses to the state of the local economy as a cause of poverty. Robert Greenhow accepted that "everyone at all conversant with human affairs, must agree, that more is required to support the poor in times of general pressure and pecuniary difficulty, than in times of prosperity" and the Overseers of the Poor of Rockingham County, Virginia, blamed an increase in pauperism in the mid-1830s on "the deranged state of the county in money matters." Others, however, believed that the existence of poor relief was actually an inducement for the poor to avoid work. The Reverend Jasper Adams of the College of Charleston believed that "many thousands have been brought to pauperism, who, aided by private sympathy . . . might have obviated the temporary difficulties of their condition by their own exertions."[96] For many of those who dealt with the poor on a daily basis the root cause of poverty was drink. The Trustees of the Baltimore Almshouse reported "that of the 623 adult persons admitted into the Alms House during the year ending April, 1826, FIVE HUNDRED AND FIFTY FOUR were positively ascertained to have been reduced to the necessity of being placed there by drunkenness, and . . . that of the great number of children who are always in the House, there is scarce an instance occurs of one being placed there, who has not been reduced to that necessity by the intemperance either of one or both its parents." It was, they thought, only drink that could explain why hundreds of people were housed in the almshouse "in a county where the means of obtaining a comfortable subsistence are so abundant, and where labour is at the same time so amply rewarded."[97] The pernicious effects of alcohol meant that all poorhouses banned their inmates from introducing "ardent spirits, or other liquor, for themselves or for their fellows." Paupers in the Wilmington, North Carolina, poorhouse were also not "allowed to go out & return intoxicated under the penalty of being expelled from the poorhouse or be confined for three days in his or her room."[98] When the steward of the Richmond poorhouse tried to confine Mrs. Wade after she had appeared "in a high state of intoxication" she "not only resisted, but with the frenzy of a tigress, rushed upon him, . . . & beat, bruised, bit & otherwise maltreated him." The board of Overseers of the Poor felt they had no choice but to direct that she should be taken before the courts "and dealt with as they, the distributors of justice should adjudge to be agreeable to the laws of our land."[99]

Regulations against drink were part of the wider principle of moral reform of paupers in antebellum poorhouses. Like their rural equivalents, urban poorhouses were meant to be places where the poor would receive basic "life support" while being shielded from the temptations of drink and their former acquaintances, and they would be reintroduced to labor. Most poorhouses limited the number of visitors that paupers were able to have, and many city authorities located their poorhouses on the edge of town precisely to make them less accessible to the wider public. The principle that all paupers who were physically able should do at least some work in the poorhouse was widely adopted. Women in the Charleston poorhouse worked as nurses, washers, spinners, carders, cooks, and cotton pickers while men worked as gardeners, cotton pickers, carpenters, and later stone-breakers.[100] Items produced by the paupers were either sold or used within the poorhouse itself, helping to keep the expenses of the institution under control. The steward of the Baltimore Almshouse estimated that in 1825–1826 the paupers had produced food and goods and undertaken work that he estimated would have cost more than $7,000 to purchase at market prices. The women had made clothes and shoes valued at nearly $1,000, while the men had undertaken significant repairs to the poorhouse as well as making furniture; together the paupers had, among many other things, grown 16,000 cabbages, raised 3,000 pounds of pork, and milked 15,695 quarts of milk from the cows.[101] Yet financial contributions, though welcome, were not the main reason poorhouses forced their inmates to work. Paupers were usually those who, for whatever reason, were unable to work to support themselves and their families. Overseers of the Poor invariably believed in the moral importance of work, thinking that it made the paupers into "better" people and perhaps gave some the skills that might enable them to support themselves outside the poorhouse. The commissioners of the Charleston poorhouse believed that "employment removes the causes of indigence, the consequent miseries of indolence, promotes health & cleanliness, and introduces habits of order, industry & frugality."[102] Robert Greenhow, chairman of the Overseers of the Poor of Richmond, Virginia, neatly summarized how important work was for the paupers in his institution: "Though there are but few of the males whose bodily state of health would admit of their labouring. Yet it is all important that they should not remain in idleness. I therefore propose that the keeper should be requested to purchase on the best terms oakum or old tarred rope, and insist upon all those, not absolutely confined to their beds, to pick or prepare it for the use of vessel caulkers. Some small profit may be derived from its sale, and if it should be productive of none, it will be of this, that they are employed."[103]

Though Richmond, Charleston, and several other cities adopted an institutional approach to poor relief, other cities continued to place their faith in the out-relief system. For most of the antebellum period the city authorities of Nashville, Tennessee, and of Montgomery, Alabama, paid for the medical care and burial of the sick and for boarding paupers with third parties in exactly the same way that rural counties did.[104] New Orleans, the most populous southern city, did not have an organized institutional system for its healthy poor until the late 1850s. For most of the antebellum era the paupers of New Orleans were able to petition the city council for help. By the 1830s such requests were so numerous that a special Committee on Relief was established "to grant relief to indigent persons, who are unable to support themselves."[105]

Even those cities that adopted the institutional solution invariably continued with out-relief in some shape or form. The new Wilmington poorhouse was constructed at a cost of $2,450 in 1853, yet despite ordering "that all the out door poor under the charge of the Wardens of the Poor be transferred to the poorhouse," the authorities continued out-relief for five people, and in 1859 one pauper successfully applied for $15 "to enable him to buy tools and leather to enable him to support himself."[106] The Montgomery, Alabama, city council approved the purchase of land and the construction of a pauper hospital in 1851, with a salaried physician on call. In 1854 the hospital cost Montgomery city taxpayers more than $1,000 to run, yet a further $246 was spent on the "relief of destitute persons."[107] In Savannah the privately run Poor House and Hospital fooled the resident British Consul into thinking that "there is no legal provision in the state of Georgia for the support of the poor." In reality, the city-funded Board of Health paid out between $100 and $200 a year in small sums of $5 or $10 to those such as Mrs. Polson "who is in a destitute situation for the want of bread, herself & children being all sick." During the 1850s between twenty and forty families were in receipt of out-relief from this source each year.[108]

In Richmond the board of overseers were well aware that "those lodged in the poorhouse do not constitute more than about one fifth part of those whose relief is by our body administered" and explained the policy of having out-relief for some while also maintaining an institution by claiming that those "not lodged at the poorhouse, [but] by monthly allowances, are assisted at an expense much less than those in the Poorhouse are." However they also admitted that a significant number of paupers simply refused "most peremptorily . . . to be sent there, . . . with a little assistance say they, we can live at our own abodes, and before we will accept of your proffered room, we will ere die in your streets. This is language to which we are all accustomed."[109] The Richmond city authorities, who provided the funding for the poorhouse, were far from happy that out-relief continued alongside indoor relief. In 1828 they publicly criticized the Overseers of the Poor for "making stated allowances to many who are permitted to remain at their own houses, thereby defeating . . . the very object for which the poorhouse was erected." Out-relief, they argued offered "a tempting bounty to all to gain a residence among us, who may desire to receive aid from the corporation and yet would be unwilling to become inhabitants of a poorhouse" while stopping it would force the poor "to rely on their own industry and economy."[110] Within five years the numbers receiving outdoor relief had tumbled from more than three hundred per year to just sixty-six and for the remainder of the antebellum era to fewer than ten. Simultaneously the numbers of paupers in the poorhouse rose steadily, from around 70 for most of the 1820s to about 150 in the 1840s and nearly 400 in the late 1850s.[111]

The clampdown on out-relief in Richmond certainly seemed to be successful, but in Charleston a similar move to concentrate relief in institutions was a total failure. Despite intentions to limit out-relief and concentrate on providing for the indigent at the poorhouse, it seems that the commissioners did not really have the heart to implement such a policy. In 1830–1831 there were only slightly more individuals in the poorhouse than on outrelief, and for the remainder of the antebellum era between 250 and 400 paupers remained on out-relief. In 1857 the commissioners acknowledged that many of the outdoor paupers were women and children and hence they found "it impracticable to carry out their policy [of institutionalization] to the extent they would desire." Commissioners even allowed one man who "supports himself in great measure, merely sleeping in the house," to continue to receive relief.[112] Furthermore, by restricting out-relief to those with at least a year's residence, which was adopted as policy in 1850, commissioners ensured that transients were not able to abuse a system that was increasingly acting as a form of income support to the poor white population of the city. It might have been policy "to prevent if possible strangers settling upon us as paupers" but no effort was made to remove "strangers" refused help, as was common in New England. Sarah Davies, for example, had not acquired a legal "settlement" when she was refused aid in April 1860, but she successfully reapplied in January 1861.[113] Even in Richmond, where poor relief policies were generally more restrictive, Overseers of the Poor admitted that "suspicious as we may be [that] paupers from other places secrete themselves until they have gained a residence," once they had done so "it becomes our duty to support them."[114] Those who desired aid applied to the Commissioners of the Poor and if successful received a "ration" of supplies to support them. Those on out-relief were often required to bring certificates attesting to illness or infirmity, or in the case of one woman, a note from the schoolmaster stating that her son had been regularly attending school. The continuance of out-relief did not mean that charity was more widely accessible than it had been before. Commissioners continued to strike off the list those whom they thought more properly should enter the poorhouse and to investigate those whom they suspected of being "an improper person."[115]

Most southern cities permitted indigent free blacks to enter municipal poorhouses. In Richmond free blacks constituted between 10 percent and 20 percent of the population of the city poorhouse for most of the antebellum period and there were certainly free black inmates of poorhouses in Baltimore and Columbia at various times. There were no nonwhite inmates of the poorhouses of Mobile and Montgomery, Alabama, when the census enumerators arrived in 1860, but this was not because of a specific prohibition.[116] In Charleston the application of free black Cupid Jones for relief prompted the Commissioners of the Poor to establish a committee to determine precisely what rights free blacks had to public poor relief. After a review of every South Carolina statute and city ordinance relating to poor relief the committee concluded that "the terms used in the different statutes and ordinances to describe and designate the poor; who are objects of relief, are of the most comprehensive and extensive signification. They are broad enough to embrace . . . not only white persons but persons of every colour, whether Indians, mulattoes, mestizoes, or Negroes; they are in fact, as wide in their import as humanity counsels and requires." Furthermore, since free blacks were "regularly assessed, exactly as white persons, for the support of the poor, it follows, necessarily as a matter of right and justice, as well as of logic and law, that their own poor are entitled to relief out of a fund to which they contribute 'equally' with the more privileged classes of the community." The committee therefore reported "that it is the mandate of law and the counsel of true wisdom and policy, as well as the dictate of sheer justice and humanity, that the aged and infirm free colored of the city and state are fit and rightful objects of public relief"; indeed, it was "an opprobrium to our city, that a place has not long since been provided for the care of the free colored paupers among us."[117] This recommendation was broadly welcomed: the *Magnolia* magazine described it as "conclusive and manly," commenting, "We should hardly have supposed that any question could be made as to the relative claim of colored and white—when starving—to the humane consideration of a Christian community. Man is the subject of the charity. Shall we ask, when he craves bread—what is his complexion? Surely not."[118] However, aware that this policy decision might cause friction among the white poor, the committee also recommended that "the free colored poor should be provided for in a place different and separated from that appropriated to the care of the white poor—the distinction of casts must be strictly and broadly preserved in slave-holding communities." The committee recommended converting the old workhouse for this purpose, and using it like a bettering house where inmates "may be compelled, if able to labour, to do some employment for the public good." As with white paupers, the board would be "administering relief only in cases of meritorious character or of actual necessity, where poverty, and old age, or infirmity of some kind, render the applicant a worthy or fit subject for public relief."[119]

The vast majority of southern cities treated orphan and destitute children in the same way that rural authorities did—by indenturing them to locals who would act in *loco parentis* until the child reached the age of majority. Certainly the Chatham County, Georgia, Inferior Court treated Savannah's public orphans in this manner, indenturing boys to local tradesmen and girls to local families who would teach them to "read, to write, to cipher, wash, iron, cook and sew." Though indentured, these children remained official wards of court. James Alexander, bound to cabinet-maker Peter Miller in 1793, returned to court two years later claiming that Miller had "not instructed him in the said art and trade of cabinetmaker." When Miller was summoned and acknowledged that he had failed to fulfill his part of the indenture, the justices had no hesitation in discharging Alexander from any remaining ties to Miller.[120] The County Orphans' Court in Baltimore dealt with far more cases than their counterparts in Savannah, about three hundred annually in the early years of the nineteenth century, but similar indenture provisions were agreed between the court, the children, and those apprenticing them regarding education, training, and freedom dues.[121] Not all city authorities earned a reputation for doing what was best for orphans. One Richmond newspaper was highly critical of a system that permitted those taking orphan children to "work them hard, feed them badly, and clothe them worse, under the pretense of taking care of them."[122]

The major exception to the practice of county courts indenturing children was in Charleston where city authorities opened the first publicly funded orphanage in the United States in 1790. Destitute children were accepted into the orphanage from a young age, and the orphanage seems to have been used by some poor families as a form of long-term child care facility. Only a minority of children were full orphans, with more than half being placed there by their mothers and fathers who were not able to support them or give them the opportunities that the orphan house offered. One father asked the orphan house commissioners to take his children since having "two boy children on my hands . . . has put me in an awkward situation."[123] Conditions inside the orphanage for the children were by no means luxurious, with expenditures kept under tight control. The fabric of the building itself was often not maintained to a high standard yet the Commissioners of the Orphan House were also capable of great humanity, on one occasion paying for a nurse to attend three particularly disabled children "with the care and fidelity which their helplessness and infirmities require."[124] The average stay in the Charleston orphanage was about five years, and during that time "salutary discipline" and "the moral influence of the establishment" was meant to encourage the "practice of generosity, gentleness, honesty, truth and cleanliness by the inmates of the house, and repress, by all the moral influence of the establishment, all selfishness, cruelty, falsehood and impurity." In order to develop "their social and religious character," the children undertook domestic chores, though when Harriet Martineau visited the orphan house in the 1830s she believed that "no active labour goes on; the boys do not even garden. No employment is attempted which bears any resemblance to what is done by slaves." By the early 1860s, however, it is clear that commissioners had become infected with the nationwide enthusiasm for physical exercise since their charges were instructed to engage in "such well-regulated muscular and gymnastic exercises in the open air as may conduce to the vigorous health and physical improvement of the children."[125] Most children also attended daily instruction, "the great agent of reform and improvement," and, as John Murray's work on the detailed records of the orphanage has demonstrated, while only 30 percent of children had basic literacy on entry, nearly all could read and write when they left. For most of the antebellum period boys and girls received similar schooling in the orphanage, but in the 1850s the amount given to the girls was reduced in favor of more training in domestic duties such as sewing to enable them "to perform the duties of life, which will in all probability devolve upon the[m]. . . when they leave this institution."[126]

In addition to the schooling that the children received, the orphan house commissioners arranged apprenticeships with local tradesmen or local families when the girls reached twelve years of age and when the boys became fourteen. These apprenticeships were intended to give the children the skills they would need in the future to support themselves but the lady commissioners who supervised the indentures of the girls in the orphan house did not always believe that apprenticeship at twelve years of age was the most appropriate course of action. In 1844 and again in 1851 the ladies protested to the male commissioners that orphan girls were "often taken by those who have no servants & who consequently expect them to act in that capacity" and suggested that instead they should remain in the orphan house until age fifteen and receive further education and training.[127] While the age of female apprenticeship did not change, in general the Commissioners of the Orphan House were willing to take into account the wishes of the children and their surviving parents when organizing the apprenticeships. On occasion the commissioners noted that a child had "expressed his willingness" to an apprenticeship, or that a particular master was "the choice of the girl." As in other cities, apprenticed children did not simply disappear from the memory of those who had indentured them. Children who felt that the apprenticeship was not turning out as planned were able to turn to the orphan house commissioners as powerful allies who could either alter the indentures or revoke them.

While the orphans were indentured to their fair share of carpenters, bricklayers, and blacksmiths, there is evidence that the commissioners also thought that some of the most able were "fitted for the higher walks of life" and they rejected offers to train boys as farmers in favor of "a position that will prove more in accordance with their wishes and views." Children were reminded that "the public have a deep store in your characters; that if you fail to improve your opportunities of becoming useful citizens you . . . defraud those by whose care you are protected and blessed." One visitor to the orphan house actually commented on "how much encouragement is here for all little boys—rich or poor—to study and improve and try to be good and great." Commissioners could think of no higher praise for their charges than that they had achieved "self-control and [an] elevated sense of propriety" and such behavior earned them a share of the "honour" so highly praised by southern men.[128] Henry DeSaussure, chairman of the orphan house commissioners took particular pleasure in reporting a chance encounter with a former orphan in 1855. This particular boy had been apprenticed to a merchant and eventually became his business partner, married his daughter, and inherited the business. "Having accumulated property for the family and myself, [I] sold out, and we all removed together to Georgia, and vested our property in lands and negroes, as planters. At this moment, and for some years past, I have been a member of the legislature of Georgia." Indeed, DeSaussure boasted he could tell of numerous boys who had become judges, military men, or businessmen, and girls who married and "became mothers of families, and respectable matrons in this city and elsewhere."[129]

This highly organized system of dealing with orphans in Charleston was not entirely static during the antebellum period. The number of children in the orphan house, for example, rose from about 100 in the early nineteenth century to more than 350 by 1860, most likely because of the increased immigration of poor families to the city in the 1850s. Yet Charleston's orphanage was a unique southern institution; no other city took such a complete interest in the welfare of poor children though the *Daily Dispatch* in Richmond thought Charleston's "judicious and enlarged philanthropy" was something "which Richmond may profitably emulate."[130] In fact, most city authorities were more than happy to cede this responsibility to private benevolent societies such as the Norfolk Female Orphan Society, the Protestant Orphan

Asylum Society of Mobile, and in Savannah the Female Asylum and the Union Society. Private benevolent societies did far more for poor children in southern cities than elected or appointed officials, though in at least some places local taxpayers contributed toward the funds of benevolent societies. Perhaps, as Barbara Bellows has suggested, Charleston's civic elite really did see themselves as proper guardians of the poor and that "those who are left heirs to the poverty and wretchedness of life should be shielded from present danger and prepared for future action."[131]

Those serving as Commissioners of the Orphan House in Charleston included some of the wealthiest and most prominent individuals in the city, and at least some of them seem to have taken their paternalist obligations to the orphans seriously. Henry Alexander DeSaussure, for instance, became a commissioner in 1827 and chaired the board from 1838 until his death in 1865. On one occasion he even gave away an orphan girl at her wedding.[132] Unlike the female benevolent societies that arranged orphan care in other cities, the Commissioners of the Charleston Orphan House were prepared to be pro-active and to remove children from parents whom they believed were "in no condition to support the child" and restrict the contact between their new charges and those "who by their vicious course of life and bad example much corrupt and lead them astray."[133] Everywhere else, those who desired public assistance were required to seek it out, either personally or by proxy: in Charleston the orphan house commissioners were evidently on the lookout for children who were neglected by alcoholic fathers or prostitute mothers. Ten-year-old Julianna Barnes, for instance, had a mother who was a prostitute and was living with a man "who treated her in so shameful a manner" that the commissioners were "obliged to interfere." Indeed, so little faith did the commissioners have in poor parents that they resigned themselves to a "continual watchfulness" over the welfare of poor white children taking upon themselves the role of the "mother's knee [and] the father's countenance."[134]

The orphan house was also intended to "distinguish us as a community" and to be an "ornament and pride of our city," since somewhere that could afford such an impressive institution with its landscaped grounds, and that cared for its needy and helpless citizens with such zeal was clearly an enlightened and cultured place. It was the "common object of our benevolence, in which all are united, and around which, as a centre, the humane sympathies of our citizens may revolve." The orphan house was one of the largest buildings in the city and visitors were clearly taken there as a matter of course. The visitor's book for January 1860 recorded the names of 146 different individuals from fifteen different states as well as Europe, Africa, and the Caribbean. If the orphan house commissioners wished their institution to be a symbol for the sophistication, liberality, and humanity of their city they evidently succeeded. Arthur Matherson from Woodstock, Connecticut, declared himself "very much pleased" with what he saw, while Sam Bridge from San Francisco though that "this institution will compare favourably with other counties which I have visited" and E. S. Williams from Massachusetts agreed: "this institution is equal to any in Massachusetts of the same kind." Edward Bradbury, from Portland, Maine, commented simply: "I wish myself an orphan."[135]

If visitors were impressed by what they saw, then orphan house commissioners also hoped that the ordinary citizens of Charleston got the same message. The orphanage, unlike the city poorhouse, was a whites-only institution. The detailed records kept by the Commissioners of the Orphan House make it clear that free black children were not objects of its charity and indeed even the suspicion of black heritage made a child inadmissible.[136] The commissioners wanted to be seen as helping and assisting the white poor, effectively giving them the privileges of race that elevated them above the thousands of slaves and free blacks that constituted such a large segment of Charleston's population. In 1848 the commissioners approved calico dresses for the girls instead of cheaper homespun, mainly because for "white persons of our cities [homespun] was unusual and peculiar." It was done, as one commissioner noted, so that the orphans would be recognized by the public "not as creatures of disgrace, but as the little ones whom it has pleased the city to bestow its protection upon."[137] The Reverend Christopher Gadsden, rector of St. Luke's Church, told the anniversary meeting of the orphan house commissioners in 1861 that "no public expense has ever been borne more cheerfully by our citizens, for they see the fruit of the outlay in such results as they are proud and happy to contemplate." This generosity arose not only because of the humane and philanthropic impulses of the city's elite but also because most understood that the institution was "necessary to our political well-being." Gadsden told the orphans to "recognize a debt to the city for her protection, which only a life of usefulness can repay,

2. Charleston Orphan House, completed 1794.

Reproduced from Edward King, *The Great South: A Record of Journeys in Louisiana, Texas, the Indian Territory, Missouri, Arkansas, Mississippi, Alabama, Georgia, Florida, South Carolina, North Carolina, Kentucky, Tennessee, Virginia, West Virginia, and Maryland* (Hartford, Conn.: American Publishing Company, 1875), 444.

and cherish in your bosoms a strong affection for the appointed guardians and teachers of your orphanage." The orphan house was therefore intended, in part, to act as a glue that bound white society together, and these bonds only became more important as the threat from abolitionism grew and possible civil war loomed. One visitor to the orphan house in 1861 observed the children singing "patriotic songs full of spirit and love for their own palmetto city" and conscious of the significance of this he commented that thus "they are taught in childhood to love their state."[138]

While Charleston's elite, with a city-supported orphan house and poorhouse, were probably more acutely aware of the relationship between public welfare and racial solidarity than those in many other locations in the antebellum South, the subtler meanings behind public welfare policies existed everywhere. The Overseers of the Poor of Rockingham County stated explicitly that publicly funded poor relief demonstrated "that a free government does not exact from its people services in time of prosperity and then cast them off upon private charity in their hour of helpless affliction." Despite rules and regulations regarding who was eligible for relief and who was not, it seems that most officials with responsibility for distributing public poor relief saw their role "humanely to provide assistance for those in want."[139] Richmond's Overseers of the Poor might have moaned about "highly coloured deceptive tales of woe" that they heard from the city's poor, but they also frequently complained to the city council that without additional funding they would be forced to turn "a deaf ear to the piteous applications for relief, day after day, made by the virtuous & really distressed applicants."[140] This humanitarian approach to poor relief can also be seen in some other cities. In Charleston, Henry Pinckney stated, "We must either aid the poor, or suffer them to perish. . . . What if charity has been sometimes misapplied, or acted as a premium to idleness and vice! These are errors or evils that may be avoided or corrected: but better that unworthy objects should deceive us, than that meritorious individuals should receive no aid."[141]

The vast majority of the funding for public poor relief came from local taxation, continuing the English principle that each community should pay for its own paupers. As the antebellum era progressed, however, this principle was weakened by state governments assuming financial responsibility for the insane, the blind, the deaf, and the dumb in centralized institutions.

Virginia's Eastern State Hospital had opened in 1773, and similar institutions were opened in Louisiana, South Carolina, and Kentucky during the 1820s and in Maryland, Georgia, and Tennessee in the 1830s.[142] State governments erected these institutions partly for simple humanitarian reasons; the superintendent of the newly opened Asylum for the Insane in Raleigh, North Carolina, reported that most of those entrusted to his care "have been tenants of poor houses, where they have been either chained to the floor of their apartments, or confined to the dark and damp room of a cellar; while the much larger portion have been kept in the cells of the county prisons." Dorothea Dix told the Alabama legislature that she had "seen thousands living in misery, wearing life slowly out in dungeons, in cells, in pens, in barns and outhouses, exposed to every variation of weather, filthy and neglected, abandoned of friends, cared for with less consideration than the oxen in the stall, or the swine in the sty; melancholy monuments of the imperfections with which society discharges its social and moral obligations." Perhaps unsurprisingly, given such an image, Alabama governor Henry Collier believed that it was the state's duty to care for insane "as objects of parental solicitude and adopt methods to make them as cheerful, rational, and happy as Providence will permit."[143]

Many southern legislatures were convinced of the curative potential of asylums. Contemporary theories about insanity often stressed the need to isolate patients from the outside world that had caused their illness. Those promoting the South Carolina Lunatic Asylum claimed that up to 90 percent of patients could be cured through isolation and proper treatment, and subsequently be returned to their families to be productive members of society. Those deemed incurable were even refused admission to the Eastern State Hospital in Williamsburg, Virginia. Dorothea Dix, who did more than anyone else to promote institutional care for the insane in the South, continually stressed that "active exercise in the open air, moderate labor in the gardens, pleasure grounds, or upon the farm, afford good results. Short excursions, resort to the work-shops, carpentering, joining, turning, the use of a good library &c. &c., are aids in advancing the cure of the patient."[144] Similarly, schools for the blind, the deaf, and the mute were not normally meant to be permanent homes but rather places where skills were imparted to enable individuals to cope with their disabilities before returning home. Those attending the Georgia Academy for the Blind, for instance, were given music tuition, "to fit them for self-maintenance; as organists, violinists, pianists, musical instructors etc." The curative nature of asylums, Dix pointed out, could ultimately save money since instead of paying to support the insane indefinitely in poorhouses, counties could look forward to receiving the taxes paid by individuals restored to health.[145]

The reformatory promise of the care offered by state institutions was only partly fulfilled. Fewer than half of those admitted to the South Carolina Lunatic Asylum were returned to their families as "cured." In Virginia the proportion was more like a third. Likewise, hopes that most patients would pay for their treatment proved unfounded. The ratio of pauper to paying patients was roughly even in South Carolina but, more typically, in Tennessee pauper patients outnumbered those who could afford to pay fees by two to one.[146] With so many paupers crowding the lunatic asylums the burdens of funding came back to the state legislatures. Robert Oliver has estimated that the Tennessee Lunatic Asylum consumed about 3 percent of the entire state budget between 1837 and 1839. Other states also spent prodigious amounts of money not only constructing their facilities but staffing and maintaining them as well. The Louisiana legislature appropriated $25,000 in 1840 to construct a dedicated building for the insane and a further $35,000 in 1854 to extend it; North Carolina's Lunatic Asylum cost the state government $22,000 to build; Georgia's Lunatic, Idiot and Epileptic Asylum cost $45,000 in building costs alone. In Alabama the state spent an enormous $280,000 between 1852 and 1861 on an insane asylum in Tuscaloosa that was unfinished when the Civil War started.[147] If these start-up costs were not enough, recurrent expenditures also ran into thousands of dollars. In the late 1850s the Georgia legislature annually appropriated $4,500 for the Academy for the Blind, $7,000 for the Asylum for the Deaf and Dumb, and $24,000 for the Lunatic Asylum.[148] Such sums were not entirely uncontroversial. The superintendent of the North Carolina Insane Asylum blithely reported in March 1861 that more than $23,000 had been drawn from the state treasury during the previous year in support of his institution. "This amount" he commented "could not be expended in a more charitable cause." This evidently caused some disquiet since two weeks later, because "a very erroneous impression prevails in the minds of many respecting the annual charge to the State of the Asylum," the superintendent had to explain that two-thirds of the state's contribution actually came from individual counties and was merely administered by the state.[149]

The institutions opened by the state were impressive buildings. Most were imposing classical structures designed by architects with domes, wings, and gardens. The Alabama Insane Asylum was designed to be more than seven hundred feet long, have two wings over four floors so that the sexes could be segregated, and even have a form of central heating.[150] Architects' plans for the South Carolina Insane Asylum show that it was equally impressive. These buildings were public expressions of the interest the state was taking in the care and health of some of its citizens. They were often the largest buildings in town, and visitors were suitably impressed by the design and scale of them. These state institutions were also remarkably alike in one other respect—they catered almost exclusively to white people. Institutions for the insane in Tennessee, Georgia, and North Carolina admitted no blacks before the Civil War, and the South Carolina Lunatic Asylum did so only after 1848. Peter McCandless has suggested that the South Carolina legislature only permitted blacks to be admitted to the lunatic asylum to demonstrate to abolitionists the humanity of their social system. In reality, few blacks were admitted to the institution before the Civil War: of more than six hundred patients during the 1850s, only thirty were black, and those who did gain admission were housed separately from the white patients in inferior accommodation.[151] Of all the southern state institutions that catered to the insane, the blind, the deaf, and the mute, it seems that only the oldest, the Eastern State Hospital in Williamsburg, Virginia, admitted significant numbers of black patients. Even here, whites formed the vast majority of the patients treated.[152]

The safety net provided by state and local authorities in the South was clearly designed to prevent the elderly, the bed-ridden, the permanently disabled, and the orphaned—those whose circumstances would have elicited the sympathies of most people—from begging for scraps of food or a slow death from neglect. Those not completely incapacitated were expected to work for themselves, and many were encouraged to do so through the continuation of out-relief even when the alternative of a stay in the poorhouse existed. Insofar as it was possible, public poor relief had a reformist agenda, since few local authorities wished to keep individuals on the relief rolls for

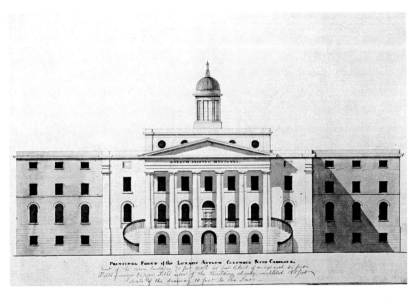

3. South Carolina Insane Asylum, opened in 1828.

Courtesy of the Library of Congress, Prints and Photographs Division, Historic American Buildings Survey, Reproduction Number HABS SC,40-COLUM, 7-10.

a day longer than necessary. It was far better to give these people the skills and assistance they needed to get themselves back on their feet as quickly as possible. Poorhouses therefore required their inmates to work and perhaps in the process learn a skill that could be used in the outside world. Those who were never going to recover their independence due to extreme age, sickness, or disability received the care and support that was appropriate to their needs. No Overseer of the Poor ever complained about the expense associated with the truly helpless.

Those who managed poor relief systems were also making a public statement about the society in which they lived. The fact that recipients were disproportionately white—and that even when nonwhites were provided with help it was of an inferior kind—sent a very clear message that poor whites were valued and respected and had a special status in this society merely because of their skin color. Elites might have looked down on the white poor as wretched, drunken, licentious, and idle, but they still proffered them more assistance than they offered free blacks. The public poor relief system in the southern states therefore existed in part to show poor whites that the state was concerned with their welfare. The fact that the wealthy were prepared to tax themselves to fund the system showed that they also were aware of the need to alleviate the most desperate cases of poverty among whites. The small numbers in receipt of public relief, however, left substantial room for organized private benevolence to complement and extend the provision made by the state. The next chapter examines the leading role that southern women took in shaping and controlling welfare policies.

2

Southern Women Assume the Charitable Role

IN SEPTEMBER 1858 the New Orleans *Bulletin* singled out the contribution that women were making during the ongoing yellow fever epidemic: "wherever there is pain to be relieved, the broken hearted to be raised up; where gaunt poverty and raging fever hold terrible carnival; where delirium and the death rattle drive men from the abode of misery, there is found woman.... Surely, these Christian ladies are doing a work that is truly God-like."[1] The *Bulletin*'s editorial merely confirms what was well known at the time—that women dominated private charitable provision in the United States during the first half of the nineteenth century. Women in the southern states, like their counterparts in New York, Massachusetts, and Pennsylvania, were the first to establish charitable societies, the first to reach out to try to help widows, orphans, and other needy individuals, and the first to provide free education. Women in Montgomery, Tuscaloosa, Nashville, Augusta, Columbia, Fayetteville, Raleigh, Wilmington, Norfolk, and Petersburg formed the first charitable societies of any kind in their communities, while those in Natchez, Mobile, Lexington, and Baltimore were the first to permit those other than society members and their families to be recipients of aid. In 1850, major cities such as Norfolk, Richmond, Savannah, and Columbia had more female benevolent societies than male ones, and if mutual-aid societies are excluded, then New Orleans and Charleston can be added to that list. Clearly southern women thought that charitable activity was something they should be involved in, and they were prepared to invest time, effort, and substantial amounts of their own money to ensure the success of their benevolent projects.

Why did American women take the lead in charitable provision in the early nineteenth century? As the introduction to this volume has outlined, prior to the American Revolution, and even for many years afterward, charity was generally seen as a government business. Private benevolent societies in the South were few in number and were concentrated mainly in Charleston. As far as records are able to tell us, women were completely absent as providers, rather than as recipients, of welfare before the 1790s. The sudden involvement of American women in benevolence in the last years of the eighteenth century arose from popular early-national ideals of women's natural role in society. Women's lives were usually centered around the home, caring for others, providing children especially with the nurturing environment vital for their future maturity. Historians of southern women such as Suzanne Lebsock, Harriet Amos, and Gail S. Murray have persuasively argued that care for nonfamily members in the form of charitable work gradually came to be perceived as a logical extension of the preexisting female role in society. As one minister put it, charitable societies were almost "designed to offer a legitimate field for labor for ladies, who being sufficiently disengaged from the more urgent claims of natural and social duty, and desirous of finding the most satisfactory employment for the time and talents which God has given them, may, without regard to worldly motives, and without the dangerous entanglement of vows or irrevocable engagements be inclined to devote themselves to a work of Christian love."[2]

The willingness of women to take on a more public role in society was not entirely uncontroversial. The managers of the Female Benevolent Society of St. Louis, for example, were "aware that objections are entertained by some, to those female associations, which bring them before the public on the ground, that they draw them from the retired sphere of domestic duty which Providence has assigned them." But it is noteworthy that criticisms of female benevolence were rarely aired in public, and far more common were editorials such as this in the *Missouri Republican*:

> As regards the propriety of females engaging in such undertakings, we would ask whether there is any thing more lovely and attractive in the female character, than the kind and humane sentiment which finds scope in these societies? It belongs to man to battle in the world to carry on its affairs and to harden his heart by familiarity with misery and sorrow in

all their shapes and grades; but it is the part of women to be kind and sympathetic and to heal the sufferings which the sterner sex inflict or pass by in silence. We assert moreover that females are better qualified to disburse charities of the kind intended by these societies than the other sex. They have more leisure, they take more interest in a tale of distress, and from this very sympathy, can more easily draw forth from honest indigence a statement of its necessities.

One correspondent of the *Savannah Morning News* declared himself "proud" of the achievements of city's charitable women, and he was acerbic in attacking "the preposterous idea that these ladies overstep the bounds of modesty, or neglect their domestic obligations in consequence of these engagements." To his mind "that man is not worth the respect and affection of his wife, who is afraid of her appropriating any portion of his wardrobe." Ultimately occasional criticisms of female charitable work were rebuffed by benevolent women who determined that they "must not be allowed to shrink from acknowledged duty, simply, because that duty is to be performed in public."[3] In this sense, therefore, southern women were entirely at one with their sisters further north who conceived of their own charitable endeavors in precisely the same manner.[4]

That southern benevolent women clearly conceived of their activities in terms of what might best be described as "virtuous Republican Motherhood" is demonstrated by petitions such as that from the directresses of the Fredericksburg Charity School to the Virginia legislature in 1803. The directresses stressed the importance of helping young girls because in the future they would be "mothers of free men, from whom the infant mind receives its first and most lasting impressions." In a similar vein the managers of the Poydras Aslyum in New Orleans described their work as spreading "motherly wings over hundreds of little unfortunates" while their counterparts in Baltimore expressed their wish to act as "mothers of numbers of such helpless beings."[5] Some charitable women adopted their active benevolent role because they simply believed that they could do it better than anyone else. The Female Charitable Association of Charleston Neck noted that "when to the evils and privations of poverty are added those of disease, the cup of human misery is full. To alleviate these complicated distresses, is the peculiar duty of females, as females alone understand and can enter into the minute details necessary to be attended to."[6]

The maternal instinct of benevolent southern women was also allied to an awareness of civic republicanism, whereby unproductive individuals who were a drain on the community would be turned into useful and productive citizens. Indeed for the founders of the Baltimore Female Humane Association "to remedy the evil in its source, to snatch the child from a fate similar to that of its mother, was considered by the ladies an important public work; for the success of any scheme to ameliorate the condition of such objects, would not only lessen the demand of the public for annual contributions, but it would actually increase the number of those whose labor would be more useful to the community." The idea that without aid the poor would only "remain in ignorance and advance in vice" whereas carefully targeted assistance should "render them useful members of society" was widely accepted by benevolent women throughout the South.[7] The managers of the Poydras Female Asylum in New Orleans told their charges that they "have your true interest and best welfare very much at heart . . . [we] can have no happiness purer than of seeing you . . . good and useful." The directresses of the Raleigh Female Benevolent Society boasted proudly that their children had been given "knowledge which may rescue them from poverty" while counterparts in Mobile cited Proverbs 22:6 "Train up a child in the way he should go, and when he is old he will not depart from it." Benevolent women to a significant extent, therefore, understood their work to have a wider social purpose than the immediate relief of want. The board of the Richmond Female Humane Association was not alone in asking, "Who can calculate the advantages to society of saving one poor child from guilt and infamy, and sending her forth to the world in purity and innocence, strong in virtuous principles, and rich in useful knowledge?"[8]

One should not underestimate, however, the purely humanitarian motivation of many benevolent women. Some simply declared that their main goal was the "promotion of human felicity" while others sought "to put into the hands of poor women the means of supporting their families" or mentioned the "relief and comfort of distressed females" and others who might "suffer under the anguish of disease and penury." The managers of the Ladies Fuel Society in Charleston were well "aware of the extreme suffering to which the poor are in many cases liable from the want of fuel, when the price of it becomes suddenly enhanced by the severity of the weather"; they believed the mere thought of the everyday suffering of the indigent "should awaken sympathy in behalf of those who are destitute" and that there was no excuse for "indifference to the calamities of those around us."[9] The humanitarian approach was reflected in the buildings constructed as female orphan asylums. Instead of the overwhelming immensity of the Charleston Orphan House, benevolent women invariably opted for a homely structure more in keeping with their aim to be replacement families for orphan children. Savannah's Female Asylum was "a three-story house, with a pretty white aspect" with the kitchen, dining room, washroom, on the first floor; school rooms, parlor, and matron's room on the second floor; and bedrooms on the top floor.[10] The homes managed by female benevolent societies in Mobile and Savannah could easily have been mistaken for the homes of wealthy citizens.

Much of this broadly humanitarian approach to the poor was molded by Christianity. Most benevolent women took seriously the biblical instruction to care for the sick and "to visit the fatherless and widows in their affliction" (James 1:27); indeed, the founders of the Richmond Dorcas Society confessed that they were "feeling deeply anxious for the interests of religion and humanity."[11] Though general religious zeal was undoubtedly crucial in the formation of female benevolent societies, it is remarkable that nearly all adopted an ecumenical approach that drew members and directresses from a variety of Christian denominations. During the 1820s the Savannah Female Asylum drew most support from the two largest and wealthiest congregations in the city—Christchurch Episcopal and the Independent Presbyterian Church—but also had a sizable contingent of members from the First Baptist Church. In Beaufort, South Carolina, membership of the Female Benevolent Society was drawn fairly equally from the only two churches in the town: St. Helena's Episcopal and the Baptist Church. The Society for the Relief of the Indigent Sick in Baltimore expressed pride that "its members embraced women who were the professed followers of Christ from every branch of his church" while the Columbia Female Orphan Society even wrote ecumenism into its constitution: "There shall be no distinction of religious denominations either in the members of the society, or in the objects whose relief it may contemplate & it is ardently hoped that it

4. Mobile Protestant Orphan Asylum, opened in 1839.
Reproduced by permission of the Historic Mobile Preservation Society Collection.

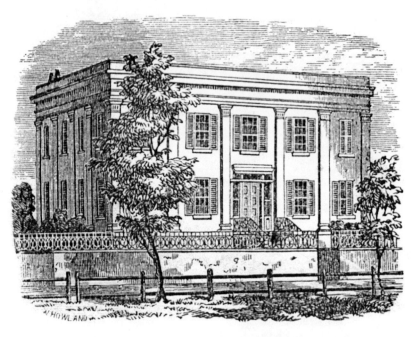

5. Savannah Female Asylum, completed in 1810.

Reproduced from George White, *Historical Collections of Georgia* (New York: Pudney and Russel, 1854), 303.

will become the instrument of cementing Christian fellowship among different denominations."[12] This ecumenical approach to benevolence in the South focused charitable women into just a few organizations and allowed a concentration of resources that permitted female charitable societies to function effectively. By contrast, benevolent women in New York and Boston were more likely than their southern counterparts to belong to faith-based charitable societies and, in many instances, they competed with each other to help widows, orphans, and the sick.[13]

Southern women clearly had a variety of motives for engaging in charitable work. The conjuncture of humanitarianism, religious idealism, maternal instinct, and civic republicanism proved a very fertile ground for the emergence of female benevolent societies. The first of these societies formed in the United States were the Female Society for Assisting the Distressed, established in Philadelphia in 1795, and the Society for the Relief of Poor Widows founded in New York in 1797.[14] In 1798 the ladies of Baltimore, "taking into their consideration the poverty, and consequent sufferings of indigent women, during the inclement season of winter, resolved to form a systematic plan for affording them relief" and formed a Female Humane Association. It is possible that the directresses of the Baltimore Female Humane Association had read newspaper reports of the activities of the societies in Philadelphia and New York and followed their example, but if they did, they failed to acknowledge the link in their written records.[15] However, there certainly was a direct connection between female charities in Baltimore, Boston, and Savannah. In December 1799 a correspondent writing under the pseudonym of "A Mother" urged the female readers of the *Boston Gazette* to imitate "the ladies of Baltimore [and] form an association for the purposes of charity to females."[16] The resulting formal organization of the Boston Female Asylum in September 1800 was noticed in Savannah where Henry Holcombe, pastor of the city's First Baptist Church, presented the idea for a Female Asylum to a group of ladies after "reading an account of a society formed in Boston for the benefit of such children."[17]

At least some east coast urban women were evidently aware of the growth of female benevolence in other cities, and their emulating these charitable initiatives suggests that northern and southern women may well have shared common charitable motivations in the early republic. Certainly many southern women who formed female benevolent societies believed that the state assistance offered to poor children, and in particular to young girls, was inadequate. The ladies who formed the Female Humane Association in Baltimore were especially concerned about "the abandoned state of the rising generation, particularly the female part thereof, many of whom were literally raised in the streets in filthiness, rags and vice."[18] Many other benevolent women were motivated to form charitable societies because of what they perceived as flaws and failings in the existing arrangements for helping the poor and less fortunate. The directress of the Savannah Female Asylum pointed out that "it is a matter of certainty, that notwithstanding the attention paid to the poor in this city, many female orphans suffer for want of early patronage." Redressing a perceived imbalance in the assistance offered by the state to orphan children became one of their main aims: "while we characteristically feel for the distressed of all descriptions, we are most deeply penetrated with the sufferings of our own sex." The same society later argued that "a boy can make his way through this cold world well enough; but the situation of a young orphan girl is one which has the strongest demand upon the best sympathies that belong to our nature."[19] The founders of the Beaufort Female Benevolent Society were even more explicit in their criticism of the system:

> It is a fact abundantly evident that notwithstanding the provisions made by the law for the relief of the poor, there are in many places numbers whose situation cannot be essentially ameliorated by the operation of the poor laws. Those young females who have been left under circumstances of suffering and destitution and to whom the means of virtuous education are not going to be extended are objects which should excite the vigilance and industry of the pious and benevolent. Their necessities finding no relief in any existing system of alleviation seem to make it an irresistible appeal to the generous munificence of their own sex.[20]

Clearly some elite women in the South took it upon themselves to ensure that poor white girls received an appropriate level of assistance in societies where female child poverty had previously been overlooked.

Women who established charitable societies aiming to rescue young girls from poverty were, in effect, combining social reform with welfare policy. Those taken from homes and families where violence, drunkenness, and prostitution were common were "rescued" from a destiny, which the ladies believed, would only lead to ignorance, "that prolific parent of evil," and vices "which they would have propagated." Indeed benevolent women often talked of "saving" and "rescuing" the poor, especially orphan children, who otherwise "like a stray waif, cast adrift life's doubtful current will perchance be lost amid its quicksands." What benevolent woman would not have desired to see children "separated from that atmosphere of moral pestilence, amidst the contaminating and baleful influences of which, such victims of early misfortunes are not unfrequently reared from the very cradle"?[21] Instead of a future that was bleak, girls were "to be employed in such useful occupations, as may enable them; in due time, to procure for themselves a maintenance."[22]

Although societies concerned with small children were perhaps the commonest of all the female charities formed in the antebellum South, they were not the only type. The sheer scale and variety of organized female benevolence in the South is remarkable. While there might not have been the number of benevolent societies in Charleston, Richmond, New Orleans, and Savannah that there were in Boston, New York, and Philadelphia, this can partly be explained by the relative sizes of the urban populations in the North and the South. The population of Charleston was just a tenth of that of New York in 1840, but the women of Charleston supported more than ten female benevolent societies in that year, compared to forty-six in New York. Anne Boylan has argued that the extent of female benevolence in the South was "much narrower" than in the North, but with the obvious exception of female abolitionist organizations, every type of charitable organization found in the antebellum North can be found in the antebellum South as well. Free school societies, often associated with, or even part of, female orphan asylums, were formed in most major cities, and the schools they opened were specifically directed at the children of the poor. Widow's societies, Dorcas societies, clothing and fuel societies, and female employment societies all sought to plug gaps in the antebellum state welfare system in the same way that they did in northern states.

Although orphan asylums were the preferred solution to child poverty in most antebellum southern communities, a few societies supported families with children in their own homes, mainly with clothing, food, and fuel. The Dorcas Benevolent Society in Baltimore supported three such families in 1842. In one, the husband "has recently broken a leg, disabling him from work"; the second was composed of five siblings "entirely destitute of food and fire. The children without shoes and stockings. Their mother was recently killed by their father in a fit of derangement." In the third, the "husband can get no employment" and there was a child who "has had three fingers casually taken off by a machine at which he was working."[23] The Fragment Society and the Ladies Fuel Society in Charleston, the Clothing and Fuel Society in Savannah, and the Female Benevolent Societies in Mobile and Tuscaloosa, all operated in a similar manner, expending between a few hundred and a couple of thousand dollars per year on supplies for the poor, but only after the ladies had been able to "investigate the claims of each applicant for relief" and used the occasion "to exhort the indolent to become industrious and the vicious to reform."[24] However, conscious of the shame that often accompanied "a public expose of their wants" and knowing that some individuals "would perhaps sink into the grave, unknown and unrelieved, rather than apply to a charitable society," these societies often worked "unostentatiously." The numbers of people assisted by them was comparatively small—one hundred people in Savannah in 1817, eighty-eight families in Charleston in 1833, and thirty-five families in Tuscaloosa in 1861—but it is likely that the support offered enabled some individuals to avoid institutionalization and some families to remain together as a unit.[25]

The female benevolent impulse even spread to girls from wealthy families who organized themselves into societies to help the poor. The Juvenile Female Benevolent Society of Columbia, for instance, was formed in 1818 by thirty-two girls between five and eighteen years of age who desired "to aid destitute children, in their clothing and education." In their annual report the girls reflected

with pleasure not only being instrumental under God of assisting our distressed fellow creatures, but also, on the benefit which we have experienced. We have been made acquainted with the manner of doing business. We have had our understanding instructed and our hearts softened. For while our hands have been employed in preparing garments for our beneficiaries, we have listed with pleasure to some interesting work which one of our number has read to us, and which has not unfrequently brought the silent tear from our eyes.... We believe, therefore, that while we attempted to benefit others, we ourselves were benefited. While we attempted to water and instruct others, we ourselves were watered and instructed.[26]

Other juvenile societies acted as auxiliaries to established organizations. The Juvenile Industry Society in Charleston made regular donations of baby linen to the Ladies Benevolent Society for distribution among poor families. The directresses of the Ladies Benevolent Society considered their young helpers to be

> like tender branches putting forth buds—which will blossom & bear fruit in due season. We doubt not it would be very gratifying to them, could they be carried sometimes to visit the smiling infants dressed in suits of their own making and giving. Would they not, when beholding the little innocents so inhabited, consider them in some measure their own—under their cares—and would not such a pleasing sight be calculated to give a zest to their employment—make them take an interest in it—and cause them to grow up in the charitable & industrious habits of a DORCAS?[27]

In such manner benevolence could be diffused among the generations and new supporters of charitable works lined up to continue work already begun.

Female-managed institutions for children existed in every major southern city, with the exception of Charleston where the city orphanage monopolized the care of indigent children, but equally common were organizations that dealt solely with elderly and sick women who could not support themselves. The Charleston Ladies Benevolent Society, formed in 1813, was effectively a pension agency for poor women in the city. In addition to providing small items of food, clothing, and fuel to needy families, it also supported eight pensioners, individuals whose circumstances were so desperate that they were totally reliant on others. Typical of the pensioners supported by the society was Mrs. Cowie:

> Mrs Cowie is an old woman, she has the leprosy. And so long, and so greatly has she suffered under it, that her hands are drawn up and deformed. Her eyes are in a high state of inflammation, and her body a perfect skeleton. She is very aged, poor, diseased, and nearly blind! She owns a superannuated negro woman, a cow, some poultry, and perhaps a little church money, but these things are insufficient to supply her necessary wants: the old negro is an expense and incumbrance. She is indeed a piti-

able object, calling forth the compassion of every beholder. In her days of youth, health, and strength, she supported herself and two children by the labour of her own hands; She did more, she educated them. They do nothing for her, having young families to support but recommend her to the continuance of your charity and to the kind care of the visiting committee, our hearts bled when we beheld her.

Other pensioners on the bounty of the Ladies Benevolent Society included Mrs. Birdie "a respectable old lady" who had formerly been a schoolmistress but who was now bed-bound. In addition to the help she received from the Ladies Benevolent Society, Mrs. Bridie was supported by her church, some of her former pupils, and the money she received from hiring out a slave boy. Another pensioner, Mrs. McIntyre, owned an "insignificant little shop which can bring her in but a mere trifle." The Ladies Benevolent Society gave her 50¢ per week even though she was also receiving rations from the poorhouse commissioners for herself and her children.[28] But while the ladies of Charleston operated an out-relief system to support elderly women in their own homes, benevolent women in many other cities preferred to offer a residential solution to elderly poor women. The directresses of the Baltimore Church Home argued that such a home might help to decrease the need for dependent carers: "place the sick or afflicted in the Church Home, and the other members [of the family] then have no excuse for not exerting themselves to get a livelihood."[29] The assistance offered by organized benevolent societies to elderly women was not generally extended to old men. All 178 recipients of fuel from the Ladies Fuel Society in Charleston in 1835, for instance, were female. This suggests that whatever the status differences between charitable women and poor women, to some extent the former felt a gendered obligation to offer help "if a sister be naked and destitute of daily food," and especially to assist widows "left to the world's cold charities."[30] Elderly men, with little or no recourse to private charity, were forced to apply to the Commissioners of the Poor for assistance.

For females who did not easily fit into the categories of innocent child or old maid, yet who still struggled to make ends meet, assistance was available in the form of a small number of female employment societies. Part of the mission of the Raleigh Female Benevolent Society was "to provide employment to such females as are able and willing to work, and who cannot meet with employers," while the aim of the New Orleans Ladies Benevolent Society was "to put into the hands of poor women the means of supporting their families" since it was accepted that "to woman, in whatever situation in life she may be placed, a proper use of the needle is invaluable."[31] Societies such as the Union Benevolent Society in Richmond; the Female Society of Industry in Fayetteville; the Society for the Encouragement of Industry and the Sisters of Charity, both in Charleston; the Needle Woman's Friend Society in Savannah; and the Protestant Episcopal Church Employment Society in Mobile were engaged across the South in trying to provide work for women who wanted it. Each of these societies recognized the particular needs of adult women who found it hard to go out to find work. Those with small children had, of necessity, to work from home, and many had been deprived of or deserted by their menfolk and left to support a family unaided. Most female employment societies recognized the insufficiency of the wages these women earned to meet the needs of a family and thus their "exertions may not be adequate to provide the positive necessaries of life." The Union Benevolent Society in Richmond lamented that poor women would "work hard all day and part of the night for 12½ cents, or even for less," yet rent alone could easily absorb all their wages; "for a miserable garret, or wet cellar, many a poor widow has to pay $2 per month." The Ladies Benevolent Society in New Orleans concurred: "the stinted pittance, granted as the reward of woman's labor, is soon exhausted by the unceasing demand for food and shelter."[32]

Charitable women who managed employment societies were therefore trying to ease the travails of poorer white women by giving them that small degree of help that might make the difference between independence and hunger. Since "for the want of proper encouragement many an indigent female is driven to vice and ruin, who might have been saved by a little benevolent exertion of the more favoured of their sex," managers of successful societies took comfort that "many aged and indigent females receive great assistance from this institution, and widows and orphans eke out their scanty subsistence from work which they obtain here." Most female employment societies accepted that "self-support is far nobler than dependence" and operated by obtaining raw materials at cost, giving the cloth to the seamstresses to make into clothing and then retailing the products at a special store opened for the purpose.[33] In theory this system provided seamstresses with steady work, and those who wished to patronize needy working women knew precisely where to come. However, patrons in many cities where female employment societies operated complained about the poor quality of work being completed. The managers of the New Orleans Ladies Benevolent Society acknowledged the work as not of a particularly high standard—"we are often ourselves disappointed and annoyed by the want of proper care and attention"—while the board of the Needle Woman's Friend Society in Savannah was forced to appeal to "the patience, forbearance and liberality" of the citizenry because "the class who are most in need of our aid are women generally unable to do other than coarse and plain work, [and are] often careless in executing even that."[34] It is hardly surprising, therefore, that female employment societies often struggled to keep going. By 1858 the number of subscribers to the Needle Woman's Friend Society was less than half the number it had been at the start of the decade and despite emotive pleas in the city press regarding the "industrious needlewomen who daily call [for work]" it languished with debts of more than $100.[35]

In essence, therefore, the charitable societies formed by the South's benevolent women before 1830 differed little from those formed by northern women. Concerns about the unfulfilled potential of poor young girls, the penury of elderly widows, and the untapped earning power of women of working age spanned the sectional divide. Southern women were just as keen as northern women to provide the republic with worthy, virtuous citizens who would do their bit to continue to advance American prosperity. As English traveler James Silk Buckingham commented, southern women "are not behind their countrywomen in the North, in the zeal with which they promote benevolent objects."[36] Only after 1830, as some benevolent women in the North became involved with abolitionism and women's rights, can a marked distinction in the work of charitable women in each section be discerned.

To carry their charitable designs into effect benevolent women knew that they needed to be properly and formally organized with a constitution, rules, duly elected officers, and quite often a charter of incorporation. The earliest extant constitution of a southern female benevolent society is the one for the Savannah Female Asylum that appeared in the *Georgia Analytical Repository* in 1802 but which in reality was an almost verbatim copy of the rules of the Boston Female Asylum that had been printed the previous year.[37] Charitable society constitutions normally set out the aims and objectives of the society (which sometimes proved useful as it allowed societies to refuse help to those whose circumstances did not qualify), the procedures by which managers or directresses were to be chosen from among the subscribers, the level of annual subscriptions, the duties of the officeholders of the society, the rules governing the disbursement of the society's funds, and guidelines for altering the constitutions in the future. Moreover, those societies that managed institutions such as asylums or widows' homes usually had additional rules governing the admission and dismissal of beneficiaries, the standard of conduct expected of employees and inmates, and the way time was to be spent in the institution. While there might be several hundred subscribing members of a charitable society, there were usually no more than about fifteen managers, including the officeholders, and in reality the first and second directresses, the secretary, and the treasurer did most of the work.

Societies held monthly or quarterly meetings of the board of directresses to approve policies, expenditures, appointments, and admissions/dismissals, though often they were approving decisions that had already been taken by the first or second directress—for example, a decision to admit a needy child. Clearly the first and second directress were the first port of call for those seeking aid, and they had significant powers. For example, the rules of the Columbia Female Orphan Society stated that "no child shall be taken onto the society without a meeting of the board of managers have been first convened to decide upon the propriety of its being done. Should however, a case of great necessity require it & a quorum of the managers cannot be obtained, the 1st and 2nd directress with any two of the managers may have the power of deciding."[38] The secretary's main job was to keep an accurate and up-to-date record of meetings, write letters on behalf of the board, and place advertisements and articles in the newspapers. The treasurer kept the accounts of the society, paid bills as they became due, and generally attempted to ensure that the society remained solvent. Each year the society held an annual meeting "for those who have contributed means to the furtherance of their institution" at which new board members were elected and the first directress presented both an annual report of the society's activities and a summary of the annual accounts. In this manner the board remained accountable to the subscribing members, shareholders in a sense, for how money was spent and for the direction that welfare policy had taken. The annual report and accounts of charitable societies were often published in local newspapers, or published separately in pamphlet form, thus ensuring that they reached the widest possible audience. As Anne Boylan has noted with regard to New York and Boston, these publications constituted the "public face" of the female benevolence, and it is possible that some reached other cities and were the catalyst for the formation of imitative charitable societies in new locations. [39]

In addition to a written constitution and annual meetings, many female benevolent societies were incorporated by state legislatures. Some sought incorporation almost as soon as the society was formed: both the Beaufort Female Benevolent Society and the Society for Orphan and Destitute Female Children in Columbia were incorporated within eighteen months of being formed. Others took their time: the Widow's Society in Savannah was formed in 1822 but incorporated only in 1837; the Norfolk Female Orphan Society was formed in 1804 but incorporated in 1816. Whether they took immediate action for incorporation or whether they only got around to it in due course, most eventually sought incorporated status because it offered them a particular legal status that enabled benevolent women to escape the restrictions of coverture. Women in the antebellum South usually held no legal status of their own, they were *femmes covert*, meaning that their husbands, fathers, and other male relatives acted on their behalf in legal matters. They had no ability to form legal contracts or to sue or be sued in court. If female-led societies were to operate successfully, this situation had to be addressed. The Richmond Female Humane Association explicitly noted that it was their "incapacity to hold property" that persuaded them to seek incorporation by the state in 1810.[40] Incorporation meant that the women who managed the charitable society could now "sue and be sued, plead and be impleaded . . . in all courts and places whatsoever"—but only in their public capacity; their legal anonymity continued for their private lives. As officers of incorporated bodies, the directresses of female benevolent societies were able to enter into proper legal contracts with workmen, suppliers, and employees, thus safeguarding the work and finances of the society. However, incorporation also acted to protect those who supplied goods and services to the society, since they could sue for the recovery of debts in the usual way. State legislatures normally made it absolutely clear that the husbands of directresses "shall not be liable . . . for any loss occasioned by the neglect or malfeasance of his wife."[41]

In Baltimore the situation was slightly different. The Female Humane Association was established in 1798 under the control of female trustees, but when the Maryland legislature incorporated the association's school in 1801 it stipulated that the society should be overseen by nine male trustees while nine female directors could manage the day-to-day running of the school.[42] When the Female Humane Association's Charity School was reincorporated in 1808 as the Orphaline Charity School the supervising male trustees remained, and indeed this model was followed for the incorporations of the Benevolent Society of the City and County of Baltimore in 1800, the Humane Impartial Society in 1811 and the Frederickstown Orphan House in the 1830s.[43] Most states did not seem to have a problem with incorporating female societies to be run by the women themselves, but Maryland evidently adhered to the tradition of female coverture. Maryland legislators apparently felt that it was preferable to appoint nine men who had accepted financial responsibility rather than having married it in the event the society became indebted to contractors or employees.

Incorporation was not something that just happened. It had to be sought, and seeking it involved presenting petitions to local representatives who had been elected to the state legislatures, and sometimes petitions to the legislature itself. The letters these women wrote are some of the earliest examples we have of women entering publicly into the traditionally male world of government and politics. While petitions were naturally couched in terms that were respectful, they also pointed out the failings of existing welfare systems and proposed means to remedy them. The managers of the Protestant Orphan Asylum Society in Mobile set out what they conceived of as the proper duty of the Alabama legislature:

> The petition of the undersigned Ladies of the City of Mobile respectfully represents to your Honorable bodies that they have seen with heart-felt satisfaction the affecting notice which the executive of the state has taken of the suffering condition of the people of this city in his annual message. They have been impressed with sentiments of grateful emotion, at the early attention that has been bestowed upon this subject, and

they can conceive of no duty that is more strongly recommended to the consideration of the sovereign power, than the exercise of that power in mitigation of the distress of a suffering community. And your petitioners cannot but believe that the legislature of a state can never be more nobly employed, nor more adequately fulfil the design of its institution than in extending its aid in relief of general and almost unparalleled calamity. . . . The ladies then of the "Protestant Orphan Asylum Society" would most respectfully ask that their appeal on behalf of destitute children should be indulgently considered. As guardians of public morals, as legislators for posterity, they would ask your assistance in their attempt to rescue these unfortunate beings not from want and bodily suffering only—but from that contamination which the heart and mind must encounter under the combined influences of necessity and neglect. The survivors among these children will constitute in time citizens of the state, clothed with important powers and bound to the performance of important duties—can they learn from want and misery to exercise the one, or perform the other? Sound policy not less than the charities of our religion demand that their condition should be considered.[44]

Benevolent women were therefore willing, and able, to express their views about welfare in ways they simply did not use regarding other aspects of public policy. Legislators evidently tolerated this interference since acts granting incorporated status to female benevolent societies were regularly passed. The female managers of the Protestant Orphan Asylum Society in Mobile reminded the Alabama legislature that benevolence, especially for children, was properly the preserve of women:

Many children of various ages were deprived of their parents, and in many cases perished all the resources of their helpless families. It is here that the appropriate sphere of female influence commences. It is here, that the sympathies of the more fortunate wives and mothers of our city should expend themselves. It is here, that the peculiar duty of their sex bids them extend the hand of protection and may the Heavenly Father of the orphan, who has made the heart of woman to thrill at the sight of infant suffering, grant them his gracious assistance in the undertaking.[45]

One historian goes so far as to describe the relationship between southern legislatures and female benevolent societies as a "partnership" whereby both worked together to relieve distress.[46] Certainly the relationship was mutually beneficial since benevolent women were able to operate beyond the normal limits of the female role in southern society, while simultaneously a social problem was being addressed systematically for the first time. Indeed, legislatures were apparently very happy for women to take the lead in providing for the poor since it obviated the need for a state-funded system of welfare and poor relief that reached beyond the "safety net" described in Chapter 1. Whether this relationship can rightly be described as a "partnership" is another matter, since the records of female benevolent societies show that *the women* actually did the work of getting involved in the lives of the poor while the involvement of legislatures often went no further than a charter of incorporation.

The process of incorporation was generally straightforward, but female petitioners were conscious that sometimes their petitions would be controversial. The directresses of the Savannah Free School Society were evidently concerned that some legislators might object to boys being sent to a school managed by women and therefore they wrote to Colonel Cuthbert, state senator for Chatham County, explaining that

> the object of the institution is to extend the benefits of education to poor children of both sexes, but if any insuperable objection can be urged against this plan, they will be willing to relinquish the boys under their care to any institution of a similar kind that be organised at a future period. To discard them at present when they cannot be received elsewhere would manifest a degree of unkindness and neglect that could not be expected from the board. It is well known we presume to yourself and the other gentlemen who represent this county in the legislature that the Union Society is the only association in this place for the education of indigent or orphan boys exclusively and from the low state of their funds we are informed but a limited number are now under their patronage. Under these circumstances it is hoped by the board that the petition they have sent to the legislature will receive its sanction.[47]

The school's charter of incorporation ultimately did contain a clause that boys at the free school would be given up to a male free school if one should ever be founded in Savannah.[48]

Although incorporations were necessary to enable female benevolent societies to function effectively, they were far from being sufficient in themselves to ensure success. Other tiers of government had to be approached and engaged in the work of benevolence for lasting change and reform of the poor to be achieved. Benevolent women approached city and town councils for grants of land and/or buildings so that orphan asylums and widows' homes could open and be of use to the community. The Savannah Free School Society obtained a prime free lot from the city council on Whitaker and Perry Streets to build their school. It surely did not hinder their cause that among the aldermen sitting in judgment of their petition were five subscribers to the school and two others whose wives subscribed. The first directress, Mary Taylor, wrote a suitably gushing thank you note to the council, claiming that "this act of beneficence is truly gratifying as it gives them the assurance of the patronage of this honourable body and encourages them to hope that their feeble exertions for the indigent will be crowned with success."[49] The efforts of the Free School Society were, in reality, anything but "feeble," but by adopting the position of humble recipient of largesse, Mary Taylor had at least left open the option of more support from the council in the future and had maintained her correct, submissive, female role. The Female Orphan Society in Columbia was less successful in obtaining a free lot from the city council, whose members stated that "their term of office would so soon end that they did not feel justified" in granting the petition; instead they donated $200 toward the eventual $500 cost of a city lot.[50]

For their benevolent aims to be met, female charitable societies required funds. Benevolent women knew this, of course, with one society describing proper funding as an "important and indispensable prerequisite," and the increasingly ingenious lengths to which some societies went to raise funds is evidence of the seriousness with which they regarded their charitable work.[51] Most societies required an annual subscription fee between $1 and $5 from members in return for voting rights at the annual meeting. Subscriptions were vital for pump-priming benevolent ventures, and many female charitable societies were able to attract 200–300 subscribers in their early years. Nathan Fiske's 1824 observation that the Savannah Female Asylum was "one of the most popular charities in Savannah" was entirely justified since its subscribing membership was twice the size of any other benevolent institution in the city. A regular income permitted boards "to form a tolerably correct idea of the extent, to which they might carry their benevolent aims."[52] Almost without exception, female benevolent societies drew their members from the wealthiest families in the immediate locality, and the money donated and subscribed by female members and their husbands was substantial. In fact, one significant difference between benevolent women in the South and their counterparts in the northern states emerges when one examines family backgrounds in depth. Unlike benevolent women in the North where the upper-middle classes took the initiative in providing assistance for the poor; in the South it was women at the very pinnacle of the social scale. The benevolent women of the South were typically in their forties, married, usually with their own children, and had the means to support more than one charitable organization at the same time.[53] The husbands of these women were commonly merchants (especially in port cities that exported cotton), lawyers (sometimes judges), planters, and clerics of every Protestant denomination. Less frequently, charitable women were married to bank presidents (three in Savannah alone), college principals and professors (especially in Columbia, home to South Carolina College), mayors and city councilmen, and other prominent public figures such as the attorney general of Virginia, the president of the Georgia Railroad Company, and the president of the Board of Merchants in Mobile.

Coupled with social prominence was substantial family wealth: Judge George Goldthwaite, whose wife was a directress of the Montgomery Female Orphan Asylum, owned $20,000 of city property in 1853, as well as thirteen slaves; South Carolina planter John Singleton, whose wife subscribed to the Columbia Female Orphan Society, owned property worth $80,000 and 123 slaves in 1850; ten years later the husband of one directress of the Beaufort Female Benevolent Society owned property valued at $320,000 including 316 slaves. Furthermore, some benevolent women controlled their own finances. Widow Keziah Brevard, member of the Columbia Female Orphan Society, had a personal fortune valued at $26,000 and she directed the labor of more than 200 slaves on her plantation outside the city. Miss Isabella Barron never married, but the thirteen slaves she owned brought her a steady income and gave her the leisure time to devote to Savannah's Female Asylum. Whether their money was their own or their husband's, the sheer wealth to which southern benevolent women had access stands in significant contrast to the assets available to benevolent women in the North. In both Columbia and Beaufort, South Carolina, the families of benevolent women owned, on average, more than twice as much wealth as other property holders and up to eight times the average wealth of a typical head of household. Similar figures were calculated by John W. Quist for the members of the Tuscaloosa Female Benevolent Society.[54]

Benevolent women in the South were therefore well entrenched as part of the social, economic, and political elite. They were almost without exception very wealthy and their husbands, brothers, fathers, and sons occupied positions of influence and power. Moreover, these women were not content merely to dip into their own pockets to fund their charitable societies. Of eighty-one people donating funds for the new Savannah Free School in 1816, the twenty-eight men with wives in the society provided half the money, with more than 10 percent of the total coming from just three men who happened to be married to directresses.[55] The managers of the Protestant Orphan Asylum Society in Mobile were up front right at the start about the need for members to "use their influence in collecting funds."[56]

Despite the individual wealth of members of female benevolent societies in the South, most organizations found that the number of subscribers could not be sustained over time. The Female Orphan Society of Columbia, for instance, took in $703 from subscribers in the first year of its operations in 1839, but by 1852 was receiving only $152. Similarly, the Savannah Free School Society had started in 1816 with more than three hundred subscribers but by 1847 had only twenty-seven.[57] In 1860 the Ladies Fuel Society in Charleston felt "constrained to solicit from the citizens generally a more systematic and sustained effort [and] . . . especially for annual subscriptions. It is to be regretted that in a society embracing all classes and denominations of the community, having in view an object in which every benevolent person can heartily unite, and where only the small sum of two dollars annually is required, there should be found not over four hundred subscribers."[58] One exception to this model was the Beaufort Female Benevolent Society that still had sixty-three paying subscribers in 1860. The healthy state of subscriptions in Beaufort was probably because the members and directresses of the society were deeply interconnected either through blood or marriage. It was common for older women to introduce their adult daughters and daughters-in-law as members, so that the work of benevolence could continue. Marianna Smith, for example, was joined as a member by three daughters-in-law and a granddaughter, while Elizabeth Barnwell Fuller's five daughters and three daughters-in-law were all members of the Beaufort Female Benevolent Society by 1860.

Another factor that influenced the number of subscribers was competition from other benevolent societies. In both Savannah and Charleston more than ten female benevolent societies competed for donations and subscribers from the female citizens by the 1850s, whereas in Beaufort the Female Benevolent Society retained a monopoly until after the Civil War. The board of the Ladies Benevolent Society in Charleston reflected in 1851 that "our list of annual subscribers is not as large as it was at the formation of our society, but the multiplication of societies since, we doubt not, is the chief cause of it."[59] The growth of denomination-specific female benevolent societies from the 1830s onward also had a significant effect on the funding available to older charitable societies. By the early 1850s the Episcopal Orphans' Home in Savannah was receiving more than $1,000 per year from the ladies of Christchurch Episcopal and a further $500 from the ladies of St. John's Episcopal. A generation earlier these Episcopal congregations had been the mainstays of funding for the Savannah Female Asylum.[60]

Few female benevolent societies were above pleading for money in their annual reports or in the city newspapers. The Richmond Female Humane Association hoped that patrons "in contemplating the good which their liberality has been employed to effect, new inducements will be felt to continue and extend that liberality." In Savannah the fluctuating income of the Free School Society—$1,200 in 1818, $3,500 in 1819, $1,300 in 1821—necessitated an appeal to the "benevolence and charity of the community," which also reminded citizens of the importance of "having the poor taught the first rudiments of our language, and regular and virtuous habits."[61] In Charleston the managers of the Ladies Benevolent Society evidently felt some disquiet about soliciting contributions, but the result was ultimately satisfactory: "the publick appeal which we made thro' the newspapers brought us a few new members & was responded to as liberally as we had any right to expect, under the pecuniary pressure of the times; & we were in some degree compensated for the pain of thus publickly proclaiming our necessities, by the kind wishes & hearty expressions of goodwill which never failed to accompany the more substantial proofs of the confidence still reposed in us as judicious stewards of the poor."[62]

The contrasting approaches toward appeals for funding adopted by the female managers of the Catholic Female Charitable Society and the Protestant Orphan Asylum Society in Mobile reflected their individual religious traditions. Catholic ladies tended to emphasize in print the heavenly rewards that donors were bound to receive for their good works. The children who had been entrusted to them by "Divine Providence" would offer up "innocent blessing[s]" for their generous patrons, and the ladies did not doubt that the "giver will be rewarded a hundred fold, both here and hereafter." By appealing to the Catholic Doctrine of Good Works, the ladies reactivated an age-old fund-raising technique, one that had served the Catholic Church well over centuries. In Mobile, Catholic women were able to generate annual turnovers that exceeded $8,000 for every year after 1850, an amount that the Protestant asylum never achieved before the Civil War, suggesting that the possible heavenly rewards of benevolence weighed particularly heavily in the minds of donors. Since Protestants believe that God alone determines who gets to heaven, there was little point in Protestant women emphasizing the heavenly rewards of being charitable. However, Protestants were supposed to lead godly lives, and the Bible expressly exhorts individuals to help those less fortunate, so Protestant women emphasized in print the biblical authority of charity, often quoting from scripture, suggesting that the word of God was good enough on its own to spur people into charitable activity.

Donations and legacies, though welcome, were also a somewhat unreliable source of income, but they sometimes enabled charitable societies to purchase lots or buildings that otherwise would have been beyond them. The Female Orphan Society of Norfolk did precisely that with a donation of $2,500 in 1816, and the Female Orphan Society of Montgomery gratefully accepted from three local businessmen the donation of a city lot where they could construct an asylum. More common were donations of $25 or $50 that just swelled the general funds.[63] While individuals were often the source of cash donations, most charitable societies also received funds from special concerts, theater performances, plays, and circus shows. The association of a public entertainment with a charitable cause probably did no harm to the overall takings for the performers and promoters, and contributed much needed funds to individual societies. Circus performers in Mobile, for instance, donated more than $500 to the Catholic Female Charitable Society and the Protestant Female Orphan Society in 1848.[64]

Not all benevolent women thought public amusements were a suitable source of income, however, and this attitude can be seen in the response of the board of the Savannah Female Asylum in 1803 to the offer from theater-owner Mr. Placide to donate the proceeds of a performance to their funds. The board published a condemnation of the event in a city newspaper, declaring that "they consider the very extensive indulgence given the players to exhibit their performances in this city as very unfriendly to religion, as it will be allowed by the candid among those who are attached to such amusements, that they more generally are the means of encouragement to vice and dissipation, than to good morals." Even worse, the players were allowed "to perform on the evening preceding the Sabbath, and on the night that our Christian congregation meet statedly in public worship in an almost adjoining building."[65] This stance was not without its critics. The editor of the *Savannah Republican* noted that "the commandment which institutes the Sabbath is equally imperative that we shall labor for six days as the seventh shall be kept . . . by what authority will the ladies justify lengthening the Sabbath?" Furthermore, in a rare public criticism of female charitable work in the South, he pointedly observed that the ladies had trespassed into a "political question, foreign to their field" by offering their opinions to the public at large on a controversial issue.[66] However, the decision to decline the money stood.

Other, less contentious, donations took the form of goods and services provided gratis. The Protestant Orphan Asylum Society in Mobile received free meat for the children from the city's butchers in 1846; two merchants donated bricks to the Savannah Free School Society to be used in the construction of their school; and Savannah merchant Andrew Low provided dresses for the girls at the Female Asylum for more than twenty years.[67] Ultimately, however, small amounts of money, or other items such as clothing for the poor, firewood, building materials, and food were only for short-term use and did nothing to place benevolent societies on a secure financial footing.

As subscriptions and donations ultimately proved an unreliable form of funding, other methods of generating income had to found. The source most readily turned to by female benevolent societies was the charity sermon. Since most early benevolent societies drew members from a wide variety of Christian denominations they felt able to call on the talents of all the ministers in the immediate locality in the hope of reaching the maximum number of local people. The boards of benevolent societies requested that ministers preach charity sermons, with a retiring collection, once a year, but if there was more than one society in the vicinity, ministers might well be asked to preach several sermons a year. Societies often published their annual accounts in the newspapers, so it became a matter of pride, even honor, that each congregation raise a respectable amount. Charity sermons thus became an important source of funding for a number of societies and some were even printed and sold, thus generating additional income.

The amounts produced by charity sermons were often substantial. The Protestant Orphan Asylum Society of Mobile raised $812 from charity sermons in 1839, and in Savannah the Female Asylum and the Free School Society each received between $600 and $1,000 per year from church collections in the 1810s. The power of the charity sermons was so great that the Female Asylum was able to raise $520 from a charity sermon at the Independent Presbyterian Church in 1820 even after Savannah had been devastated by fire only five months previously.[68] The majority of this money was provided by the congregations of Christchurch Episcopal and the Independent Presbyterian Church, which were the wealthiest in the city and which also provided most of the board members of female benevolent societies.[69] While most ministers willingly expounded on the virtues of charity, some were less forthcoming. In 1840 a Presbyterian minister in Columbia, South Carolina, claimed that he needed permission from the synod before preaching a sermon on behalf of the Female Orphan Society, though no other Presbyterian minister had ever made such a claim before. In 1845 the Female Orphan Society in Norfolk sent a rather impertinent note to the minister of the Methodist church "reminding him that no collection had been received from that church the past year & asking his immediate attention to it."[70]

Aside from charity sermons, which were always a variable source of income depending on the economic conditions of the times (the female managers of the Savannah Female Asylum termed this source of funding "precarious and disagreeable" in 1829), some female benevolent societies were more proactive in raising money.[71] Some, such as the Protestant Orphan

Asylum Society in Mobile and the Female Orphan Society of Norfolk, based most of their financial strategy on personal collections by members in their neighborhoods. The directresses of the Raleigh Female Benevolent Society, however, confessed that "the business of collecting is laborious and irksome, as many give with such evident reluctance that it mortifies those who receive."[72] Other societies, such as the Nashville Protestant Orphan Asylum or Union Benevolent Society in Richmond, had an adjunct male society with the sole purpose of collecting money to support the activities of the female benevolent society. This strategy worked, up to a point. Such organizations could function, but only in a limited manner, and the Protestant Orphan Asylum in Mobile, the Female Orphan Asylum in Norfolk, and the Union Benevolent Society in Richmond were not large organizations dealing with hundreds of paupers every year.

The most successful female benevolent societies in terms of sums raised and numbers helped had to raise money on an altogether different scale. Several societies organized fairs, where the women "devoted much time to preparing a great variety of goods, both useful and ornamental," selling cakes, fancy goods, lace and other luxury items; others organized dances, balls, and soirees. The income from these events was impressive: $3,500 from a fair for the Savannah Female Asylum in 1829; $3,767 from a three-day fair for Mobile's Catholic Female Charitable Society in 1858; and $4,000 for Savannah's Catholic Orphans in 1859. It was this profitability that attracted increasing numbers of southern benevolent women to the idea of fairs. The directresses of the Savannah Female Asylum confessed that their own fair was "in imitation of our sister cities, Baltimore, Washington and Boston, where fairs have been held in behalf of similar organisations with great success."[73] The publicity given the fair in Mobile by the city press suggests that it became something of a highlight of the social calendar. Reporting on the New Year fair of 1843–1844 the *Mobile Register* described a "brilliant and interesting scene. Bright lights, gay music, happy faces, pleasant greetings, beauty and wit enlivened one of the fullest gatherings of the season." A few years later the *Register* even went so far as to describe the fair as "the favorite gala of the season."[74] The Savannah newspaper, *A Friend to the Family*, waxed lyrical about a similar event organized by the Female Seamen's Friend Society in 1849: "We had seen cakes before, but we had considered them hitherto merely as matters that were to come under the operation of our masticatory organs, and gratify one sense only. But here we saw what delighted our eyes more than ever our palate was gratified in the days of our boyhood. We saw flowers, formed by hands, almost as cunning and skilful as nature's own, and full as fair. We fancied we would inhale the aroma of the japonica, the oleanda, and the rose, when in fact silk and tiffany were the components."[75]

When female benevolent societies received large sums in one lump, such as the receipts from a fair, they usually invested it in one of four ways: deposited the money in the bank, loaned the money out to local planters or merchants at a set interest rate, purchased rentable property, or invested in stocks. The Protestant Orphan Asylum Society in Mobile believed that the Planters and Merchants Bank was the best place for its money even though "it does not draw interest." The decision makers in the society acknowledged that "these funds might have been more profitably invested in individual securities, but in consultation with the Managers of the Society, it was decided that the safety of its resources was not to be hazarded for the chance of making an addition to them, through the interest of loans." The societies that preferred to lend money in the community received an average of 6 percent interest, but they had to be very certain of the bona fides of the borrower to prevent an individual from absconding with the money. It was probably for this reason that the Columbia Female Orphan Society, for instance, only lent money to members and their immediate families. Those who accepted loans were effectively donating money by paying interest on the capital they held even though they often had no use for it. Widow Lucy Green, for example, who served as the first directress of the Columbia Female Orphan Society for a number of years, paid $35 per year in interest on a $500 bond, even though she was worth about $80,000 in 1860 and owned one hundred slaves.[76] The Poydras Orphan Asylum in New Orleans had been given a large amount of property by its eponymous founder and continued to see property as its best investment for the remainder of the antebellum period. In 1855 the ladies came up with an ingenious solution to a difficult problem. Wishing to build a newer and larger asylum, but not wishing to sell the property bequeathed by Poydras, the ladies raised more than $40,000 by selling long leases but retaining the freehold of their land, and thus were able to finance their expansion.[77]

Many other societies, however, chose to invest their money in bank stocks and city, state, and U.S. treasury bonds, receiving average yields of about 5 percent a year. The income from these investments was significant: the forty shares in the Planter's Bank owned by the Savannah Female Asylum generated an annual income of more than $200 throughout the 1810s, roughly 10 percent of the society's budget, and the portfolio of shares held by the Savannah Widow's Society and the Ladies Benevolent Society in Charleston generated between a third and a half of their annual income in 1860, with the latter's total investment in shares being $21,559.[78] Not content with merely investing in bank shares, these two societies ventured further into the capitalist marketplace by purchasing railroad stocks. The Savannah Widow's Society already held six shares in the Central Railroad worth $600 in 1854 when it invested a further $4,100 in the Southwestern Railroad. The obvious reason for investing in railroad stock was that the potential return was far higher than with bank stock. Instead of a meager 5 percent, the Widow's Society earned 13 percent from the Southwestern Railroad stock in 1860 and an impressive 35 percent from its holding in the Central Railroad. Of course, such investments were risky because railroad companies could fail, but the capital injected into local infrastructure improvements by female benevolent societies was substantial and encompassed a variety of internal improvement companies. The Benevolent Society of the City and County of Baltimore owned forty shares in the Frederickstown Turnpike Road company while the Ladies Benevolent Society, the Ladies Fuel Society, and the Female Charitable Society of the Upper Wards all held shares in the Charleston Bridge Company. And sometimes even bank investments were not an absolutely safe investment. The Ladies Benevolent Society in Charleston, for example, lost $3,522 that it had invested in stock of the United States Bank during the financial crisis of 1837.[79]

Whatever the female managers decided to do with their investments, the financial records of charitable societies demonstrate that the ladies kept an extremely close eye on where they had placed their money so as to generate the best return. In 1830 the Beaufort Female Benevolent Society "resolved that $400 be transmitted to Charleston for the purchase of shares in the Planters and Mechanics Bank. Resolved that all the surplus funds of the society be invested in Bank stock, in preference to private loans in future." Yet just two years later the board resolved to sell its bank stock and lend its money to local planters since they calculated they would earn an extra $25 a year in interest by doing so. The secretary noted in the minutes that "it was thought advisable to make a transfer of the funds, so as to secure all possible profit on the property of the society."[80] While retaining its faith in the value of stocks and shares, the Charleston Ladies Benevolent Society systematically sold off its 6 percent U.S. government stock between 1824 and 1827 in favor of shares in the Union and South Carolina Banks that offered a better return.[81]

A smaller but no less significant element in the funding available to female charitable societies came from a variety of state, county, and municipal bodies. Many local authorities came to the same conclusion as the Common Council of Norfolk, which suggested to the directresses of the Female Orphan Asylum "that the ladies should receive into the asylum such young Female Orphans as are at present in the poor house, or may in future have legal claims on the corporation for support, offering for the board &c of each such child, the sum of sixty dollars per annum." The Beaufort Female Benevolent Society not only took in girls paid for by the town of Beaufort but also those from neighboring St. Luke's parish, with their board paid for by the Commissioners of the Poor. The city authorities in New Orleans placed more than 150 children in more than ten different asylums between the start of 1853 and the end of 1855, sorting them not only by sex but also by religious affiliation and ethnic background. Payments from government authorities could either be a set amount per child, as in Norfolk and in Nashville, or a simple lump sum, as in Richmond and New Orleans, that might vary according to the economic circumstances of the times.[82] Such payments were an acknowledgment that the care and support offered by female benevolent societies to young girls was more appropriate than that available in the local poorhouse. An exception to this policy of civic funding of private charitable societies can be found in Charleston. With their own city poorhouse and orphanage to fund, and despite the urging of some citizens that an annual appropriation to societies such as the Ladies Benevolent Society would "prove a real saving to the city," city councilmen spent city money elsewhere.[83]

Where states had literary or poor school funds, as in South Carolina, payments were often made to female benevolent societies to fund the salary of a teacher or the school fees of the children if they were sent to a private school. In 1818 the Free School Commissioners in Beaufort, South Carolina, offered to back-date their contribution to the Beaufort Female Benevolent Society by two years on production of receipts, and in 1830 the society was able to persuade the Free School Commissioners to pay one of the older girls to teach others inside the asylum.[84] In both instances, cash payments to female benevolent societies were an easier, and cheaper, solution than providing alternative care or schooling. When added together, the state support for the work of female benevolent societies made a real difference. More than a third of the annual budget of the Poydras Asylum in New Orleans came from the city or the state in 1827. In 1851 the Catholic Female Charitable Society received $500 from the Mobile County Commissioners, $195 from the city council, and $375 from the school commissioners, amounting to about 10 percent of its operating budget for the year.[85] State funds were not always offered, as they were in Norfolk; sometimes they had to be fought for. In November 1824 the directresses of the Savannah Free School Society wrote to the Georgia legislature outlining the "very precarious" state of their finances and requesting a regular annuity. The legislators responded with remarkable alacrity, passing "An act to vest the poor school fund in the county of Chatham in the Savannah Free School Society" on December 20, 1824. The income from the poor school fund amounted to about $500 a year, though it was not always promptly paid, and the ladies had to agree to allow three justices to examine their books to attest that the fund was being spent on "beneficient purposes."[86]

The last, and sometimes most important source of income, was that earned by the ladies or their charges. The nuns who managed the orphan asylum for the Catholic Female Charitable Society in Mobile also ran, in tandem, single-sex schools that took in fee-paying pupils. In 1850 the citizens of Mobile paid $2,339 to have nuns educate their children, a sum that constituted more than a quarter of the operating income of the orphan asylum.[87] The Poydras Orphan Asylum in New Orleans and the Augusta and Savannah Female Asylums all recorded small amounts of income generated through the sale of sewing done by the girls in their care.[88] For other female benevolent societies, especially those concerned with adult women, the income generated by the women themselves could be substantial. The Ladies Benevolent Society in New Orleans recorded income of $1,378 in 1854–1855 from "sales and work" done by those in their care, and the Raleigh Female Benevolent Society earned three-quarters of its income in 1823 in this way.[89]

The substantial amounts of cash raised by benevolent women is a testament to their perseverance and dedication but also to the generosity and support of the wider communities within which they operated. Only by making themselves indispensable to the community could female benevolent societies survive. For all the arm-twisting that might have gone on behind closed doors to open pocketbooks, it is doubtful that many of these societies would have lasted as long as they did if they had not been perceived as fulfilling a vital role. Benevolent women used all the wiles at their disposal to obtain the funding to support their charitable work. With the requisite finances in place these women set about reforming poor children into useful and productive citizens, assisting mothers back into employment, and tending the sick and elderly in their declining days.

Although the vast majority of benevolent women were experienced managers of labor, their benevolent work differed significantly from their domestic arrangements because those employed as matrons, teachers, and contractors were free (and white) rather than enslaved. The directresses of the Beaufort Female Benevolent Society, for instance, on average belonged to families owning more than sixty slaves; Harriet Fripp's husband, William, owned 316 slaves in 1860.[90] Of course, Beaufort was in the heart of South Carolina's rice district and surrounded by large plantations, but even urban benevolent women in Savannah, who did not generally belong to planter families, owned more than five slaves each. These slaves would have normally been under the direction of the mistress, who was responsible for the smooth running of the household, and would have been punished by whipping and by other means if their work was not satisfactory. When these same women employed white women as matrons they had to adjust to working with free labor that was not so easily directed, controlled, and disciplined. The experience of benevolent women with female employees was mixed, and many had significant problems obtaining the services of "proper persons" whom they respected and trusted.[91] The Protestant Orphan Asylum Society in Mobile went through four matrons in its first eighteen months and the records of female benevolent societies are littered with employees being summoned before boards of directresses to answer for their behavior and conduct. After their own "committees of inspection reported that they saw, most shameful neglect of the children—in every respect, with the exception of their diet" the board of the Savannah Female Asylum summoned

Mrs. Robertson, the governess, and "informed her that unless she altered her mode of conduct as Governess to the Female Asylum, that she must be displaced. Mrs Robertson then agreed to try and give satisfaction to the board, by her attention to their orders." A second inspection three months later found that "Mrs. Robertson was unfit to take charge of the children" and she was therefore dismissed.[92] Also in Savannah the Female Seaman's Friend Society dismissed the landlord of their Sailor's Home after he had "proved unworthy" of their trust.[93]

Given the problems associated with getting good staff, it is not surprising that when female benevolent societies found someone they were happy with they tried to keep that person for as long as possible. The Savannah Free School Society went through numerous teachers between 1816 and 1834 until they finally settled on a local man, Emmanuel Sheftall, who served the school until the Civil War. And when matron Mrs. Jakeman resigned her post after seven years with the Norfolk Female Orphan Asylum the board praised "the diligence and affectionate fidelity with which she has uniformly discharged the duties of her office."[94] Catholic charities were often able to circumvent the problem of finding suitable employees by using women from religious orders. The Catholic Female Charitable Society in Mobile, for instance, obtained the services of six Sisters of Charity from Maryland to whom they handed "sole control of the interior of the asylum" in 1841. Not only did the society get six people for less than the price of a matron—as the nuns required no salary, only an annual contribution to their mother house and their board and lodging—they also got the dedication and devotion to duty that was singularly lacking in many paid employees. The nuns brought a stability to the Catholic asylum that permitted the managers to concentrate on fund-raising and expansion, not on minor administrative details.[95]

Allegations of mistreatment of the children by matrons were taken extremely seriously, even if most proved unfounded. When one mother complained to the board of the Savannah Female Asylum that the matron "had whipp'd and otherways ill treated her child," the board called in witnesses who disproved the charge and eventually it was the child who left the asylum, not the matron. The Protestant Orphan Asylum Society in Mobile reacted strongly to what it thought were remarks casting doubt on the character of superintendent Mr. Benjamin. The *Mobile Tribune* reported that Benjamin had been charged by the Mayor's Court with "Cruel Treatment to a child" and while the case had been dismissed the newspaper commented, "It is not necessary for us to give the entire evidence in the case, as it is a case in which the community at large are more or less interested and let them investigate the matter and judge for themselves." The directresses believed that this last sentence was an "intimation that cruelty to children is practised by the persons in charge of them (and allowed by the managers)." They cited the unpublished evidence from a doctor, from several inmates, and from the girl herself, all of whom testified to the "kind parental care" of Mr. Benjamin. As a direct result of the ladies' robust defense of their employee, the newspaper was forced to concede that "there was no intention on our part to fly in the face of the decision of the court."[96] The matron of the Beaufort Female Benevolent Society, Mrs. Salinas, could have done with a similar level of support from her employers in 1827. An anonymous note sent to the board after the death of one of the children claimed to have seen "marks of violence on its body after death and [it] had been hardly treated during its illness." Discussions with a number of independent witnesses disproved the charges, yet within a year Mrs. Salinas had been dismissed. When she requested an explanation for her dismissal the board informed her "that their reason for parting with her, is not the disapprobation they themselves feel with her, but that the public mind has been so much prejudiced against her, that the board could not consistently with their duty to the society continue her in office." Directresses commented privately that "the present matron had become so unpopular as to injure the interests of the society" and clearly the continuance and prosperity of the society was paramount.[97]

Apart from the treatment of the children the most common reason for disputes between employees and boards of directresses concerned salaries and benefits in kind. The Norfolk Female Orphan Society twice refused requests for a salary increase from their matron since "the salary at present allowed Mrs. Latham being deemed a sufficient compensation for her services," and on two other occasions actually reduced the amount per child she received "in consequence of the fall in the price of provisions."[98] This society was fortunate that Mrs. Latham tolerated salary cuts since employees of other societies did not. The Savannah Free School, for instance, lost a teacher in 1832 after the board refused his request for a salary increase, and the matron of the Beaufort Female Benevolent Society resigned in 1823 for the same reason.[99] Boards of directresses were particularly worried that their employees might be taking advantage of them. The Norfolk Female Orphan Society refused to allow Mrs. Latham's daughter to reside at the asylum during her confinement, perhaps because they feared that she might stay for a long time, but they did permit Mrs. Latham to go and stay with her daughter providing she found someone else to take care of the children.[100] Mr. and Mrs. Batchelor lost their position with the Protestant Orphan Asylum in Mobile because they had housed their three sons with them without the board's permission. In their place the board stated their wish to appoint those "whom we shall expect to obey more promptly, and cheerfully, the wishes of the board."[101] Ruth Jones, matron of the Beaufort Female Benevolent Society, consistently tried to make a little extra money by teaching local "coloured girls" to sew but her employers ordered to her to stop the practice in 1841 stating that it was "quite inadmissible." Yet, perhaps because they were otherwise very pleased with her, the board reversed their position by the 1850s, stating that those "who had owners residing in the town" could be taught.[102] The treatment of Ruth Jones suggests that boards of directresses sometimes had to be flexible if they wanted to retain the best staff.

Boards of directresses normally had to deal with matrons and teachers in person, and without outside assistance, but when they had to deal with lawyers, businessmen, and builders, boards frequently turned to men for advice or to act as intermediaries. The Female Orphan Society in Columbia asked John Bryce, husband of one of the directresses, to obtain quotes for the building of their asylum in 1842 and even managed to persuade him to superintend the work.[103] The Catholic Female Charitable Society in Mobile always used one of the Catholic priests in the city to negotiate contracts with builders.[104] In March 1851 the regular meeting of the Widow's Society in Savannah was attended by "several gentleman friendly to the institution [who] proposed that we should sell the lots now occupied by the widows being a very desirable part of the city & would sell to advantage & purchase other more suitable & appropriate the surplus fund together with the amount out at interest to the building."[105] Female managers of benevolent societies sought and accepted such advice most likely because they acknowledged the greater experience that their husbands, brothers, and fathers had in these matters. Moreover, the intermediaries would probably get a better deal with suppliers and tradesmen than the ladies would themselves. Of course, seeking out the advice and counsel of men lessened the independence that female benevolent societies had always sought to preserve. Martha Richardson objected on just such grounds to a proposal for gentlemen to join with the board of the Savannah Female Asylum in 1839 to oversee the construction of a new asylum. She was happy for the board to "consult" the gentlemen but was adamant that the final decisions should be taken by the ladies alone.[106] The Savannah Female Asylum had a long tradition of excluding men from decision making; in 1802 the first published rules of the Asylum had stated plainly: "Gentlemen cannot be members of this society"; one visitor was informed that the Asylum was "the fruit of female benevolence . . . wholly managed by females." The board of the Norfolk Female Orphan Society displayed a similar streak of independence over its new building in 1847. Despite declaring their "entire confidence in the committee of gentlemen" who advised the ladies to sell their existing lot and build a new asylum elsewhere, eventually the ladies determined to rebuild on their existing lot.[107]

Southern benevolent women therefore had to fashion their own relationships with white employees and contractors, and most found that their previous experiences did not prepare them well for the encounter. White labor was not so easily directed as the slave labor the ladies were generally accustomed to managing. Indeed their benevolent work probably brought white women into contact with a far wider range of individuals than would otherwise have been the case. Given their mission to relieve want and hardship, benevolent women inevitably came into contact with the poor on an almost daily basis. Some societies, such as the Ladies Benevolent Society in Charleston, operated a "visiting" system that one southern newspaper likened to "hunting," wherein the ladies walked through the poor neighborhoods, identifying individuals in need, searching for "needy children," and providing assistance as necessary.[108] Other societies dealt with indigent parents who wanted an education for their children or simply a place that was warm and dry for them to sleep in. The work of benevolent women constantly brought them face-to-face with poverty and suffering that otherwise would most likely have remained hidden to them. But for benevolence, few elite women would have ever felt the need to leave their genteel neighborhoods and set foot in Charleston Neck or in Yamacraw where whites and blacks intermingled promiscuously and where grog-shops and brothels were more common than grocery stores. One minister in Mobile commented that "nothing but the dire necessity of a funeral could induce him" to visit those on Widow's Row.[109] By contrast, the visitors of the Ladies Benevolent Society in Charleston had beheld "scenes of distress, want, misery, and woe, scarcely to be conceived by those who have never entered the frail and un-sheltered tenements of this city, where poverty, sickness and wretchedness dwell," and the ladies of the Female Charitable Society of Charleston Neck observed "scenes of haggard wretchedness" on their visits to the homes of the poor. The visitors of the Union Benevolent Society in Richmond described "sorrow which our eyes have seen, over which our hearts have bled."[110] Only by actually encountering the poor did these women gain any real insight into the misery of their lives, and such encounters often elicited sympathy, especially for abused or abandoned women. One of the lady visitors of the Union Benevolent Society in Richmond was asked to visit a poor woman in the Basin district of the city:

> She went, and found the woman on a bed of straw, nursing an infant only a few days old. The entire furniture of the room consisted of a part of an old chest and a broken chair. Misery and wretchedness were stamped on the inmates and the abode. The husband was a drunkard, whose ferocious appearance and horrid oaths might have frightened the most resolute man, much more a defenceless female. But the visitor was not to be deterred from her errand of mercy, though he ordered her to leave his house, and declared that if his wife should take anything from the visitor, he would kick both downstairs. The visitor was compelled to leave with-out giving anything to the wife, but left money to relieve her wants with one of her neighbors, whom the husband would permit to come into his house, and by such means her immediate necessities were supplied.[111]

However miserable the lives of the poor, most benevolent women made judgments as to the character and suitability of the individual to receive relief. Those deemed "worthy" for assistance were invariably the ones who had led blameless lives, who were "industrious" but who still could not earn enough to support themselves and their families, and who were victims of circum-stances. The Savannah Widow's Society decided to pay Mrs. Burroughs's rent because they perceived her to be "an industrious woman with a large

& sick family," but at the very same meeting they denied assistance to Mrs. Hart since, "after a strict investigation into her present condition [they] do not think her an object of charity when there are so many who are much more in want."[112] In a similar manner, the New Orleans Ladies Benevolent Society only provided the poor with assistance "after making ourselves acquainted with their needs and worthiness" and the Columbia Female Benevolent Society confined its care to "objects worthy of the attention of the society."[113] The Female Charitable Society of Charleston Neck drew a "line of discrimination . . . between the virtuous & decent poor & those who are otherwise & when the V[isiting] C[ommittee] shall be called to attend on vagrants or persons of intemperate habits & infamous lives such persons shall generally be dismissed." The directresses firmly believed in the benefits inherent in personal visits to the homes of the poor: "It is a great thing for the wretched poor to be visited by refined females. Their children look up to these visitors as beings of a superior order and where a few words of religious or moral instruction are added it seems almost to supply a want of the soul as well as the body."[114] Such sentiments were echoed by the Ladies Benevolent Society in Charleston: "Every system of charity, which takes the rich among the poor, must be particularly efficacious and beneficial; it improves the condition of one party, the feelings of the other, and the virtues of both."[115]

Most female benevolent societies were therefore anxious to be perceived as selective to avoid charges that charity actually encouraged and facilitated idleness. If the wider community had believed that assisting the poor did nothing to alter their behavior for the better, and in fact sustained them in their dissolute ways, then the money that funded the work of these benevolent societies would have evaporated quickly. The Raleigh Female Benevolent Society stood against this trend. Answering a charge that they should provide help only to the deserving poor, the ladies replied "that the most deserving may not be the most necessitous, and although evil may previously have been committed, yet who shall say what has been resisted?" Instead they preferred to think that their help contributed toward the reform of those "who before trod the path which leads to destruction."[116] More typical of the attitude of benevolent women toward the poor however was the annual report in 1843 of the Ladies Benevolent Society in Charleston that set out clearly what they understood to be their mission:

Where the poor are blessed with health & strength we would excite them to industry by withholding pecuniary aid, except as the reward of labour; we would offer them work & encourage them to do it. But the society whose anniversary we this day celebrate has no such pleasing objects in view. Our visitors go the hovels of the poor, not to stimulate them to employ their strength while they have it, but to minister to them when that strength is gone, when consuming disease has laid them low & bodily pains are rendered more acute by the sad thought that their families are suffering from their inability to labour for them. They go & examine into & satisfy themselves as to the actual case of each recipient of your bounty, they carry to them the simplest comforts, not luxuries.

Those who, after a visit, did not meet the criteria of "worthiness" were refused help, and from 1844 the Ladies Benevolent Society kept a list of "such persons as have been found unworthy of the assistance" so future applications could be denied without a visit.[117]

Directresses of several other female benevolent societies placed an equal store on "worthiness." The female managers of the Dorcas Benevolent Society in Baltimore found in the poorer parts of the city "some very worthless, but so extremely indigent, that assistance might, in some instances, have been, not improperly rendered; but was declined in order efficiently to meet the wants of the more deserving." Elsewhere, the directresses of the Nashville Protestant Orphan Asylum did refuse admission to an illegitimate child, though it ultimately provided some financial assistance to the family, and the board of the Savannah Female Asylum declined the application of Mr. Fisher to have his two daughters taken into the asylum due to "his wife being an improper character [and] it would be impossible to prevent her from having intercourse with her children . . . her example and precept would be an injury perhaps to the other children in the institution as well as her own."[118] But for the most part it was far more common for benevolent women to deny help for practical economic reasons, especially to those whom they believed were already supported elsewhere, rather than for moral ones. The Columbia Female Orphan Society denied help to Emma Craig in 1844 "as she resided some distance from the town & had a present protection." Mary Jane Nithercote was refused admission to the Mobile Protestant Orphan Asylum as the ladies knew that "the father of the said Mary Jane was a mechanic engaged in the exercise of his trade, and as it appeared able and willing to support his child" and two other children were turned away since "the mother was in good health she was the proper person to have charge of her children." Similarly the Beaufort Female Benevolent Society turned away a "little girl by the name of Slowman [who] had both parents living and one of them with a trade. The society could not consistently with their object, which was to assist the orphan and destitute child, receive her" and the same society offered only education and not residency to the daughter of Mrs. Ike since "many of the members present were of [the] opinion that the mother in this case, was so well qualified to train the child properly, that it would be rather a disadvantage to remove her from her care."[119]

Since female directresses had worked so hard to raise funds to sustain their benevolent enterprises, it is not surprising that they wanted to ensure that they assisted those most in need. The board of the Savannah Female Asylum censured one of its founder members, Mrs. Hannah McAlister, when it found that a child represented by her as indigent was actually "then under the protection of one, who could provide for it." A shamed Mrs. McAlister agreed to support the child herself "as long as she remains in the asylum" and then tendered her resignation. The visiting committee of the Savannah Widow's Society reported that they had "visited Mrs. Hart & after a strict investigation into her present condition do not think her an object of charity when there are so many who are much more in want & as she is assisted by other societies who are abundantly able to relieve her wants. After the above statement was made before the ladies a resolution was passed that after the present month she must not expect further assistance from the society." Sadly the reaction of Mrs. Hart to this outcome was not recorded.[120]

Successful applicants were often able to demonstrate a previous willingness to support themselves. One request for assistance from the Poydras Asylum came from a widow with five children who "has tried hard to support them, but in vain, & now appeals to your charities for an asylum such as she, even by the hardest labour cannot bestow on them." The directresses of the Beaufort Female Benevolent Society were impressed by an application from a child "who had been trained by its widowed mother, Mrs. Murdoch, to habits of industry, but whose poverty precluded the possibility of education," and they agreed she "should receive the patronage of the society." Mrs. Burroughs had her rent paid by the Savannah Widow's Society mainly because they perceived her to be "an industrious woman with a large & sick family." When applications were beyond existing finances, the Mobile Female Benevolent Society relied on the judgment of the Reverend McLean, who testified "to the worthiness & great need of Mrs. Blackburn it was resolved to give her the preference over Mary Donaldson who is already cared for by the church & has many friends."[121]

Since most female benevolent societies had their own criteria for who constituted a "proper object of charity" it became the responsibility of the poor to try to meet those requirements, or at least to convince the directresses that they had met them. Applications for admission into orphanages from single parents with small children, in particular from widows, were normally approved, as the ladies were conscious of the burden of children on women who had "nothing to support them, but the labour of her hands." The directresses of the Beaufort Female Benevolent Society admitted Eliza Cobler since her mother was providing full time care for her father and therefore it was "impossible for her to pay the attention to her daughter that she required," and later justified their admission of the daughters of overseer Mr. McNull as they "had been recently left by the death of their mother, quite destitute of female care and attention." Reports of abuse or neglect also usually led to relief. The directresses of the Savannah Female Asylum accepted a German-born child "whose father is in the habit of locking up his child when out at work himself," and other children who were left alone all day during "their father's absence at work," while the managers of the Tuscaloosa Female Benevolent Society provided help to Mrs. Coker in 1860 who had a "drunken husband." The destruction of families through death and their reconstruction by remarriage provided a ready supply of needy supplicants for assistance. Catherine Williams was offered a sanctuary at the Beaufort Female Benevolent Society in 1836 following the death of her father as "her mother was not permitted by her present husband to give her the shelter of her roof."[122]

Even those who were deemed worthy of aid frequently created problems for directresses by their attitude and behavior. For adult women who had managed to support themselves and their families for decades, being forced by infirmity and old age to accept charity involved coming to terms with issues of personal pride and dignity. For some it was too much to take. The board of the Savannah Widow's Society was informed "that Mrs. Woods had her things brought to the home a few days after the last meeting, but on being told that she could not keep her dog in the room with her, put everything back in the wagon & declined to remain in the house." The same board was also forced "to call together the inmates of the home, [to] let it be distinctly understood that no person who was guilty of rudeness & disrespect to the matron would be allowed to remain in the building."[123]

Many "worthy" recipients of aid were still regarded with suspicion by benevolent women. Most orphan asylums had a rule stating, "No children shall be entitled to the bounty of the society but such as shall be exclusively given up by their parents or guardians to the control of the society." There were several reasons such a rule was necessary: first, directresses often had a low opinion of indigent mothers, fearing that "the morals of the children would probably be corrupted by remaining any portion of their time with their mothers." After the ladies of the Female Humane Association in Baltimore had observed "scenes of complicated misery" in the homes of the poor, which they attributed to an early exposure to "filthiness . . . and vice," their solution was "to remedy the evil in its source, [by] snatch[ing] the child from a fate similar to that of its mother."[124] Second, female benevolent societies did not like being used as a form of temporary child care when children were deposited periodically only to be taken out again when it suited the parents; and third, societies usually wanted the children to be in their care long enough to receive the education and training that might make them "useful" future citizens.[125] The rule requiring parents to sign away all rights over their children to benevolent societies caused more friction between parents and directresses than anything else. By signing the indentures the parent lost any right to see or communicate with the child, and for many, once they learned that this was the condition of entry, it was too high a price to pay. The minutes of orphan asylum societies have frequent references to children who were admitted but who never actually arrived because the mother "was reluctant to part with her." A mother's attachment to her child was only natural, and no doubt many mothers could not face the prospect of hardly seeing their children again for perhaps ten or more years. Girls at the Savannah Female Asylum, for instance, were permitted to see their parents or friends only "once in three months, and then in the presence of the matron," and the board told the mother of one applicant "that upon no occasion shall she be allowed to visit them at the asylum or that they be permitted to go to see her, except in case of her extreme illness certified by a physician. The board being aware that her character and examples are such as to render these precautions necessary." Unsurprisingly perhaps, the mother refused to admit her child under those conditions. Others only wanted care for a child while it remained nothing more than an extra mouth to feed; once the child reached an age when it might be productive, either in the home or the workplace, many mothers wanted their children back. Mrs. Thrower, for instance, was able to persuade the Savannah Female Asylum to return her daughter Elizabeth since she "was old enough to assist in her work." Given the trouble associated with parents it is not surprising that an attempt by the Natchez Female Charitable Society to extend their relief to non-orphan children in 1826 was swiftly abandoned "owing principally to the interference of the parent."[126]

As the above case demonstrates, the boards of benevolent societies were not above returning children to parents or relatives if they believed it was the best thing for the child, but they needed to be firmly convinced that it was. The Norfolk Female Orphan Society returned Jane Holsey to her mother as they perceived the mother to be "a respectable woman & now able to provide for her support" and the Protestant Orphan Asylum Society of Mobile approved an "Application from Mr. Lyman Dunn for his three children, who had been placed in the asylum by his wife, who had deserted him."[127] The Savannah Female Asylum, on the other hand, believed that it offered better care than many mothers and refused a number of requests to have children returned to their parents: "Mrs. Atkinson made application to take her child from the asylum—but the ladies knowing her character to be very bad it was unanimously resolved not to give up her child to her." Even when permission was granted, the board sometimes stipulated that "should it hereafter appear to the directress that this child is not properly brought up, they retain the power to demand her return to the asylum" and required some mothers to sign bonds accepting such conditions.[128]

Mothers who were refused permission to take their children out of asylums or who knew they would be refused were not above taking matters into their own hands. The directresses of the Protestant Orphan Asylum of Mobile were informed that "one of the children had been decoyed away by its mother, & a similar attempt made upon another"; and Mrs. Atkinson did not accept her refusal by the Savannah Female Asylum as the final word, taking her daughter without their permission less than a month later.[129] When children were taken without permission, the boards of female benevolent societies were left with two options: accept the fact that the child did not wish to stay and use the money saved to support a more willing child; or seek recovery of the child through the courts. When proper indentures had been signed by the mother, boards of directresses were able to obtain a warrant from a magistrate for the child, who was returned forcibly to the asylum.[130] Of course when the ladies had not obtained a formal indenture, they were effectively powerless. Rebecca Larissy, "whose parents were too indigent to afford her any instruction," failed to return to Beaufort after visiting them; when it was "well understood that her parents did not intend to send her back" the ladies gave her up, "no written agreement having been made with the society."[131] Children did not just flee orphanages to return to their parents; some simply ran away from the regime imposed on them. Seven boys fled the asylum of the Protestant Orphan Asylum Society in Mobile between 1856 and 1860, four of whom were orphans and had no parents to offer an alternative means of support. Most runaways were in their early teens, though John Carpenter was only seven when he ran away with his twelve-year-old brother William in 1857.[132]

Running away was not the only way for the children to express their dissatisfaction with their situation. In 1828 the matron of the Savannah Female Asylum "complained of the conduct of the large girls, particularly Nelly Gill, Diana Kirkland & Selina Smith, their conduct was represented so highly improper that the board conceived it their duty to reprove them in the presence of the matron, when they presented her with a whip with directions to use it, whenever their conduct made it necessary." The board of the Protestant Orphan Asylum Society in Mobile was informed of a fire "caused by one of the little boys throwing hot ashes on some dry materials under the cowshed, that together with the wood house & privies were consumed."[133] While the ladies were unsure if the action was deliberate, they had to find $300 to replace the lost buildings. The willfulness and naughtiness of some children was often blamed on the "utter want of discipline and untidiness in person and dress observed in the families . . . from which the children come."[134] The managers of the Poydras Asylum in New Orleans went so far as to outline a sequential punishment regime for children who misbehaved: "To stand alone in some conspicuous place; to wear a foolscap; to be sent earlier to bed; to be deprived of their play. Whipping should only be resorted to for lying, stealing, using profane or vulgar language, running away, or when other punishments have no effect."[135]

Given the regime adopted by most orphanages it is not surprising that some children rebelled against authority. Most female directresses would have agreed with the managers of the Alexandria Orphan Asylum who described their institution as "a public blessing; a school of Christian morals; of propriety of deportment; and of fixed habits of useful industry." Their counterparts in New Orleans announced their intention "to instruct the children in good morals and behaviour, in all such knowledge as shall tend to make them useful members of society, in all useful labor, and the rudiments of science."[136] To accomplish the required reformation of behavior the children normally rose and retired early, spent most the day in the schoolroom, and were forced to devote a significant portion of their "free time" doing household chores. Morning and evening prayer started and ended each day; matrons were responsible for Bible instruction and for taking the children to the various nearby churches in rotation. Most asylums also had children baptized when their parents had neglected to do so. The purpose of religious instruction was to ensure that the children absorbed "moral examples and habits of industry" that would direct them in their future course of life. For the same reasons, practical training was included in the curriculum.[137]

The path of reform on which the children were set necessitated personal cleanliness and outward signs of order and neatness. They were bathed at least once a week and were to "be neatly and comfortably clothed." Most female benevolent societies were anxious to ensure that the children all dressed alike in some kind of uniform or "plain, simple attire." Uniforms had two distinct purposes: they publicly demonstrated that a particular child was under the control and direction of a particular society, and they prevented the children from wearing clothing that was unsuitable or unseemly. The Beaufort Female Benevolent Society refused a request from the uncle of two children for them to be permitted to wear their own clothes "as they would allow no difference in dress among the children." A good public impression was vital if female benevolent societies were to continue to attract donations and subscriptions. The lady managers of the Catholic Female Charitable

Society in Mobile would no doubt have been pleased with the *Register's* description of their girls as "comfortably and tidily clad in warm winter garments and white aprons."[138] To maintain this kind of orderly dress, boards adopted rules that prevented children wearing "at any time any article of clothing but what has been provided by the society. Namely, homespun & calico frocks" and directed that they "never be allowed to wear other dresses than those provided or approved by the board." The board of the Savannah Female Asylum, unable to refuse with propriety a gift of white cotton dresses from merchant Andrew Low, decided the best course of action was to withhold the dresses from the children as it might give "them a taste for dress which the board deem it proper to discourage."[139] Where orphans mixed with other children—for instance in the schools operated by nuns in Mobile, Natchez, and several other cities—uniforms served a third purpose by removing any visible distinction between the two groups of children. One newspaper noted approvingly that "it was impossible to distinguish them [orphans] from other children in the establishment, who are blessed by their parents' protection, and on whom the hand of worldly fortune has bestowed more prolific favors."[140]

The concern with suitability of dress was part of the future that managers of female benevolent societies imagined for their charges. The directresses of the Female Humane Association in Richmond clearly envisaged a future as wives and mothers for their girls, directing that they "be taught reading, writing, arithmetic, needle work, knitting, spinning and every kind of domestic business."[141] In Beaufort directresses of the Female Benevolent Society ordered that their charges not only "be required to exhibit a specimen of nice yarn when they leave the society" as proof of their competence but also that "special attention be paid to housework of every kind, (except scouring floors) [and] that the larger children be made to attend to such work attentively so that in case they have no turn for needle work, they may be qualified to earn a maintenance by housekeeping."[142] Benevolent women saw it as part of their purpose to prepare children for their later working lives. If they had done their job properly, their charges would be able to support themselves, and their families, through their own industry and labor. Contrary to what some mythic portrayals of the South might have us believe, there was no disdain of work among the vast majority of white women. In rural areas white women worked on family farms and in the towns and cities they diversified into housekeeping, needlework, and shop-work. More than a third of white women in Savannah in 1860, for instance, had occupations ranging from servant to teacher to cotton planter. Even Beaufort, South Carolina, with a white population of only a few hundred, provided employment opportunities for white seamstresses, mantua-makers, teachers, and storekeepers.[143] Given the cross-membership of most female benevolent societies, it is likely that those trying to help children were acutely aware of the work of other societies aiming to help adult women. The first and second directress of the Female Benevolent Society in Mobile, which provided residential accommodation for widows, together with five other managers were also members of the Protestant Female Orphan Society in 1860. Similarly, eighteen board members of the Needle Woman's Friend Society and the Widow's Society in Savannah during the 1850s were involved with one or more of the several benevolent societies dealing with children. These women saw firsthand how poverty could afflict women throughout their lives and could begin to think of strategies that might help prevent the causes of pauperism.

Female managers of orphanages placed great faith in the system of apprenticeship, whereby children reaching their mid-teens were taken by sober, industrious, and pious individuals who would teach them a trade and hopefully continue their education. The female managers of the Benevolent Society of the City and County of Baltimore declared their intention "to procure a station superior to that of common domestics for those children who may have shown extraordinary capacity and merit."[144] Ideally, offers to take children came from adult women already working as seamstresses, milliners, and mantua-makers; they would not only impart the skills of their trade but would also provide a role model for their charges. Where better to learn the life skills that would serve them in adulthood than with those who were already supporting themselves and perhaps their families through their own labor? The problem was that such situations were hard to find. The board of the Beaufort Female Benevolent Society gratefully accepted the offer of Mrs. Irvine, "a milliner of respectable character," to take two of the girls and train them as milliners, but most female benevolent societies were unable to find suitable working women to take the children.[145] Consequently, it was far more common for children to be bound out as domestic servants where they would learn the basic housekeeping skills they would need in their own households as adults and which might provide them with employment if required.

The main criterion used by the boards of female benevolent societies, when judging where to place the children in their care, was the suitability of the family. The Norfolk Female Orphan Society reported proudly in 1819 that "we have bound out four of the children to service in respectable families where they are likely to be well brought up" while the Protestant Orphan Asylum Society of Mobile stated that children had been placed only with families "whose character and circumstances justify the belief that an advantageous arrangement has been made for their present comfort and future welfare."[146] Applications for children from wealthy individuals or from professional people were generally welcomed. When Judge Bridges approached the Protestant Orphan Asylum Society of Mobile for a little girl the board readily acceded, "it being thought a very desirable situation . . . and permission was given him to select one of the age and character he desired."[147] In a similar vein the Beaufort Female Benevolent Society delivered Eliza Cooler to Captain Dennis whom they knew to be of "respectable character," but only after receiving written confirmation "that she should be sent to school until 14 years of age & be further taught some suitable business."[148] By contrast, situations were refused if the board did not believe they were to the best advantage of the child. The board of the Protestant Orphan Asylum Society in Mobile rejected the application of Mr. W. G. Johnson for one or two of its girls "as it was understood he wished them as servants."[149]

Like county courts, female benevolent societies did not simply wash their hands of their former charges once they left their care. In Nashville directresses of the Protestant Orphan Asylum initially placed their girls out on trial and only formally indentured the child "if the ladies were satisfied with her treatment of her, and were assured of her remaining permanently in Nashville."[150] In fact, the evidence suggests that most boards of directresses kept a discreet but close eye on those who took in orphans and were willing to intervene when matters did not turn out as they had hoped. In 1818 the board of the Savannah Female Asylum directed the secretary to "wait on Mrs. Monrow and inform her that the board cannot continue Mary Ann Flynn any longer in her service, as they have every reason to think, that she is kept for the sole purpose of attending on her child, and never allowed to go to a place of worship." The following year the same board took Julia Wilson away from Mrs. Nevil after receiving "information that she had been cruelly whipt, . . . the cruelty of the treatment which Julia received makes it incumbant upon them to take her again under their protection." The Norfolk Female Orphan Society similarly deemed Mrs. Smith "unworthy of the charge" of Peggy Jones and removed her from Mrs. Smith's home.[151]

A more common cause for the breakdown of the indenture system, however, was misbehavior by the children. Those who took children but who found them difficult to control, or in any way unsuitable, were faced with two options. Some such as Mrs. Hodges, who claimed Mary Vincent had "given great dissatisfaction," simply transferred her indentures to another individual and merely informed the board of the new situation.[152] Others took the more straightforward option of simply returning the child. When Mrs. Taylor found Eliza Cheery "not qualified for the services required" she returned her to the Norfolk Female Orphan Society and took another girl instead. Some female benevolent societies accepted returned children while others, like the Savannah Female Asylum, stated "that it is against the rules of the society to receive back any child that had been bound out by them." In circumstances like this it is not clear what happened to the children. Mrs. Savage, for instance, tried to return Mary Wright after she had "behaved in a most improper manner to her," but the refusal of the Savannah Female Asylum to accept her back left both Mrs. Savage and Mary stuck in a relationship that probably neither wished to continue.[153]

It is evident that both the boards of female benevolent societies and those accepting children had issues with the indenture system. The Savannah Female Asylum went so far as to declare "that it being found by experience that the children derived no actual benefit by being bound out in families, and so much trouble arising there from, it was resolved unanimously to keep the children in the asylum . . . until they were old enough to support themselves."[154] Yet there were two other parties to indentures who also had significant misgivings about the system: the children themselves and their parents. Parents often tried to influence where their children were placed and report suspected abuses and problems to boards of directresses in the hope that they would intervene. One mother, for instance, complained to the board of the Poydras Orphan Asylum in New Orleans that the man who had taken her daughter "beat her most every day for no fault whatever [and] abused her person by threatening her with anything but good."[155] Most boards felt bound to investigate the claims made by mothers, but without physical evidence they normally sided with those who had taken the child and not the parent. When Mrs. Sanderlins appeared before the board of the Savannah Female Asylum with her daughter Sarah, having removed her from Mrs. McLeod's service and alleging ill-treatment, the board duly followed up the claims but swiftly concluded that "there was no just cause of complaint against Mrs. McLeod and the child Sarah Sanderlins [was] ordered back to her service."[156] The Beaufort Female Benevolent Society, presumably to avoid this sort of situation, required parental consent to an indenture if a parent was still living. Most mothers acceded to the placements found for their children, accepting the opportunity offered as a good one, but some found it impossible to face a long separation. Mary Barnet's mother, for instance, initially agreed to let her daughter travel with Mrs. Tabor from Beaufort to St. Augustine, acknowledging that it was an "advantageous offer." But within a few days she had changed her mind "on account of the distance," and the managers of the Beaufort Female Benevolent Society "did not think it advisable to send Mary against her mother's wishes and entreaties."[157]

In addition to at least listening to, and sometimes being influenced by, the views of mothers, boards of directresses were also sometimes forced into taking into account the views of the children. Sarah Suares found her placement with Mrs. Plumb "not agreeable" and left her service while fellow inmate of the Savannah Female Asylum, Susan Hutchinson, refused to be bound to Mrs. Williams in the first place and also later ran away. In the latter case the board resolved "to take every legal measure" to secure her return. Five years later the same benevolent society dealt with the case of Mary Ann Flynn who "had left Mrs. Munro and placed herself under the protection of Mr. Hutson." While it is doubtful that the board would have approved of the actions of Mary, when presented with a fait accompli they "unanimously agreed" to let the situation remain as it was.[158]

Several boards of directresses refused applications to take particular girls from the asylums because "the services of the larger girls are much needed."[159] Using the older inmates as support staff for the matron, as teachers, cleaners, and cooks, saved the boards of female benevolent societies significant amounts of money. The Savannah Female Asylum was candid enough to admit this in 1834 when they refused an application from Mrs. Stiles to take Jane Wilson as she was "essentially necessary . . . if they gave her up they would be compelled to hire a servant in her place." While they regretted "to refuse so good a situation for her" ultimately the needs of the asylum came first. When Jane reached eighteen the following year the board resolved to pay her $3 a month to keep her employed at the asylum, and upped this to $5 a month in 1836 to prevent her from being poached by a local family. This was not the first time the board of the Savannah Female Asylum had paid an inmate to remain in the asylum beyond her age of majority. In 1829 they had paid Eliza Tullis $3 a month "on account of her excellent example and useful services" and such was the high regard the board had for her that when Eliza left to get married two years later the board sent her a tea-set as a wedding present.[160]

Ultimately, whether by agreement or not, children did leave the care of female benevolent societies and entered the wider world. In the antebellum South the most likely outcome for a child at an orphanage was to be bound out. More than half the children at the Norfolk Female Asylum, the Columbia Female Orphan Society, and the Savannah Female Asylum were indentured. Of societies with adequate surviving records, only the Protestant Orphan Asylum Society of Mobile and the Poydras Asylum in New Orleans bucked this trend by returning more than half of their charges to parents or other relatives.[161] Most female benevolent societies had fulfilled an important community function by providing for children who otherwise would not have had access to proper nutrition, clothing, or education, and might well have died from neglect. No doubt many ladies took a private pleasure that so many of their charges were now "worthy members of the community, . . .[who] have married respectably, and reared . . . up families who have done them credit."[162] A study of the "outcomes" for indigent children in Savannah who were assisted by one of the benevolent societies revealed that, on the whole, most followed the path that had been mapped out for them. Many engaged in precisely the "suitable" artisanal occupations that they had been indentured to, and few, according to the federal census records at least, were "servants" or "domestics."[163] One Savannah directress remarked, "That they are not *all* a credit to the Institution after they leave it, is to be lamented, but is no fault of the system—nor is it to be wondered at when it is recollected who they often are, and the *haunts* from whence those children are rescued. And here I would mention that in a recent review of this very matter, it was ascertained that the *average* number of those girls who had been trained in this Asylum *& a credit to it in after life*—far exceeded the opposite calculation."[164] Girls who had spent time at the asylum included Charlotte Sawyer who was working as a milliner and dressmaker in 1860. Having been married and widowed by her mid-30s, it is a credit to her, but also to the upbringing that she received at the asylum, that all three of her own sons were working in 1860. Alice Gordon who had spent time in the asylum in the 1840s was by 1860 married to John Kennedy, a clerk in a hardware store, and the mother of five children. The story was the same elsewhere. Adeline Bucknor, for instance, had left the Beaufort Female Benevolent Society in 1853 at the age of seventeen, and seven years later she was working as a schoolmistress in Gillisonville helping to support her brother and two sisters.[165] The directresses of female orphan societies must have taken particular satisfaction from life stories such as these.

Of course, the upbringing of future citizens and the mothers of future citizens was inevitably targeted at whites. Proper education and a grounding in religious morality would fit white orphans for whatever role fate had in store for them, whether as a carpenter, a planter, or a mother. Although the records of female charitable societies were not explicit about the issue, it is clear that all female benevolence in the South, whether for children or adults, was highly racialized. The managers of the St. Louis Protestant Orphan Asylum might have declared in 1843 that "our asylum is open to all," but what they meant was that white children of any religious persuasion would be accepted, not that they would accept black children.[166] In fact the organizations discussed in this chapter, regardless of whether they dispatched visitors to the homes of the poor or provided a residential home for elderly women or children, invariably offered aid only to whites. In some locations separate benevolent societies, formed by free black women, existed that worked within their own communities. The Union Female Society, founded in Baltimore in 1821, the Female Union Band Society in Washington, D.C., and the Coloured Female Benevolent Society in New Orleans were mutual aid societies that also dispensed smaller amounts of charity among the free black poor. Free black female religious orders such as the Oblate Sisters of Providence (Baltimore, 1828) and the Sisters of the

Holy Family (New Orleans, 1842) provided free tuition for free black children, well aware of the empowering nature of education. In each case the Catholic church provided a protection against state authorities seeking to restrict free black access to learning. While secular schools for free blacks were being closed down during the 1840s and 1850s, religious schools were usually left alone. The Sisters of the Holy Family in New Orleans also aided the sick and elderly in the black community, opening the residential Lafon Home in 1848. It is no coincidence that Washington, D.C., Baltimore, and New Orleans had the largest free black populations in the South, each numbering over 10,000. They had the critical mass of people and a free black elite with sufficient wealth to support such benevolent organizations. No other southern city had more than 3,000 free blacks; consequently, most free blacks were left without recourse to privately organized benevolence.[167]

In New York and Boston, white women organized and managed orphanages for free black children from the 1830s onward but in the South only Charleston had white-run societies that were prepared to assist free blacks. Perhaps it was the absence of a female free black benevolent society in the city that persuaded the Ladies Benevolent Society and the Female Charitable Society of Charleston Neck to take it upon themselves to aid "real objects of commiseration" among the free black population. In 1825 the Visiting Committee of the Ladies Benevolent Society reported on the circumstances of three free black female pensioners: "as they have been a long time on the bounty of the society; as their supplies are very trifling, and as they cannot be received into the poor house, not being insane;—under all these circumstances, and as they have grown old upon our hands, we recommend that they shall be continued on the bounty."[168] After 1836 the Ladies Benevolent Society and the Female Charitable Society of Charleston Neck jointly administered the Hopkins Legacy which provided an income of about $900 per year to support indigent free blacks. However, despite these efforts, the majority of those supported by both societies throughout the antebellum era were white. In a city evenly divided between white and black, the Female Charitable Society of Charleston Neck helped nearly one hundred white women in 1857, for instance, but only twenty-five free black women.[169] The very public interest taken in the lives of the white poor by elite white women throughout the South therefore continuously reaffirmed the solidarity of racial ties. The message was clear: white people suffering privation and hardship deserved better merely because they were white. Free blacks and countless slaves did not.

Southern women had set the agenda on benevolence and charitable reform for half a century. Admittedly, outside major towns and cities female benevolent societies were rare and their impact on the rural poor was limited to those who lived within a short distance of a town. Yet within urban areas women had been the first to take poor young white girls and try to give them the education and training that might lift them from a life of poverty and misery. They had also acted to provide adult white women with employment, if the women were well enough, and if they were not, with fuel, food, medicine, and sometimes lodging. For much of the antebellum period, southern benevolent women had stepped out from behind their husbands and into the public world of workers, employees, and finance to create and sustain an effective system of welfare for urban poor whites.

3

The Male Response

By ALMOST ANY MEASURE, women dominated private benevolent provision for most of the antebellum era in the South, but they did not monopolize it. In several eastern cities such as Richmond, Charleston, and Savannah, male benevolent societies predated female ones by several decades. This chapter explores why southern men formed benevolent societies, how their charitable motivations differed from those of southern women, and how their charitable impulses evolved during the antebellum period.

Several male benevolent societies had been formed in the colonial South but in truth they bore little resemblance to the new breed of male benevolent society that appeared in the last decade of the eighteenth century and the first decades of the nineteenth century. The philanthropic and readily available benevolence of organizations such as the South Carolina Society, the Fellowship Society, and the Union Society gradually gave way to inward-looking organizations more concerned with their own membership than with the general relief of hardship. Many of these new associations can most accurately be termed mutual-aid societies since they restricted assistance to a particular ethnic or national group. German Friendly Societies, for instance, founded in Charleston in 1766 and 1832, Baltimore in 1783, and Savannah in 1837, and later in Louisiana, Alabama, and Tennessee, accepted members among or provided assistance to those who were of German nativity or descent. The German Friendly Society School that opened in 1802 in Charleston admitted only the children of members, and the rules of the German Friendly Society in Savannah limited charitable help to "members of the society requiring assistance in consequence of sickness or personal injury" and to the widows and orphans of deceased members. Those who sought help from the society were subject to "careful investigation" by the

Committee on Charity as to their eligibility for relief.[1] Similarly, the St. Andrew's Society in Baltimore stated in its constitution that "none but natives of Scotland, their widows and children ... [will] be entitled to any part of the charity [of the society]."[2]

The Irish were the most numerous immigrant group in the South and like their German counterparts they quickly organized themselves for mutual aid and to assist immigrants. Those of Irish descent organized Hibernian Benevolent Societies in Charleston (1799 and 1817), Baltimore (1803, 1824 and 1830), Savannah (1812 and 1847), Mobile (1822 and 1854), New Orleans (1824), Atlanta (1858), and Richmond (1859) particularly to provide food and shelter to newly arrived Irish immigrants. The founders of the Hibernian Society in Savannah stated clearly that their intention was to aid "indigent and exiled Irishmen" as well as "indigent widows and orphans of Irishmen and their descendants." In conformity with their stated aim of "providing men with work and subsistence until they could establish themselves in the New World," the Hibernian Society secured many jobs for immigrant Irishmen on the Ogeechee canal project during the 1830s and hired lawyers to prevent their exploitation by employers. The Hibernian Society of Baltimore used the legacy of a past president to establish a school initially "for the education of poor children of every religious denomination" but later limited it to "poor Irish children."[3] If the records of the Charleston Hibernian Society are typical of other Irish societies in the South, the amount of charity actually dispersed was quite small. Between 1827 and 1847 no more than $150 per year was spent on the relief of, at most, eight indigent Irish people in the city, and normally it was under $100. This parsimonious attitude was not due to lack of means—in 1846 the Charleston Hibernian Society had assets of nearly $70,000—but might have been either a result of the rules that restricted help to members and their families (who clearly did not require that much assistance), the existence of well organized city-funded relief, or the unsuitability of those who came to ask for help. Without more comprehensive records, the reasons must remain speculative.[4]

Jewish congregations in the South also organized themselves into Hebrew Benevolent Societies extending charitable help to those of the Jewish faith. The earliest, in Charleston, was founded in 1784 and while most large towns and cities had a Hebrew Benevolent Society by 1860, smaller towns like Galveston (1852), Montgomery (1852), Shreveport (1854), Houston (1855), and Macon (1857) often followed suit. It seems that wherever a Jewish community existed then some form of organized benevolence automatically followed. In the largest towns and cities there were often several different Hebrew Benevolent Societies with some operating solely as mutual aid societies while others operated orphanages, schools, and burial associations. Of course, when so many southern benevolent societies were decidedly Protestant or determinedly Catholic, it is hardly surprising that the southern Jews decided to organize themselves within their own communities as far as they were able.

Not all organized ethnic charities were completely inward-looking; the Association of the Friends of Ireland in Savannah, for instance, collected funds to assist in the cause of Catholic emancipation in Great Britain in the late 1820s, and the Irish Union Society sought to help famine victims of the 1840s. Normally, however, German, Irish, and Hebrew societies were far more concerned with their own memberships than with alleviating poverty more generally. The same charge can be levied at the many tradesmen's societies that appeared in every settlement of any size in the early national South. Once again Charleston's citizens pioneered this particular form of benevolent organization with a Master Taylors' Society (1765) and a Carpenters' Society (1783), but such organizations quickly spread among southern working men. Savannah had a House Carpenters' Association by 1802 and a Grocers' Society by 1811, but more common were the all-encompassing Mechanics' Benevolent Societies that were founded in towns and cities such as Augusta (1791), Savannah (1793), Charleston (1794), Baltimore (1796), Norfolk (1811), Milledgeville (1816), New Orleans (1821), and Petersburg (1825). These trade-based societies were essentially mutual-aid societies, desirous "of establishing by their united exertions and contributions, a lasting fund for the relief and support of such of their unfortunate brethren, or their families, as are or may become objects of charity."[5] The assistance offered to members who were sick or who left dependent wives and children on their deaths was effectively a form of social insurance in an era when the state safety-net was generally reserved for the elderly or incapacitated. The members of the Charleston Mechanic Society explained the necessity for such an arrangement thus: "From the nature of their employments, and the smallness of their capital, they are more exposed than any other class of citizens to the inconveniences and distresses arising from sickness, and such other unavoidable accidents as may deprive themselves and families of the benefit of their exertions." The founders of Charleston's Carpenters' Society added, "It is observable amongst men of all occupations, that the most industrious are not always the most successful—that designs planned with skill, and executed with perseverance, are often frustrated by unforeseen contingencies—and that through the instability of human affairs, families in comfortable circumstances, are frequently, without any fault of their own, reduced to indigence and distress." The fees paid by members therefore bought them peace of mind by guaranteeing some form of income if they became sick, without having recourse to the poorhouse.[6]

Some mechanics' associations went beyond the narrow confines of their original aims and tried to further the cause of working men more generally. The Petersburg Benevolent Mechanic Association sought "to alleviate the wants of the unfortunate, to prevent poverty, by furnishing the means of employment to those who are becoming idle and poor for the want of those means; to discountenance immorality and vice, in whatever form it may appear; and to advance the peace and prosperity of the community." It set out to do this first by encouraging its members to take on apprentices and "teach and instruct them in all those principles of morality and religion, which have a tendency to make them useful and respectable among men." Apprentices who had demonstrated "sober habits, and fidelity" were rewarded with a certificate attesting to their good character at the end of their apprenticeship. Second, "having seen and considered with sentiments of deep regret the too general neglect which prevails among persons exercising the various mechanic arts in regard to general improvement in useful knowledge," the members successfully solicited donations for an apprentice's library. Within six months the association had also founded a night school for about fifty apprentices who worked during the day, a development that earned "on the part of our fellow citizens a very general expression of pleasure and a strong disposition to further the object in view." The early operation of the school was marked by "the orderly conduct of the boys who attended" but while the "the improvement of the minds and morals of youth" was something to be lauded, the small number of pupils was not. In October 1825 members were told "the school has been but thinly attended by the scholars and [we] very much fear many of them have no desire to embrace the opportunity afforded" and two years later the school committee felt "compelled to make known their regret at the little inducement held out by masters to their boys to attend." Attendance at school was clearly seasonal, with more pupils in the winter and fewer in the summer when "their evenings were their own."[7] Throughout the antebellum era attendance at the school was patchy, most likely because much of the instruction offered was not particularly practical and many masters were not zealous in sending their apprentices regularly. James Watkinson's study of the members of the Petersburg Benevolent Mechanics Association demonstrates that masters who were themselves of meager backgrounds were far more likely to compel their apprentices to attend the school than those with wealth and status. The wider prejudices against any form of freely provided education in antebellum Virginia, discussed at length in Chapter 5, clearly had some influence among Petersburg's mechanics.[8]

Perhaps as a consequence of their limited access to state welfare, mutual-aid organizations were also the most common benevolent society formed by free black men. The Perseverance Benevolent and Mutual Aid Association was founded by free blacks in New Orleans in 1783 while Louisiana was still under Spanish control. Similar organizations were formed in Baltimore and Washington, D.C., but by far the greatest concentration of these societies was in Charleston where the Brown Fellowship Society (1790) was followed by the Free Dark Men of Color (1791), the Humane and Friendly Society (1802), the Friendly Union Brotherly Association (1813), and the Friendly Moralist Society (1838). Each operated much like white mutual-aid societies but tended to be more exclusive as to their membership. The mulatto members of the Brown Fellowship Society, for instance, designated themselves "free brown men" mainly to distinguish themselves from non-mulatto free blacks. Unlike some other free black benevolent societies, the Brown Fellowship Society was willing to help "any poor colored orphan or adult, being free, whose case requires needful assistance" but the numbers helped were very small.[9]

Mutual-aid societies were certainly the most common form of organized male benevolence during the first thirty years of the nineteenth century, and their inward-looking nature stands in stark contrast to the outreach of benevolent societies, orphan asylums, and school societies organized by southern women. However, perhaps because the medical profession was an exclusively male one, charities that provided free health care to paupers were organized and managed solely by men. Some hospitals were built by state or local authorities and therefore funded by taxpayers, but others, such as Savannah's Poor House and Hospital, were founded and administered as private concerns. Many of the persons who required medical treatment in Savannah were well able to pay the normal fees of $12 for the first week and $8 per week afterward; therefore only the indigent received free care. Part of the "great utility" of the hospital for "the community at large," boasted the managers, was that "no longer [do] beggars infest the doors of the citizens, or unseemly objects of human infirmity assail their senses in the streets."[10] The need for a proper hospital in Savannah, and in many other port cities, was partly driven by the need to care for the large number of visiting sailors who became sick while in the city. The charter of incorporation of the Poor House and Hospital explained that as "a commercial city, much resorted to by the citizens of this state, and adventurers from the different parts of the world, [Savannah] is exposed to the burthens of those afflicted with poverty, disease, & infirmity, in much greater degree than the other counties of this state; that no adequate provision has yet been made for their succor and support in times of accident, sickness and distress." Those behind the formation of the institution in Savannah were also well aware that "three fourths of the seamen, buried in this place have died for the want of suitable diet, and nursing when sick. For no sooner are they indisposed, than the proprietors of the houses where they board, stow them away in a close garret, without paying attention either to cleanliness or anything else necessary for their recovery."[11]

For most of the antebellum period visiting sailors constituted the largest single group housed in Savannah's Poor House and Hospital. About half of all admissions during the 1810s were sailors born in other states, and a further third were foreign sailors. No more than 20 percent were natives of Georgia.[12] The United States treasury refunded the expenses of each American sailor at the rate of $4.50 per week, and during the 1810s this brought the hospital an average income of $1,500 per year. The British consul in Savannah paid for the care of British sailors at a similar rate and it is likely, given British naval supremacy, that British-born sailors dominated the foreign-born in the hospital.[13] Government funding was not as reliable as it might seem. The managers of the hospital informed the mayor in 1821 that unless more funding was forthcoming from Washington they would "reject all seamen as paupers." Furthermore, "when it is considered of what importance Savannah as a commercial city is, it surely ought to be a subject worth the attention of government to have the seamen arriving in this port well provided for . . . many poor seamen will be destitute and of course suffer exceedingly if this proposition is not accepted." Treasury secretary William Crawford was not able to find a cheaper alternative in Savannah, so the managers were informed they would receive the additional funding they had requested; however, it was not immediately forthcoming.[14] In April 1822 a public meeting was held in the city to debate whether the city should assume the debts of the Poor House and Hospital, then amounting to $21,000. An editorial in the *Georgian* explained that the debts were primarily due to tardiness of the federal treasury in paying for American seamen and the failure of the state legislature to provide for those Georgians from outside Savannah who were housed there. Indeed, "were the expenses of the Hospital confined only to the objects which require its aid from the city, its finances would be in a different situation from what they are now," but since "benevolence is universal" the managers had decided that "it would be inhuman to drive from its doors the diseased and miserable because they do not reside within its immediate vicinity."[15] Despite a sympathetic city council and letters in the press arguing that failure to assume the debt would mean the poor would be thrown onto the private charity of individuals where they would "invade our recesses" and "press their claims in the bosoms of our families," the city, meeting on April 19, refused to assume the debt.[16] The following year the city council again put the idea of an annual appropriation of $2,500 for the hospital to a public vote, arguing that "whilst the poor are increasing, the means of assistance proportionately decreases and the period has at length arrived when public appropriations are required to supply the deficiency of private donations." The special committee of council even published a proposed city budget showing how this appropriation was affordable within the existing revenues of the city, but once again the citizens voted against it.[17] Without financial support from the city the Poor House and Hospital closed on May 1, 1823. The building was purchased from creditors by the Planter's Bank and the Marine Insurance Company, and in 1825, it was resold to the city council. Two years later, believing that "there is a strong disposition on the part of the inhabitants of the city to place the Poor House & Hospital upon its former footing," the city council handed "the entire control & superintendence" to a new association of subscribers.[18]

The altered status of the Poor House did not mean that the city intended to become its main source of income. Accounts from 1832 show that payments by the federal government for sailors, and subscriptions from private citizens constituted more than two-thirds of its annual income.[19] Like their benevolent female counterparts, the managers of the Poor House and Hospital gradually moved away from private subscriptions and toward investments, purchasing, for instance, $1,600 of stock in the Central Railroad in 1842. During 1850s the hospital's permanent fund of investments grew from $34,500 to $57,600, with money invested mainly in railroad stocks, bank shares, and Savannah city bonds. By the 1850s the hospital was clearly not in any kind of financial need. When John Tipton, a pauper patient, died in the hospital in 1858, the steward discovered nearly $200 in gold and notes on the body, but rather than deduct any fee for his care the managers sent the full amount to his sister in Pottsville.[20]

Because local authorities failed to make their own arrangements for housing the poor, Savannah's Poor House and Hospital also received part of the county poor tax, which in the late 1850s amounted to $600–700 a year. The number of pauper patients was initially quite small, only 22 of nearly 200 admissions in 1810; but it rose rapidly during the antebellum era, numbering 330 in 1841—more than two-thirds of the total inmates during that year—and staying at roughly that level until the Civil War.[21] While some of the paupers were sent to the hospital by the Inferior Court of Chatham County others applied in person to the managers for admission. Catherine McGolrick begged Dr. John Grimes to take her "sister who is in a very low state of health and suffers for the want of proper assistance in regard to nourishment as well as medicine." Having tried to care for her sister herself, McGolrick sought help because "I have two small children and [am] sick myself and have no other support but what I get by my industry and what I am able to do now is hardly sufficient to keep my family from want."[22] Although it is not known if McGolrick's application was successful, it is clear that managers of the Poor House and Hospital in Savannah, like their counterparts who managed public poorhouses elsewhere in the South, had to make decisions regarding the suitability of applicants. The President of the Board of Managers in Savannah was "authorized to exercise his own judgement in reference to poor and indigent persons applying for the benefits of the hospital" and in 1843 he admitted two elderly women for "as long as they live" since they "are of excellent character & respectably connected in Savannah." Another successful applicant was Mrs. Neville, who informed the board "that her health is so delicate and precarious as to deter [her] from using those exertions at her needle for her support," but Philip Lamp was refused admission since it was known "that he has children in good circumstances in Jefferson County."[23]

In general, the board of Savannah's Poor House and Hospital held a low opinion of the poor, commenting in 1841 that "by far the greater proportion of paupers admitted are men of decidedly intemperate habits." On another occasion the steward of the institution was overheard describing the Irish-born patients "as being the most dirty, obstinate and troublesome in the institution." Managers clearly intended to keep a tight rein on the inmates since the rules of the hospital stated that patients were not permitted to come and go as they pleased, to enter the kitchens, or to visit wards reserved for the opposite sex; they were not permitted to drink alcohol or "to play at cards, dice, or any other game of hazard, within the hospital, or to beg any where in the city of Savannah, on pain of being discharged for irregularity." Furthermore, "such pauper patients as are able, in the opinion of the physicians, shall assist in nursing others, washing and ironing the linen, washing and cleaning the rooms, and such other services as the steward or matron shall require." In 1851, in order to recoup some of the costs incurred in caring for the poor, the board resolved that the free labor of the poor should not cease with their recovery but "that pauper patients may be required by the steward to remain at the hospital after recovery from sickness, & render services to the institution in nursing or other work about the house at the discretion of the steward to the amount of the expenses incurred in the hospital as patients."[24] Despite these rules the board tried hard to make the hospital a pleasant place for the sick to be treated and to convalesce. The hospital had running water, gas lighting and heating, and a small garden with shade trees "where the patients can daily take such exercise as may conduce to the restoration of health."[25] Clearly the gentlemen who managed the Poor House and Hospital had a genuine humanitarian purpose where moral reform and better self-discipline was part of the care/cure on offer.

Male charitable societies were not immune to the staff problems that often plagued female-run orphanages. On two separate occasions the board of Savannah's Poor House and Hospital had to intervene to protect its slaves from abuse by the steward. When one slave appeared before the president of the board "covered in blood," the board informed the steward that he should use "less hard measures with the servants" while accepting that no doubt the slave had given "serious provocation by impudence or otherwise." When the board intervened again in 1858 the steward complained "that the president sided with the servants rather than with him in such conflicts," but the board stated unequivocally that all slaves "whether owned or hired are under the protection of the board." The president further confided his hope that the young Irish-born steward, James Shore, "would improve as he learned the true mode of management of servants."[26]

Even though Charleston already had a hospital attached to its poorhouse, members of the Medical Society of South Carolina worked in conjunction with the city council to establish the new Roper Hospital in the 1850s. Aware that the legacy of Thomas Roper was insufficient to establish a hospital on its own, the trustees petitioned the city council for help, informing them that "the [existing] combination of a hospital and poorhouse under the same roof works badly. It deters many from asking aid at the hospital, least they be considered paupers. This feeling is strong among our own citizens. Accordingly the hospital is mostly filled by strangers . . . the necessary mingling of the honest, but unfortunate sick with the degraded and vicious reprobates sent to the same house for temporary punishment is another evil to which the system there exposes its inmates." In answer to the objection that the Shirras Dispensary provided for the worthy poor, the trustees responded that outpatient care could not provide the good food, clean bedding, new dressings, and proper clothing necessary for recuperation. As a result of this petition the city council granted $20,000 and a city lot for the construction of a hospital, together with $1,000 annually. During the yellow fever epidemic of 1854 the hospital treated 180 patients despite not being fully built, but in normal years it treated about thirty people gratis per month.[27]

Other medical charities were organized by southern men in response to a particular crisis to provide immediate nursing care as well as food and clothing for widows and orphans. The Can't Get Away Club was established in Mobile by a small group of merchants, bankers, and lawyers who had been

6. Savannah Poorhouse and Hospital, opened in 1808.
Reproduced from George White, *Historical Collections of Georgia*
(New York: Pudney and Russel, 1854), 314.

unable to "get away" from the city during its first major yellow fever epidemic in 1839 that claimed more than 600 lives. After the epidemic was over the club became dormant, but it was revived with every fresh outbreak of the disease in 1843, 1853, and 1858. After the 1853 epidemic, the worst in Mobile's history claiming 764 lives, the club was incorporated and more formally organized. The doctors and nurses whose salaries had been paid by the club during 1853 were retained and were sent to Savannah in 1854 and Norfolk and Portsmouth the following year to provide emergency medical care during further outbreaks of the disease.[28] The Montgomery Relief Club, founded on similar principles in 1854, raised funds for medical purposes and so "that this society shall always be ready to meet the necessities that may arise . . . a certain number of its members will be detailed for each night's service."[29] Perhaps the most common of these relief organizations were the Howard Associations that were formed specifically in response to yellow fever epidemics in New Orleans (1837), Galveston (1845), Charleston (1854), Richmond (1855), and Norfolk (1855). These societies provided food, shelter, and medical care to the sick, and they also coordinated the distribution of relief supplies that often flooded into the affected cities at a time when the normal civil authority was weak or even nonexistent. Members' names were published in the newspapers once it was clear an epidemic had begun, and the sick were directed to contact a member for medical help and other supplies. Members of the Howard Association in Charleston were permitted to spend up to $2.50 per week on each patient when the patient produced a doctor's certificate, but "persons disorderly in conduct or of intemperate habits, or having no reputable means of support when in health, shall be regarded as proper inmates of the poorhouse & shall not be attended by our visitors." The president of the association was proud to report following the epidemic of 1858 that members "have shrunk from the performance of no task assigned them, and have been found in every quarter of our city, including the lowly and the unseemly hovel of filth and disease."[30]

Although not termed a Howard Association, the Savannah Benevolent Association fulfilled a similar function during the yellow fever outbreak in the city in 1854. First formed as a "Young Men's Benevolent Association" on September 12, 1854, at a time when the epidemic was at its height, the members raised more than $3,000 in a matter of days from the remaining residents of the city for the relief of suffering and want. A thousand loaves of bread were ordered from Macon and distributed among the hungry, and those found without anyone to care for them during their illness were either moved to a newly opened hospital or offered nursing care. A member was assigned to each city ward with instructions to report back daily to the association with the number of new cases of yellow fever, the number of deaths, and the measures that had been taken to relieve the worst cases up to a maximum cost of $5 per individual. As in other cities the benevolent association took on the trappings of a civic government during the crisis, undertaking a census of the city for the mayor and accepting and distributing donations totaling more than $22,000 from other cities as well as from local residents. Even the mayor, when money was sent to him, would frequently pass it to the treasurer of the benevolent association.[31] Not content with merely administering to the wants of the sick, members also acted as a form of moral police publicly condemning "to the execration of every member of the community," for instance, the "cruel, unchristian, unmanly, and inhuman" actions of Dennis Haley, a local landlord who evicted a widow and her child "for the non-payment of rent, turning her into the street, and endangering the life of the child." The *Morning News*, commenting on this case, believed that "the paltry pittance of rent has cost [him] vastly more than it was worth."[32]

Once the epidemic was over, the Savannah Benevolent Association effectively became dormant, refusing an application for help from Mary Harris in March 1855, for instance, "it not coming within the constitution of this association." Over the next few years the association quietly accumulated more than $8,000 of stocks and shares, and on its resumption of "active operations" during the next yellow fever outbreak in September 1858, it was able "to raise upon pledge of the stock of the association such funds as may be necessary for the uses of the association during the epidemic." The moral dimension to the charitable work of the Savannah Benevolent Association was again evident in 1858. With a young girl in their care whose mother had succumbed to the disease, the association wrote to her "putative father, requesting him to provide for the child, and if he refused, the association would take steps to compel him to do so." The father never replied to this letter, and when the child died the following summer she was buried at the expense of the association.[33]

In general, before about 1840, southern men associated themselves together for a small number of distinct benevolent purposes, most commonly to offer some kind of support to members of a common ethnic, religious, or trade group, but also to offer limited free medical services to the most indigent members of society. There were exceptions to this generalization of course. The Society for the Prevention of Pauperism was established in Baltimore in 1821 to combat the easy availability of strong liquor, which it had identified as the main cause of poverty, vice, and crime in the city. However, its attempts to control the sale and consumption of alcohol were fiercely resisted by citizens who characterized its work as an "inquisition." The so-called "Tribunal of Liberty" urged the citizens of Baltimore to "defeat the Grand Inquisitor, and those familiars of the brotherhood, who would destroy your rights, interrupt your trade and worldly pursuits; mature a system of grinding taxation, and make your beautiful city a den for howling fanaticism, the abode of intolerance, persecution and hypocrisy; who would deprive you of all social pleasures, and of all amusements connected with the improvement, or which, in themselves, constitute the graces and the elegancies of the intellectual world."[34] With such vilification it is not surprising that the Society for the Prevention of Pauperism lasted barely a year.

Another exception, at least before 1840, was the Lancastrian School founded in Richmond in 1816. The funding for the school came from three sources: paying subscribers; the Common Hall of Richmond, which contributed $600 annually; and fees from the pupils, "it being understood that none but really poor children are to be exempted from said fees."[35] Aside from the fact that the school took paying as well as free pupils there was little to distinguish it from the Savannah Free School founded in the same year. Both were organized on the monitorial system advocated by Joseph Lancaster, which was believed to be "the cheapest way, ever devised, of teaching the elements of learning." Furthermore, both sought to give children a clear moral compass that would sustain them as adults. Richmond's *Christian Monitor* believed that "scenes of turbulence and riot, the indulgence of disorderly passions, the irregularity and confusion of vice, will be very likely to disgust rather than seduce a youth accustomed to the strict discipline, and perfect order, of a well conducted Lancastrian School." Consequently "the scholars shall be required to be cleanly in their persons and clothing, punctual in attendance, diligent and attentive in school, obedient and submissive to their teachers, affable and kind to each other, and quiet and orderly while at play." Just as Charleston's Orphan House was shown off to visitors as an example of the city's sophistication, the founders hoped that the Lancastrian School would "be worthy of the city, and worthy of the state. Let it be an institution that the stranger will enquire for when he comes to Richmond, and that the wise legislator will contemplate with pleasure and admiration."[36]

The Lancastrian School in Richmond was actually more akin to the free schools of South Carolina and Virginia, where local school commissioners identified the "poor" and offered them free tuition, than a genuine free school. Elite men were accustomed to this role in Richmond and elsewhere, and therefore the only difference between this school and many others in the state was the method of teaching and the number of poor children taught. The Chatham Academy, a school in Savannah that charged tuition, also took in a small number of pupils free of charge throughout the antebellum era, though this charity was strictly limited. When Mrs. Davis applied "to educate her children at the academy at a lesser charge than the regular rates of this time, upon the investigation of her pecuniary circumstances it was determined by the unanimous vote of the trustees that Mrs. Davis could not be considered an object of charity" and in fact no more than twenty children from poor families received free tuition at any one time. This is not to decry the achievements of some Lancastrian Schools. The Anderson Seminary, founded in Petersburg in 1821, also operated along Lancastrian principles primarily because it would allow "all the poor children of our town to partake of the advantages of education." In its first decade of operation the seminary taught about 400 pupils, "the greater part of them, without the facilities which this school affords would be without the means of daily instruction. . . . Many who were taught in this seminary are now pursuing trades and occupations; and the greater part promise to be useful members of society."[37] In comparison to female free schools, however, the efforts of men were modest. Savannah's Free School enrolled nearly 250 children in 1823 alone, and the schools run by Mobile's Catholic Orphan Asylum taught between 600 and 700 children a year in the 1850s.[38]

Free black children were excluded from charity schools managed by white men and women as well as from state-funded common schools; therefore, several male free black benevolent associations attempted to redress the balance. The fifty members of the Minors Moralist Society, founded in Charleston in 1803, gave 20¢ a month in addition to the $5 joining fee, to pay for a teacher for free black children. However, the majority of the free black children taught at the expense of this and other institutions, such as the Bonneau Library Society (Charleston, 1830), the Catholic Society for the Instruction of Indigent Orphans (New Orleans, 1847), and the Resolute Beneficial Society (Washington, D.C., 1818), belonged to free black elite families and were not truly indigent. The men who founded these schools were well aware that education and literacy distinguished them from most enslaved people and helped to preserve their free status. The work of such societies was therefore to some degree conservative since social mobility for the poorest free blacks was rarely their main aim. Census records suggest that the vast majority of free blacks remained illiterate throughout the antebellum period.[39]

A small number of male charitable organizations dating back to the eighteenth century continued their charitable work throughout the antebellum period. Originally designed to be a mutual-aid society, whereby paid-up members received the security of knowing that their relatives and widows would be cared for in the event of a member's untimely death, the mission of the Union Society in Savannah gradually expanded to include assistance for any poor or disadvantaged child, regardless of whether the child's parent had been a member of the society. To secure their control over the children, the Union Society demanded that living parents or relatives sign indentures legally binding the children to institutions, just as they did elsewhere in the South.[40] The managers of the Union Society were absolutely explicit in their justification of this position: "Whereas it may happen that children who have been schooled by the funds of this society, may afterwards be taken away by their parents, guardians or friends, and instead of being put to some useful trade, or occupation, may be permitted to pursue vicious courses, whereby both they and the community, may be deprived of those advantages, which it was the design of this institution to procure."[41] The Union Society clearly aimed to take disadvantaged children from meager backgrounds and to give them the tools to become independent adults. Boys taken in by the Union Society were expected to "learn habits of industry and usefulness, become familiar with the use of tools, and with farming and mechanical operations and . . . receive strict attention in their schooling."[42] On reaching about fourteen years of age they were normally apprenticed to a "suitable trade or profession" such as printer, carpenter, cabinetmaker, blacksmith, saddler, or tailor. The Union Society managers took their responsibility seriously, genuinely trying to find positions for their charges that would lead to a sustainable employment in later life. Concerned in 1817 that "the printing business was not of sufficient importance," managers recommended that boys should instead be apprenticed to "some respectable carpenter, bricklayer or some other mechanic," perhaps recognizing that Savannah was unlikely to support enough newspapers to give work to so many apprentice printers.[43] The involvement of the Union Society did not cease abruptly when a boy was apprenticed, since on several occasions the boys were later sent to a different master to learn a different trade. The minutes do not record, however, whether these moves were due to the death of the original master or dissatisfaction of either the boy or the master with the existing arrangement.[44] The charity of the Union Society was limited, however: no more than ten boys were on the bounty of the society at any one time. The female equivalent of the Union Society, the Savannah Female Asylum, by contrast, housed between twenty-five and thirty-five girls at once.[45]

The Winyaw Indigo Society, founded in 1755, provided free schooling for up to twenty children in Georgetown, South Carolina, throughout the antebellum era, and spent more than $1,000 on a new schoolroom in 1854.[46] Similarly, the Fellowship Society of Charleston created a school fund for the education of poor children in 1804. Parents of poor children could apply for aid and by the 1820s the society was spending more than $400 on the education of thirteen indigent children. When the city established its public school system in the 1850s the Fellowship Society closed its own school and contributed $3,000 toward the cost of a new city high school.[47] However, the Fellowship Society continued to expend the greatest amounts of its funds on the support of the widows of former members. There were normally about twenty-five widows supported in any given year, and they usually received between $100 and $150 each. Absolute destitution was not a prerequisite for relief; nine of twenty-four pensioners in 1829 owned slaves and several owned their own homes. The cash provided by the Fellowship Society was in many cases a supplement to support from other charitable societies, such as the South Carolina Society or the St. George's Society, as well as income from hiring out slaves. In no instance did the Fellowship

Society insist that slaves be sold before relief would be granted, accepting that in many cases these slaves were actually more "an incumbrance...either from age or infancy" than an asset.[48]

Although several male benevolent societies provided assistance to poor children and widows in their respective cities, they tended to work on a far smaller scale than comparable female benevolent societies. Not only in Savannah did the care offered by female societies outstrip that offered by male ones. In Charleston, the Fellowship Society might have been aiding twenty-five widows, but the Ladies Benevolent Society assisted more than 300 needy families each year.[49] Male benevolence in the South, therefore, tended to be limited in scope, and it was rare before 1840 for a male orga-nized society to expand either the number of its beneficiaries or the nature of the care it offered.

However, men definitely took the lead in the care and reformation of sea-men. Bethel unions, and marine and port societies were common in nearly all southern coastal cities, starting with the Baltimore Charitable Marine Society (1797), and the Charleston Marine Society (1806) and continuing with Bethel unions in Richmond (1821), Charleston (1822), New Orleans (1823), Louisville (1830), and Mobile (1836); there were port societies in Charleston (1823), Mobile (1835), Savannah (1843), and Galveston (1858). Despite their different names all these societies tried to provide a religious ministry to visiting seamen and sailors, and it was the religious goal that attracted both finances and members in support of Bethel societies, that tended to lead prayer meetings, and port societies that focused their atten-tion on providing the services of a minister. The Richmond Bethel Union drew support from all of the city's protestant denominations seeking to "ex-tend to seamen the instructions of the gospel, to persuade them to become reconciled to God, and generally to promote their temporal and eternal welfare." For the Richmond Bethel Union this meant leading religious worship on the decks of visiting ships, and distributing Bibles and religious tracts to the seamen. And while they took heart that most were "orderly, serious, and attentive," they were conscious of some "restlessness" and "pre-mature retirement."[50] Savannah's Port Society also drew members from ev-ery protestant church and declared its intention to "furnish seamen with the regular evangelical ministration of the gospel and such other moral and religious instruction as may be practicable" and nothing pleased them more to see "the rough and unlettered seaman bowing humbly before his maker in the lowest attitude of prayer."[51]

Aware that only a minority of the hundreds of sailors visiting Savannah every year attended services in the mariner's church, the managers of the Port Society blamed the sailor's boarding houses where drink and easy women were readily available. The obvious way to combat this was to finance a sailor's home where they could "hold out every proper and reasonable inducement for the inmates of the house to attend divine worship on the Sabbath." Perhaps uneasy at taking on the domestic management of the sailor's home, the Port Society enlisted the assistance of the Female Seaman's Friend Society to furnish the house that had been rented for sailors. The numbers of sailors using the new home was small because of "the active opposition constantly made by common sailor boarding housekeepers, whose pecuniary interests depend in a great measure upon the suppression of the sailor's home and for the accomplishment of which active runners, as they are called, are employed to decoy and seduce the poor sailor." At the end of 1846 the Port Society passed the entire management of the home to the Female Seaman's Friend Society, preferring to concentrate on the ministry of the Bethel Church, commenting that Savannah had many charities providing temporal relief "but how much more worthy is that charity that seeks the good of immortal souls."[52] The Port Society members were not entirely happy with their decision to give up the sailor's home as the 1850s wore on. In 1851 the managers concluded that "whereas the objects of the Mariner's Church and the Seaman's Home are intimately connected, and that the proper management of the latter is essential to the success of the former," it was therefore necessary to work more closely with the seaman's home to try to get those who stayed there to attend the mariner's church. A year later they censured Captain Parker, superintendent of the sailor's home, for "not acting in concert with the Mariner's Church."[53] Between 1852 and 1861 the Female Seaman's Friend Society held only two meetings, in 1856–1857, and the virtual collapse of this hitherto staunch supporter forced the Port Society to take on more responsibilities itself. In early 1860, "the president was requested to make inquiry of the Ladies Seaman's Friend Society respecting a transfer of the Savannah Home to the Port Society" and the inability of the Female Seaman's Friend Society to reconstitute itself during the 1850s was a total reversal of the situation that had persisted between 1845 and 1850, when the fund-raising capabilities of Savannah's women had sustained the work of the Port Society.[54]

Almost exactly the same development occurred in Charleston. The Female Seamen's Friend Society was founded in 1826 with the express purpose of managing a sailor's home, and for more than a decade it worked closely with the Port Society and the Bethel Union to house more than 200 sailors annually. However in 1839 the Port Society purchased the sailor's home from the Female Seaman's Friend Society for $8,500 and set about actively recruiting sailors by employing six runners who visited all newly arrived ships "to procure boarders for the house." Such tactics were evidently effective as in 1850 more than 500 sailors boarded at the home.[55]

By moving into residential care that had previously been a female monopoly, the managers of the port societies of Savannah and Charleston were crossing a line, but they were not alone in this. The twenty years after 1840 saw southern men increasingly involved in benevolent work, such as the management of orphan asylums, that had previously been almost exclusively female. Admittedly some male societies had cared for orphan boys for a long time. The Union Society in Savannah, for example, could trace its roots back to 1750; but crucially, it did not run an orphanage as the children it supported were housed with local families or relatives and not in any institution managed by members of the society.[56] One of the first orphanages built, maintained, and managed by southern men was the Asylum for Destitute Orphan Boys opened in New Orleans in 1824. Local protestant men contributed $10 each toward the project, but they were seven years behind their female counterparts who had opened the Poydras Orphan Asylum in 1817, and nearly a century behind the Ursuline nuns who had taken in orphan girls since 1727.

Little is known about the Asylum for Destitute Orphan Boys in New Orleans, but the House of Refuge that was opened in Baltimore in 1830 was, at least implicitly, a criticism of preexisting orphanages such as that managed by the Female Humane Association. Founded by "respectable" citizens of Baltimore "for juvenile delinquents," it was supposed to "redeem youth from temptation and ruin, and after a course of moral apprenticeship, to send them forth to usefulness, as honest and industrious members of society." Those taken into the house could expect "education, employment and instruction in some useful trade; constant association with men of character and purity; frequent exercise in religious duty; rational amusement . . . cleanliness in dress and person; the absence of falsehood and profanity" and the watchful eye of a "task-master."[57] While many of these aims and objectives were identical to those professed by female managers of orphan asylums, clearly Baltimore's men felt that they needed an institution under their own direction to achieve the desired social transformation.

The foundation of the Charleston Benevolent Society in 1827 can also be interpreted as a criticism of the existing charitable endeavors in the city, and principally those of the Ladies Benevolent Society. Its target group was precisely the same as that of the Ladies Benevolent Society, namely, "aged and helpless females in the lowest condition of poverty and distress" whom it would identify by means of a visiting committee and relieve through the provision of food and clothing. However, the Charleston Benevolent Society was not simply intending to join in the existing charitable labors of the Ladies Benevolent Society; rather, it demanded a more discerning approach to benevolence "by judiciously discriminating between the truly indigent, and the shameless abuser of public sympathy—between him, who by the force of irresistible circumstances, had been made to sink under the chilling frosts of adversity—and him, who by a long course of indolence, intemperance, or extravagance, has reduced himself to penury."[58] The men who created this society commented that "they have long observed, as well as experienced the gross impositions which are daily practised upon the liberal and open handed members of your community, by persons assuming the air and appearance of suffering mendicants, without having any claims however either in point of fact or of merit to pecuniary or other relief." A more hard-nosed approach would permit funds to be concentrated on those who truly deserved it, "thus cherishing and promoting the cultivation of virtue" while making life harder for "this class of individuals who solicit aid from door to door and from day to day." In perhaps the ultimate snub to the Ladies Benevolent Society, Peter Shand, secretary of the Charleston Benevolent Society, claimed that "several ladies of great respectability, who, with many others of their sex, have expressed their desire to become members."[59]

It is hard to measure the impact of this particular society and others like it, such as the Humane Society of Louisville, which in order to prevent "deception . . . [and] artful tales" required "indubitable evidence of the distress to be relieved." The first annual report stated that more than 150 people had been assisted with food and clothing, all of whom were not only "deserving" but also of "the lowest situation of indigence and desertion."[60] However, the number of subscribers, and therefore the income of the society, was small, suggesting that it did not catch the imagination of Charlestonians as much as the managers had hoped. Its slightly mean-spirited approach to benevolence seems to have gone against the grain of charity in the city. Henry Laurens Pinckney, addressing the Methodist Benevolent Society in 1835, declared, "What if charity has been sometimes misapplied, or acted as a premium to idleness and vice! These are errors or evils that may be avoided or corrected: but better that unworthy objects should deceive us, than that meritorious individuals should receive no aid."[61] Given the city council's willingness to fund a city poorhouse and a magnificent orphan house, it is more likely that it was Pinckney who was typical of Charleston's male elite and indeed of benevolent men elsewhere in the South. Charles Button, editor of the *Lynchburg Virginian*, asked his readers to accept that "there are always some who find it exceedingly difficult to obtain even the necessaries of life." Furthermore, although the "idle, dissolute and depraved" would be found among the poor, "we should not be too rigid in any case."[62] Perhaps unsurprisingly, no references to the Charleston Benevolent Society exist after 1830.

Another male-organized charitable society that failed to captivate the populace of Charleston was the Episcopal Church Home, founded in 1851. Deciding that "the church had too long neglected a solemn duty," Episcopalians opened a home that would "provide a retreat for destitute and deserving females, in which they may be employed in industrial pursuits"; it also accepted orphan girls "to train them up in industrial pursuit, to give them a secular education suited to their sphere in life, and above all, to afford them a religious education on the principles of the Church."[63] The problem for the church home was that Charleston's Orphan House and Poorhouse adequately provided for the poor of the city and therefore most citizens did not see the need for a new facility offering residential care. In fact, the suspicion among the city elite was that the women entering the institution "spend their days in unnatural rites or indolent pietism" and consequently those who might have supported the venture looked "coldly" upon it. Their fears were apparently confirmed in 1854 when the Reverend J. Barnwell

Campbell condemned the Commissioners of the Orphan House, some of the most respected citizens of Charleston, because their "Chapel Door is open to every sect under heaven, from the Unitarian to the Universalist; and the commissioners of that institution, eligible from all creeds, may claim to teach those children all their religious errors." Perhaps aware that this kind of rhetoric was part of the reason that their institution was not flourishing, with only a handful of adult inmates and about twenty orphan girls, the managers had become far more conciliatory by 1858 stating that "the Home has no rivalry whatever with any other charitable institution. It has its own peculiar features, which we deem of great value and importance. Other institutions have, in most respects, a different sphere of action, and fill each by itself a want or even a necessity of our community."[64]

Another reason for the low fortunes of this home was the attitudes of some of the poor toward the regime inside. Despite believing the discipline within the home to be "gentle, steady, and firm," the managers were forced to report each year that some of the girls had either absconded or been removed by their relatives without proper permission. Even among those who remained in the home the managers reported "the absurd prejudice against labor, existing quite as strongly among the poor as among the rich. It has often happened that the surviving parent has given serious annoyance to us by telling the child, that she ought not to do this or that kind of work."[65] The managers were happy to report in 1858 that "considering the ignorance and degradation from which many of them were rescued, the indolence, vice, and disorderly lives into which many of their parents (when they have any alive) are plunged, and almost certain prospect before them, had they not been rescued by this charity of ours; of growing up not only in poverty but in open vice, we cannot but look upon the ruddy countenances and smiling faces of these interesting little ones with lively gratitude"; however, it was obvious to everyone who knew the work of the city's orphan house and poor house that the achievements of the Episcopal Church Home were modest in the extreme.[66]

Richmond's male elite also formed their own benevolent societies in the 1840s, not in competition with preexisting female equivalents but rather directly because of their encouragement. The Gentlemen's Benevolent Society was formed in 1844 as an "adjunct" to the female-run Union Benevolent Society (founded 1835). With "our visitors entering the abodes of want and suffering only on the summons and as the attendants of lady visitors," it mainly concerned itself with raising money to be spent by the ladies.[67] The Male Orphan Society, founded in Richmond in 1846, was a direct result of the directresses of the Female Humane Association persuading their husbands to start a benevolent society for boys complementary to their own for girls. Tobacconist Frederick Bransford's wife, Charlotte, had long been a member of the Female Humane Association, as had Dr. James Bolton's wife. Both men were among the first managers of the Male Orphan Society. Other possible contributors were encouraged by editorials like this in the Richmond *Daily Whig*:

> It is believed that the liberal and benevolent of our citizens could not more judiciously bestow their favors than by the establishment of an asylum for destitute and orphan boys. What an incalculable amount of good might be produced by thus saving from vice and degradation, and leading into the paths of virtue, industry and knowledge, the unfortunate beings of that description? Now suppose some two hundred gentlemen should commence an association for this laudable object with contributions of ten dollars each; can there be a doubt as to the noble undertaking so commending itself to the patronage of our citizens, so as to ensure its permanence and usefulness? Boys thus saved from ruin and vice, could in due time, be instructed in suitable branches of the mechanic arts during their abode in the institution, and at their majority, be prepared as men to undertake with efficiency their duties and responsibilities.[68]

Once open, the orphanage accepted "orphan boys, and boys with a parent, or parents who are morally or physically unable to provide for their children, between the ages of six and twelve." Like most other orphanages, "for the well-being of the boys, and proper management of the Home, all the boys shall be under the absolute control of the superintendent, . . . and no person outside the Home shall have any communication with any boy, except and by consent and in the presence of the Superintendent or Matron." Even letters written to and by the boys were vetted by the superintendent who alone determined if they were delivered.[69]

Funding for Richmond's Male Orphan Society in its first years came principally from donations and subscriptions with a civic allowance of $40 per year for each boy taken from the city's poorhouse. The Richmond *Whig* was enthusiastic about this development, believing that "a necessary tax which vice and idleness impose upon the community is thus by the aid of this society, converted into a boon to the objects of public charity; and the city actually confers upon them the blessings of education and moral culture for what she expended in maintaining them in a state of pauperism."[70] However, just as female benevolent societies had found a generation earlier, the large numbers of initial subscribers quickly dwindled, leaving the subscription income insufficient to meet expenses. In 1851 the board resolved to establish a $10,000 permanent fund, to be invested in stocks and shares, that would provide the necessary annual income. This idea evidently caught the imagination of Richmond's benevolent elite, and the sum was raised relatively quickly. With its finances secure the Male Orphan Asylum increased the number of boys in its care from fifteen in 1851, to twenty in 1854 and thirty in 1856. When numbers reached thirty-nine in 1859 the managers decided to construct a new asylum that would house up to seventy-five boys. This required a fresh appeal to the liberality of local citizens, but such was the attractiveness of the cause and so well connected were the managers, that $14,000 was raised within a very short period.[71]

The Manual Labor School in Baltimore experienced a similar increase in interest and support during the 1850s. Founded in 1840 on a farm just outside the city, the school took in orphan and other destitute boys and provided them not only with free education but also training in agricultural skills. The report of 1849 showed the institution in some disarray, with eight boys absconding during the year, the main building consumed by fire, and the society in debt. The directors hoped that publicity regarding their perilous state would revive "that steady and increasing interest, which they had hoped would have, ere now, more widely pervaded this community."[72] By 1855, however, not only was the school free from debt, but it had also increased the number of boys from thirty-one to fifty-five while rebuilding the school bigger and better than before. The directors were able to take pleasure that they had spared their charges "from the evil influences that surround them" and at the same time were able to "afford them a home, to feed, clothe, and instruct them in moral and religious duties, and at suitable ages, to place them out to respectable trades or professions, to fit and qualify them to become useful members of society." Much of this transformation can be attributed to the increased income from subscriptions that nearly doubled in the space of six years enabling the society to embark on expensive building projects and to increase the scope of its work among the poor.[73]

Another society that grew rapidly in the last decade of the antebellum era was Baltimore's Association for the Improvement of the Condition of the Poor, founded in 1849. Those organizing this association were particularly concerned with reforming the existing outdoor relief system used by the city, which they declared was "not only defective and inadequate to the honest discharge of the highest obligations imposed on us by the relations of society, but is in itself radically vicious, producing in many instances pauperism, idleness and vice, whilst in many others it fails to reach the homeless and helpless widows and destitute orphans, the really poor and needy."[74] Of particular concern, poor whites were reduced to true desperation to survive. While accepting that "the calamities of poverty are an incident of our race," the founder members saw it as their role to facilitate "the social and physical elevation of that class of society, usually calling for the interposition of charitable aid, and the discouragement of pauperism and vagrancy."[75] Members of the public were encouraged "never to give to strangers at your doors . . . but in every case to visit the applicants in their homes and learn their true character and condition before granting relief or send them to the visitors of the association." Visitors were instructed to show the indigent "the true origin of their suffering when these sufferings are the result of imprudence, extravagance, idleness and intemperance or other moral causes which are within their own control and endeavor by all appropriate means to awaken their self respect, to direct their exertions and to strengthen their capacities for self support." While those reduced to poverty through no fault of their own would receive assistance as well as "that sympathizing counsel which re-enkindles hope," those who were paupers as a result of their own vices "should not live so comfortably . . . as the humblest independent laborer." To this end the visitors were instructed to "give assistance both in quality and quantity inferior, except in cases of sickness, to what might be procured by labor." In an attempt to break the cycle of poverty in which many families were trapped the association strongly encouraged parents to send their children to school. While they contemplated removing children from unsuitable parental influences by force, the association agreed that "it would be better to open the way for the children to participate in the benefits offered by our schools" by providing suitable clothing for the children who were willing to go.[76]

The ability of male benevolent societies to raise significant amounts of money in the late antebellum era is in complete contrast to female counterparts. Few female benevolent societies were able to tap into large amounts of additional funding, and most were content in the 1850s to have built up a reasonable portfolio of investments that ensured continuation of their normal day-to-day activities. The increased activity of male charitable societies from about 1840 onward was partly in response to the increasingly fractured nature of female benevolence in the South. Before the 1830s it was unusual for female benevolent societies to compete with each other for beneficiaries. Once a female orphan society was formed, no one else tried to set up an alternative. Rather, new societies extended the scope and reach of benevolence in a particular community. For example, the next society formed in Savannah after the Female Asylum (1801) was the Dorcas Society in 1816, which provided out-relief to the poor, followed by the Free School Society (also 1816), and then the Widow's Society (1823). With the Dorcas Society defunct by the 1830s, its place was taken by the Clothing and Fuel Society in 1838, and as one newspaper editor commented, "This society seems to be a connecting link in the chain of benevolent institutions with which Savannah abounds." Each of these societies catered to different sections of the population and complemented rather than competed with each other. Indeed, the small charity fund kept by the Female Asylum was given up shortly after the formation of the Dorcas Society since it was now "unnecessary," and in 1841 the board declined the offer of a fund-raising oratorio performance by the Singing Society, saying that money should instead be "given to the Widow's Society, which was very needy at the present time."[77] A similar cooperative approach to charity can be seen in Charleston where the Charity School (1805) was complemented by the Ladies Benevolent Society (1813), the Fragment Society (1820), and the Fuel Society (1832); in Norfolk where the Female Orphan Society (1804) was joined by the Dorcas Society (1822) and the Infant School Society (1829) as well as in other southern cities. Benevolent women in the early decades of the nineteenth century therefore constructed benevolent webs that tried to assist as many poor individuals and families as possible, and sought the greatest good for the community rather than pursuing any specific ethnic or religious agenda.

Over time, however, this cooperative dimension to female benevolence gave way to an increasingly sectarian approach. Much of this was due to the desire of Catholics to provide care and education for the large number of Irish immigrants who flocked to the South from the 1820s onward. Only in New Orleans were Catholic charities really well established in the South before the 1830s. John England, Bishop of Charleston, started to change this with the formation of the Sisters of Our Lady of Mercy in 1829 who took in poor children and provided free education. According to England, an alternative Catholic education was necessary so that "prejudices will be removed and many conversions will follow; or at least the way will be opened through the good ladies educated by the nuns to exercise a very powerful influence on the whole mass of society."[78] The Sisters of Mercy were, of course, in competition with preexisting charitable societies in Charleston such as the Ladies Benevolent Society, the Fragment Society, the Ladies Society Charity School, and the Sisters of Charity.[79] This pattern, of a new Catholic society being formed to compete with preexisting societies, was eventually copied all over the South. In Natchez, the Female Charitable Society, in existence since 1816, was challenged by the formation of the Catholic St. Mary's Orphan Asylum in 1848; in Richmond the Female Humane Association (1805) had its monopoly broken by the St. Joseph's Asylum in 1834, and in Savannah the Female Asylum (1801) and the Free School (1816) faced new competition from St. Vincent's Home after 1844. These new Catholic charities had an immediate impact on the older ecumenical societies. The Savannah Free School, for instance, reported in 1845 that "there have been some removals since the establishment of the Catholic Asylum in this city of children belonging to that denomination" and with fewer children attending the free school, pleas for increased subscriptions and donations seemed somewhat hollow.[80]

In many cities, the response of Protestant women to the growth of Catholic female benevolence was to form their own, distinctive, charitable societies, even if these simply added to the competition that more established societies would face. The word "Protestant" appears in the names of female charitable societies only after it became necessary to distinguish them from existing Catholic charities. In Louisville the Protestant Episcopal Orphanage was founded four years after the Catholic Orphanage in 1831, and in Mobile only eighteen months elapsed between the formation of the

Catholic Female Charitable Society in early 1838 and the Protestant Orphan Asylum in late 1839. This fracturing of female benevolence occurred in most southern towns and cities and the net effect was not only to increase the amount of help on offer to the poor (though this did happen) but also to weaken the stature of female benevolence. Of course, female benevolent societies did not completely wither in the 1840s and 1850s: the Charleston Ladies Benevolent Society, the Poydras Asylum in New Orleans, and the Savannah Female Asylum all continued to operate and make a real difference in their communities. Yet, taken as a whole, it cannot be denied that female benevolence in the South was but a shadow of its former self by the 1850s.

Into the vacuum left by the weakened state of some female charitable organizations stepped new male societies. As the funds of the long-established Lynchburg Dorcas Society dried up in the 1850s, for instance, a new male-run Relief Society emerged to take its place. During the 1850s male charitable societies were generally far more dynamic than the older female benevolent societies. New orphan asylums, operated by men, were opened in New Braunfels, Texas (1846), Augusta (1852), Portsmouth (1856), and Norfolk (1856). Unlike earlier male benevolent societies that had almost exclusively drawn upon working men for membership, these new male benevolent societies brought merchants, bankers, judges, newspaper editors, ministers, and planters into the work of benevolence for the first time. While grocers, blacksmiths, and carpenters were still to be found in the membership records of male benevolent societies, this infusion of new blood brought new ideas and, most significantly, new sources of money for charitable uses. Physician Robinson Miller, who became a member of Mobile's Can't Get Away Club in 1855, owned $12,000 of real estate and had a personal estate valued at $5,000 in 1860. Merchant Isaac Davenport, First Vice-President of Richmond's Male Orphan Asylum Society, owned $50,000 of property in the city and had personal wealth valued at $6,000.[81]

Wealthy new members also permitted older benevolent societies to expand. In Savannah, the Union Society had persisted in its policy of housing orphan boys with local families until the 1850s but by 1854, finding that the boys "do not make that progress in intellectual or moral attainments that it should be our aim to have them do," they decided to build an asylum for the boys "where they could practice gardening and various other employments

7. West Texas Orphan Asylum, opened in New Braunfels in 1846.
Courtesy of the Library of Congress, Prints and Photographs Division, Historic
American Buildings Survey, Reproduction Number HABS TEX,46-NEBRA.V, 1-1.

conducive to their comfort, health and support, and where they could have a teacher devoted to them exclusively." In a neat piece of historical circularity the Union Society purchased the original orphan house tract where George Whitefield had constructed Bethesda in the 1740s. The total price for the land, and for the erection and furnishing of the buildings, was more than $7,000, but the Union Society was able to sell some of its shares in the Planter's Bank and in the Central Railroad to finance the move. The number of boys supported by the Union Society grew from nine in 1851 to fifteen in 1855 and to forty-nine by 1861, surpassing the number of girls of the bounty of the Female Asylum for the first time. This rapid expansion in the scope of charitable provision offered by Savannah's men was partly funded by the donations of the city council (two city lots worth $7,000), past president Joseph Fay (85 acres adjoining the Bethesda site), numerous wealthy members (up to $500 each), and the free provision of supplies, advertising, and medical care by local merchants, printers, and doctors. The rapid growth of the Union Society inevitably deprived some of Savannah's older female benevolent societies of funds, with some elite women donating money toward the cost of new facilities at Bethesda who might previously have concentrated their charitable donations in female-managed organizations. The justices of the Inferior Court split the poor school fund of the county, previously channeled in its entirety to the Savannah Free School, between the Free School, the Union Society, and the new city-managed primary schools. The assault on the funding of the Free School had started in 1848 when Union Society members George Hunter and Francis Bartow had written to the directresses of the Free School "respecting the more equal distribution of the poor school fund." The ladies were able to rebuff this attempt, but in 1853 city officials suggested that their Massie School should also receive part of the state poor school funds. With the original Free School destroyed by fire in 1852 it was now proposed that since the Massie School was to be constructed in the southeastern section of the city, the new Free School should be built in the southwestern wards, with the indigent children of the city divided between them. After taking legal advice the ladies decided that such a plan would be a "surrender of their chartered rights" and a breach of the "sacred trust" they had been engaged in for nearly forty years. Almost as if to demonstrate their independence, they built the new Free School only a few city blocks from the Massie School. Despite their unwillingness to participate in this new scheme, however, the funding changes went ahead during the 1850s and severely affected the work of the Savannah Free School. In early 1855 the board was informed that "the school is not so large as it has been owing to 20 having left for the Public School." Despite their long association with the provision of free education in Savannah, women were effectively marginalized by the actions of the city's men.[82]

Though a contribution from the Inferior Court was no doubt welcome, in truth the Union Society hardly needed it. The assets of the society grew by more than $10,000 between 1855 and 1860, and plans were well advanced to erect new buildings on the site to house upward of a hundred orphans "who are constantly applying for admission" when secession came. Even more remarkable than the increase in numbers of orphans on the bounty of the Union Society was the doubling of the subscribing membership, from 394 in 1858 to 784 in April 1860.[83] The new members of the Union Society were not simply drawn from the wealthy families who had long supported its work. Frederick Augustus Habersham followed his father and his grandfather, and numerous uncles and cousins, in joining the Union Society in 1859, but hardware merchant William Lattimore and grocer Barnard Tilden, who joined that same year, were the first male members of their families to join.[84] Clearly benevolence was increasingly attractive to a cross section of Savannah's men in the last years before the Civil War, at a time when the number of children assisted by the Savannah Female Asylum was static, and the membership of that august institution, as well as that of many other female benevolent societies, was actually falling.[85]

It is possible that the newfound interest in charity among Savannah's male population arose from a growing awareness of the role that benevolence might play in easing social divisions among whites. Alonzo Church, president of the University of Georgia, told his predominantly male audience at the Georgia Historical Society in 1845 that

> the object of society is mutual aid—the great business of society is to prepare its members for the full discharge of individual duty, and to enable them to enjoy the highest degree of individual happiness. Or it may be said, with propriety, that the business of society is to educate men for society. To do this effectually, men must be taught the relations which

they sustain to each other—they must be made to feel the obligations which arise from these relations—they must be able to trace the direction to which the virtuous emotions of the heart point, and to find the objects of benevolence upon which the virtuous sympathies of our nature should fasten.

Church singled out for praise those individuals "who have devoted their lives to the happiness of their fellow men . . . their virtuous deeds should be held up to the view, and for the imitation of all" and especially those who have "been benefactors to their race."[86] Although Savannah's elite men were unique in the antebellum South in opening an infirmary expressly for "the relief & protection of afflicted and aged Negroes," the vast majority of their charitable works were aimed at poor whites. The Georgia Infirmary never treated more than six blacks at once, and most of those were paid for by slaveholders. "Afflicted and aged Negroes" might have received the benefit of the infirmary, but in reality masters also gained since their slaves were cared for at less expense than if they had been treated at home.[87] Orphanages, schools, and out-relief organizations demonstrated clearly to the white poor in Savannah and elsewhere that the elite were concerned with their welfare and would continue to look after them.

It is clear that charitable associations organized by men differed considerably from those established by women in the antebellum South. Men came comparatively late to the ambitious and broadly philanthropic benevolence that had characterized female charitable endeavors since 1800. That this type of charity, rather than mutual-aid societies, became the most popular way for men to organize their benevolent labors is on the one hand a generous acknowledgment that southern women probably had it right all along and that the white poor needed protection from the worst that life could throw at them. On the other hand, though, men's new entry into the world of orphanages and visiting the poor in their homes effectively undermined and weakened the position that benevolent women had occupied for more than a generation. Men had better access than women to local and state governments and the pockets of other men who would fund their efforts, so instead of complementing female benevolence men were effectively supplanting it. Benevolent men did not do this because they felt women were doing a poor job; in fact, they were generous in their praise of what women had accomplished. One minister lauded the role of women "as wives and mothers—nay, in a great degree as workers together with us for the good of society."[88] Sentiments such as these suggest that men increasingly recognized that the work of benevolence was too large (especially with high levels of immigration) and too important to be left to women alone. Charity, especially for the young, could be used to shape the attitudes of the white poor so that they understood the proper relationships that should exist between white and black, and between the enslaved and freemen. As early as 1824 an audience in Charleston had been informed that only charity could take young boys and turn them into "men, wiling to shed their blood in defence of your laws, your families, and your country." It would also, it was hoped, encourage the poor to "manifest a proper sense of gratitude" to those who assisted them.[89] Benevolence, in this sense, had a political as well as a humanitarian purpose.

On April 23, 1861, barely four months after Georgia had seceded from the union, Frederick W. Sims, owner of the *Savannah Republican* and vice-president of the Union Society, presented the boys at Bethesda with a confederate flag telling them, "We all owe it our allegiance, as a child to a parent, and it is appropriate that you, my dear children, whose parents are gone to rest, and who can only claim our country for a father, should become familiar with its emblem. . . . It is an emblem of our nationality, and is entitled to your warmest love and admiration." It would be difficult to find a clearer example of how benevolent men understood the political importance of their work. Sims did not realistically expect the conflict to last long enough to draw in the boys before him "but should it be otherwise, think of this day and that emblem, and strike with the arm of a giant and heart of a patriot." Ten-year-old Edward Wall replied on behalf of the boys, accepting the

> proud banner of our own South—just baptised in glorious victory—in it we recognise the symbol of a regenerated nationality—of the virtue, chivalry, honor, and civilization from which springs that true philanthropy to which we, the orphan boys of the Union Society, are so greatly indebted. . . . we are young and helpless today, and unable to share with you, our kind benefactors, the perils of the approaching conflict. In defence of the banner of the South it shall be our aim to cultivate principles

which will render us in manhood's years worthy to stand beneath its folds. We will not forget the fealty we owe our generous South, and imbued with love and gratitude for our paternal home we will emulate the noble example of Capt. Samuel Mercer, a beneficiary of the Charleston Orphan House, who, having won rank and distinction in the service of his country, obedient to the impulse of a patriotic and grateful heart, resigned his command in the United States Navy rather than turn his sword against the country which had nurtured and protected him in his helpless orphanage. [90]

It is likely that this speech was written by one of the managers and not by Edward Wall himself, but the sentiments expressed were not completely out of line with the views of some recipients of the bounty of the Union Society. At least twenty former orphans fought on the confederate side during the Civil War, with Thaddeus Fisher reaching the rank of captain in the 1st Georgia Infantry Regiment. Among those to serve was Cornelius Long who, as a twelve-year-old, had spoken on behalf of the boys at the anniversary meeting of the Union Society in 1857: "I hope we may appreciate the many blessings we enjoy here, and that we may never disgrace it by our conduct, but rather, that we may live to do honor and credit to those who have sustained us." The managers of the Union Society would indeed have seen Long as "worthy of the care bestowed"—he was killed in action during the Civil War fighting to defend the South that he had been taught by charitable men to love and cherish.[91]

4

The Personal Touch

ORGANIZED CHARITY, both private and public, was ubiquitous throughout the antebellum South. The elderly, sick, crippled, orphaned, and in some
instances the unemployed were supported with food, clothing, indentures,
and instruction from county officials or the well-intentioned (mainly civic)
elite who invariably managed both male and female benevolent societies.
Yet, as the chapter on state welfare made plain, the proportion of the population who actually received public poor relief, particularly in rural areas,
was incredibly small. In part this was because of a widespread reluctance
among the indigent to seek out institutional forms of aid and therefore accept the status of "pauper." Pride, of course, did not put food on the table.
Those living marginal existences on small farmsteads were always only one
stroke of bad luck away from real privation. How did these people survive
when disaster struck or when circumstances overtook them? Those need-
ing assistance after a poor harvest or having to rebuild after a house fire or a
storm were forced to rely on the informal community or neighborhood ties
that had been built up over a lengthy period. This assistance might come
in a variety of forms: free food or livestock, free labor, or even cash. Some
wealthier planters shipped their poorer neighbors' produce to market with
their own crop; others lent the stud services of a stallion or a bull, or permitted the free use of specialized equipment for processing cotton, sugar, or
rice. Examining the significance of these informal, personal, acts of charity
is the purpose of this chapter.

By its very nature informal charity in the antebellum South is not quan-
tifiable in any meaningful way since few individuals kept detailed records
of their day-to-day dealings with their neighbors. Mary Anna Claiborne,
member of a wealthy Richmond family, was one of the few who kept a re-

cord of her charitable giving, noting in 1863, for instance, that she had doled out to a "Poor widow $5" and to a "Poor woman, sugar, tea etc, $1." There were others, however, who recorded their general sympathy for the sufferings of the poor. Keziah Brevard, one of the wealthiest widows in central South Carolina, wrote in her diary that "I feel for the poor people who have large families to struggle for. We who are able ought to help them." In addition to any personal gifts she might have made, Brevard was also a member of Columbia's Female Orphan Society.[1] In an address before the Orphan Asylum and Free School of Alexandria, Alexander H. Stephens recalled his own childhood as a poor orphan boy in Georgia "with no home or roof to shelter his head." He was fed and cared for by a local planter and this act of kindness "inspired him with fresh courage to battle with the obstacles of life." As an adult he was able to repay the kindness he had been shown as a child by successfully taking on the case of the widow of his benefactor, now in straitened circumstances, whose lands were at risk from creditors.[2]

Most of the personal interactions between the wealthy and the poor described in this chapter were local, between neighbors, and it seems clear that neighbors in the antebellum South were generally willing to help out each other, if only because no one knew when he would need assistance himself. Alexander Stephens took particular pleasure in helping the widow of his former benefactor precisely because they had done him a kindness in the past when they had the means to do so. As one southern newspaper put it: "the man who has competency today, may be plunged into the depths of poverty tomorrow." The experience of Thomas B. Chaplin, a planter on St. Helena's Island, serves as a good example of the vagaries of fortune. In 1846 he gave money to a man whom he thought was "deserving of charity" and later he lent his cousin "a cow & calf, so that he can get a little milk to put in his coffee" but a series of mishaps and misjudgments left him struggling. In 1851 his land rent was paid for him by his uncle, something he "suffered much mortification" about, and he confided to his journal, "We never were so hard up for something to eat."[3]

When fortunes went downhill, having good neighbors could make all the difference. One resident of Cherokee County, Georgia, recalled that "all the charity in the settlement came from friends and neighbors" while Charles Darby, having recently relocated to Murfreesboro, Tennessee, wrote, "I am much pleased with the place; the society very good, and every one appears to be busy and attentive to business, the people generally are very moral, and the able are ready to assist those in need."[4] Community bonds like this were not only based on residency; kinship groups often lived in proximity to one another so that siblings, cousins, and in-laws might be the first port-of-call for assistance. Most of the landowners on St. Helena's Island, for instance, were related to each other by blood or by marriage. Membership in the same church or a trading relationship might also be the basis of personal ties between individuals. Crucially, these relationships were only formed among whites and did not include free blacks.

Many of these individual acts of kindness were exactly that: friends helping each other out of difficulties or through hard times. Tools, food, and even people (both slave and free) would be lent and borrowed on a needs basis. As one man remarked, "borrowing... was neighboring."[5] Some interactions, however, were not between social or economic equals and served to reinforce and define status differences between individuals. Mary Boykin Chesnut recalled numerous poor white women who came "again and again" to the kitchen "ready to carry away anything they could get." These women were clearly not of the same social standing as the elite families they hoped would help them, but "they were treated as friends and neighbors, not as beggars." Chesnut believed that her mother and grandmother treated these supplicants well because "their husbands and sons, whom we never saw, were citizens and voters" and certainly the political dimension to personal benevolence should not be ignored.[6] James Henry Hammond invited all his neighbors to an annual feast on his South Carolina plantation, and while his guests were no doubt well fed and watered, they were also subject to a very public demonstration of Hammond's wealth and resources. One guest recalled that Hammond acted the part of "the great feudal landlord" on such occasions. William Gilliland did the same in Charleston when the poor came directly to him, and in his case the $1 or $2 they received was partly intended just to get rid of the supplicant. Gilliland wrote rude remarks about the paupers he had helped in his journal such as "I don't believe much in her" or "I don't like her looks or her talk," yet it still suited him to distribute charity because it helped him to maintain the image of the benevolent patriarch.[7]

Hammond and Gilliland's patrician-style benevolence was not typical of the relationship between the poorer and the wealthier members of most southern communities. Most individuals, even those with significant assets, simply did not have sufficient personal wealth to throw community parties or dispense cash freely to the poor. Daniel Turner, resident in south Georgia in 1805, remarked, "I suppose in all Cambden County there is scarcely a planter with a hundred dollars by him and perhaps his plantation and slaves worth a hundred thousand." Since very few people had significant amounts of ready cash, the southern economy, in rural areas at least, can accurately be described as a credit/debt one. An itinerant trader in Virginia in 1807 confided to his diary that "it appears that cash seems to become scarcer every day, this certainly the worst season for cash, the planter having spent the amount of his last crop, and the present not being sent, or in readiness for market, and also prices of produce dull therefore no encouragement to hurry their produce; credit sales out to be brisk, and is in those articles which are necessary." In upcountry South Carolina, Charles Ball confirmed that white people "almost always require[d] credit" at the local stores since most were only able to settle their debts following the harvest. Indeed, many stores acted as factors for small farmers, ensuring that store debts were paid first.[8] Debt and credit were a normal part of economic activity in the antebellum South, but they were also at the crux of relationships between individuals, and especially between rich and poor.

Throughout the South wealthier individuals extended credit to their poorer neighbors, sometimes in return for goods and services but more commonly in the form of cash to enable the poor to purchase supplies or extend their credit at the local store. How far was this personal extension of credit an act of charity and how far was it just part of the normal economic activity of the period? The distinction is a little unclear, but instances where credit was given and repayment never subsequently sought suggest that at least some of these transactions had a wider social significance than the merely financial. Loans tied the non-elite to the elite with bonds of obligation since by accepting credit, debtors entered into a patron/client relationship with lenders. The cultural significance of credit, debt, and gift giving has not escaped the interest of historians. Craig Muldrew has argued, with regard to early modern England, that the existence of a debt created an obligation in the borrower toward the giver, making the debtor "a servant to the lender." He calculates that, at 5 percent of total yearly expenditure in the wealthiest 15–20 percent of households, "income redistribution through

the forgiveness of debts was massively higher than positive [charitable] giving."[9] Margot Finn's study of credit and debt in eighteenth- and nineteenth-
century England has argued that nonfinancial criteria were sometimes paramount in determining whether a debt should be pursued. In other words,
the social gain from leaving the debt unpaid was at times greater than its
monetary value.[10] Bruce Mann's work on debt and bankruptcy in early national America largely conforms to the framework established by Muldrew
and Finn. Debt, he argues, was not only "an integral part of daily life"; it
was also in many parts of the United States "governed by common law, local custom and private negotiation." While Mann believes that there were
some regional variations in the social role of debt—suggesting, for instance,
that loans in the southern states "rested on complex perceptions of honor
and personal autonomy"—he does not explore in depth how southerners
regarded personal debt. Was the antebellum South a place where "forebear-
ance was the rule and demands to pay . . . were affronts to the debtor's honor
and integrity?"[11] Or were debts primarily economic relationships between
individuals with little wider social meaning?

Paramount in the decision of whether to lend money in the South and
elsewhere was the reputation of the recipient, and many lenders stated their
intention to lend only to those they considered to be "good men." Asheville,
North Carolina, merchant James Patton urged his children to adopt the
stance of a benevolent paternalist in financial matters. Viewing wealth as
a blessing, he was critical of those who did not use their resources to assist
others: "I find fault very much with wealthy men, for not taking poor young
men by the hand, and putting them in a way to do well, when they find them
honest, trusty and capable."[12] The sure way to become a "respectable member of society" was therefore to "be charitable to your poor relations and
neighbors." Naturally help should not be offered to "spendthrifts"; instead,
"you should exercise a good degree of judgment in determining who are
proper objects of charity, and who are not." But by assisting "sons of honest
and respectable farmers," advantages would accrue to the lender since "these
will consider themselves, in a great degree, dependant on you for their advancement in life."[13] The lending behavior of James Patton's son, James W.
Patton, and two of his wealthy Asheville contemporaries, James McConnell
Smith and James Alexander, provides us with an insight into the operation of
the credit/debt system on a personal level. All three lent money to a wide range

of individuals throughout Buncombe County (which surrounded Asheville) and analyzing their lending behavior lets us draw some conclusions as to what wider purpose they believed loans served.

Located in the Appalachian region of western North Carolina, Buncombe County's relatively small, generally agricultural population was spread over a wide and geographically remote area.[14] Most families lived in small neighborhoods, or townships, centered on the fertile river valleys, like Swannanoa, French Broad, Flat Creek, Hominy Creek, and Reems Creek. The only town, Asheville, was an important staging post on the trading routes that linked farmers to the north and west with markets in South Carolina and Georgia, and was home to about a thousand residents when the Civil War broke out.[15] As an administrative center it had a more diverse economy than the county as a whole and boasted a professional class of lawyers, doctors, and clerks as well as a significant cadre of artisans. It also had over twenty stores and businesses, a courthouse, a jail, several schools, and churches. To provide accommodation for visiting traders and to service the significant tourist trade, Asheville also had three large hotels.[16]

Prominent among Buncombe County's elite were James W. Patton, James Mitchell Alexander, and James McConnell Smith. Patton and Smith were the two wealthiest men in the county according to the 1850 census, while Alexander was the sixth wealthiest.[17] All three owned considerable amounts of land both in the county and in Asheville itself, while Smith and Patton also owned stores. Furthermore, all owned hotels in the county: Alexander's hotel was located north of Asheville; Smith's Buck Hotel and Patton's Eagle Hotel were both situated in the heart of the town. In addition to their financial muscle, Smith, Patton, and Alexander were also highly visible members of the community. Smith and Patton served as town commissioners in 1849, and Patton went on to chair the county court and serve as both a Superintendent of Common Schools and as a Warden of the Poor.[18] Alexander donated the land on which the Methodist and Baptist churches were built in Asheville, while Patton did the same for the Presbyterian and Episcopal churches.[19] These three men were at the very pinnacle of Buncombe County's antebellum society.

The elevated status of these three men evidently earned them a reputation as those to whom the cash-strapped could turn in times of need. The estate inventories of Smith (1856), Alexander (1858), and Patton (1861) between them contained 669 credit notes for uncollected debts at the time of their deaths. Some of those debts were probably the normal extensions of short-term credit to those who would repay in time. Joseph Eller's note for $80, for example, became due for repayment shortly after Smith's death in the summer of 1856. Had Smith lived there is no reason to suggest that this note would not have been repaid: Eller was worth more than $12,000 in 1860. Debts were classified by estate administrators as "good," "doubtful," and "desperate" suggesting that not all debts were the same. The terminology used by administrators to classify debts is of itself quite revealing, although the criteria used to make such judgments was not specified and was most likely subjective. Since most debts labeled "good" had been signed by leading citizens or businessmen of Asheville, it seems most likely that administrators based their judgment of whether notes were likely to be honored mainly on reputation. Those whose debts were considered "good" by James McConnell Smith's administrators possessed a mean personal estate of $10,890. Notes from those whom the administrators had never met and who might be dead or have moved out of Buncombe County or from those who were known to have no assets were probably classified as "desperate" because the administrators felt there was little or no prospect of recovering the debt. In Smith's case, only four out of 221 individuals whose debts were classified as "desperate" possessed personal property valued at more than $1,000.

"Desperate" debts were usually older than debts considered "good," dating back in some instances more than forty years; they were usually for much smaller amounts than "good" debts and there were more of them. Of the 669 debts listed in the estate inventories of Smith, Alexander, and Patton, 457 were classified as "desperate," 98 as "doubtful," and 114 as "good." The mean value for desperate debts was $29.90, though a more accurate reflection of the size of these debts is the median value, which was only $3. Good debts, by comparison had a mean value of $327.18, and a median value of $99.58. There are several possible explanations for the existence of desperate debts. Creditors might simply have lost track of an individual who owed them money and without an identifiable residence in the county, or some other form of visible property, it was hard to pursue a debtor for repayment. On several occasions when suit was actually brought for the repayment of debts in the county court, the sheriff reported back simply "not found"—

in other words the debtor was no longer a resident of the county. Other debtors might have died leaving no obvious heirs to pursue for repayment. Throughout the South "desperate" debts such as these were fairly common. Two studies of antebellum Georgia concluded that between two-thirds and three-quarters of inventories contained such notes, and the proportion in Asheville was roughly similar.[20] Since inventories tend to overrepresent the wealthy, there being little point in appraising the estates of those who possessed little or no property, it is not surprising that the wealthiest citizens often carried a significant number of debts with them to the grave that chance had dictated they would not be able to collect before death.

However, there were plenty of "desperate" debts where failure to repay the loan cannot be attributed to chance, death, or departure. Farmer Jonathan Bradly, for instance, borrowed $9.40 from James Alexander in 1849 and had not repaid the debt by the time of Alexander's death in 1858 despite being resident in the county throughout the 1850s. Similarly, laborer T. C. Drayman borrowed $1.50 from James McConnell Smith in 1851 and had made no effort to repay the money by 1856 when Smith died. Some "desperate" debts were more than forty years old: in January 1815, and again in March 1818, James Bassett had borrowed money from James McConnell Smith. During the 1820s Bassett did not repay these debts, nor did Smith pursue recovery through the courts; in fact, Smith lent Bassett more money in 1831. When Smith died in 1856 these debts remained outstanding and there is no evidence that Smith ever made any effort to recover his money through the legal system. The financial relationship between all of these debtors and their creditors raises many interesting questions. Why, for example, had these individuals not repaid the debts they owed, and why had they never been pursued in the courts for repayment? Of course it is possible that in Bassett's case his death or migration made recovery of the debt more difficult, but this does not explain why Smith extended Bassett more credit in 1818 and 1831 when his first debt from 1815 had not been repaid.

There is some evidence that James W. Patton, James Alexander, and James McConnell Smith were well known in the community as men who were willing to lend money, and that they consequently attracted the most interest from people in need. There were about fifty heads of household in Buncombe County during the 1850s who owned more than ten slaves and who collectively accounted for between a quarter and a third of the county's total wealth.[21] They might reasonably be described as the county's elite. Twenty-two of those heads of household have extant inventories of their estates, but only fourteen of those inventories contained "desperate" debts. The concentration of "desperate" debts was more marked than even these figures suggest: Smith, Alexander, and Patton collectively accounted for more than half of all "desperate" debts in the county.[22] It is logical that people would come to the richer individuals for money, but the concentration of "desperate" debts suggests that Patton, Smith, and Alexander had earned a reputation for their "ever readiness to relieve the distressed."[23]

Although there is no comparable evidence for Buncombe County, we know that elsewhere in the South some seeking loans would write in fairly humble terms to those with the ability to assist them. R. B. Brodnax hoped Alexander Stephens would "help a poor man that is in want" and sought $20 "to help my buy sum corn [*sic*]," while the Smith brothers told Georgian David Burrow "if you will lend some money do it immediately and sent it in a letter you will oblige your suffering friends bye so doing."[24] Others, perhaps lacking the literacy to write to ask for a loan might have made an application in person knowing that some planters found it more difficult to refuse a personal application than a written one. Linton Stephens, for instance, recalled the visit of one poor man to whom he gave $30 "to buy bread, tho' I could ill spare it" while Mrs. Brantly turned up at the Wadley household "to get a little money" but left empty handed due to their being "no money in the house."[25]

Whether the loan was in the form of cash or goods, such as the forty bushels of corn owed by W. C. Hay to James Alexander, or the six bushels of wheat provided to William A. Cobb by James McConnell Smith, in each instance the lender would have made a judgment of the credit-worthiness of the borrower. James W. Patton certainly placed great store on reputation: in 1861 he sent Asheville brickmason William Waight to work for his son, stating that "his steady habits, or sobriety, industry, and agreeableness, in every way makes him more desirable than strangers, or one that we have not known."[26] South Carolina rice planter Robert Allston evidently surprised himself that he had lent a local teacher $20, "stranger as he was," especially since he "found little difficulty in asking for money." Allston spent the rest of the month regretting that he could not turn the loan into an advance of tuition fees for his daughter Adele.[27]

This emphasis on personal knowledge of the applicant was a central part of the decision-making process; indeed, it might have been far more relevant than the potential future ability of a debtor to repay the loan. There is evidence that Smith, Alexander, and Patton each used nonfinancial criteria when determining whom to lend money to. Numerous debtors such as miller Stephen Fore, blacksmith William Edmonds, and hatter Enoch Ward, all indebted to James Alexander, possessed no property according to the federal census. Indeed, only about half of those with "desperate" debts to their name owned any land and between 75 percent and 80 percent had a total worth of less than $1,000.[28] Therefore, the majority of those with "desperate" debts had little or no means to repay the money they owed, even if that sum was just a few dollars. Their poverty and lack of means should have been obvious to Patton, Smith, and Alexander at the time they loaned the money, suggesting that all three used more than just hard, cold financial judgment when deciding to make loans.

The most crucial criterion used by Smith, Patton, and Alexander as to whether to lend money to an individual appears to have been residency. The evidence from inventories and census records shows clear geographic boundaries between the lenders and a geographical relationship between lenders and debtors. By the 1850s, James Alexander had a large house in Asheville and had been running his hotel ten miles north of Asheville for over twenty years. The hotel, built on the eastern bank of the French Broad River and incorporating a tanyard, blacksmith shop, grist mill, and sawmill, was also close to his farm.[29] His presence in Asheville and north of the town clearly played a large part in determining whom he came into contact with in the course of his business and social life, and it is not surprising that the men who owed him money lived in these places too. Most of his debtors lived in Reems Creek and the nearby Flat Creek, which were both close to Alexander's hotel.

While Alexander tended to lend to residents north of Asheville, James W. Patton did the same in Swannanoa, Leicester, and Dick's Creek, all to the east of Asheville, and James M. Smith focused his attention on Hominy Creek west of the town. Only in Asheville itself did the three creditors overlap since all owned at least some property there. In addition to the family home and farm in the Swannanoa Valley to the east of Asheville, James W. Patton owned several town lots, including the Eagle Hotel on Main Street, and spent much of his time in the town working for the county court and the Wardens of the Poor. James M. Smith owned the Buck Hotel and a fine house. Regular visits to and periods of residence in Asheville meant that Smith, Patton, and Alexander had the opportunity to come into contact with a wide range of town residents as well as those who visited the county seat on business. If, as seems likely, personal contact was crucial in forming the debtor-creditor relationship, then these three men had ample opportunities to make such connections. James W. Patton clearly would have known James Stradley when he lent him more than $100 in 1857 since Stradley was the county jailor and poorhouse keeper while Patton was both a magistrate and president of the Wardens of the Poor. Meanwhile, James McConnell Smith extended credit to those actually resident at his hotel, lending money to G. W. Demerst, a tanner; and L. M. Williams, a laborer; though it is not known if they were guests or employees.

Patton, Smith, and Alexander sat at the pinnacle of society in Buncombe County, and providing small loans to those who sought their help reinforced their elevated social status within their community. Those who borrowed money placed themselves in a dependent, beholden position with their creditor. In this sense, as J. William Harris has ably pointed out, credit in the antebellum South was a "social as well as [an] economic exchange" just as it was in rural parts of New England and in England. Thomas Belk approached future Confederate vice-president Alexander Stephens for a loan in 1852 telling him that "if you will condecene to assist me that much this one time of need I will be under the greatest obligation to you at all times."[30] The debt relationships outlined here for Buncombe County and by Harris for middle Georgia can be found in most places. Steven Tripp's study of antebellum Lynchburg, Virginia, for instance, found that the elite used "credit networks to strengthen the ligaments of community with their less wealthy neighbors." The records of businesses in Lynchburg demonstrate that debtors were normally permitted to clear their debts over a lengthy period of time, regardless of previously agreed dates for repayment and without use of the courts.[31]

Dependent relationships were normally formed between the wealthy and the poor, but not exclusively so. James Alexander advanced credit to wealthier citizens of Buncombe County, men whose means more than covered the debts they owed. Farmer Joshua Heron, for instance, owed Alexander $51.58

from as far back as 1847, despite an estate valued at over $1,000 in both 1850 and 1860.[32] Alexander did not even get back $1.40 from W. G. Shoope, despite the fact that Shoope was worth $1,000 when repayment was due the following year. Similarly James McConnell Smith never received the $3.88 owed by harness-maker Enoch L. Cunningham who owned two slaves and had a total estate valued at more than $10,000 in 1860. James W. Patton, Asheville's wealthiest man, was even more likely than Smith or Alexander to allow credit to those with the means to pay him back. Asheville's mayor, Isaac Sawyer, worth more than $5,000 in 1860, and lawyer Marcus Erwin, owner of eleven slaves and an estate of more than $15,000 in 1860, were both indebted to Patton at the time of his death in 1861.

Debt and credit relationships clearly bound Buncombe County's society together in complex ways, and although none of these three men used their patronage to secure political power for themselves at a state or national level, they had debt relationships with several men who were politically significant. Marcus Erwin, for example, was not only a lawyer but was also a Methodist preacher and editor of the *Asheville News*. During the 1850s he was elected to the state legislature and later held the post of assistant attorney general of the United States. By forming debt relationships with a variety of men, Patton, Smith, and Alexander created ties of dependency that bound an entire community together. Of course, the dependency of poor whites who genuinely lacked the ability to repay loans differed markedly from those who could have paid but did not. Yet, even among those able to pay, the credit offered and accepted from Patton, Smith, and Alexander forged relationships that were fundamentally unequal.

One might think that Patton, Smith, and Alexander had an aversion to using the court system to recover debts. Certainly elsewhere in the South, using the courts to enforce repayment, something that might involve the sale of land or personal possessions, was often seen as unneighborly and therefore not an option. Virginian newspaperman Joseph Addison Waddell lamented to his diary that even during "hard times" when the number of insolvencies was growing rapidly, and "we shall lose a good deal in the aggregate by these failures . . . I cant harass and persecute people however hard it is to have to bear these losses."[33] One Georgia artisan complained, "I have got notes and accounts aplenty if I had the money for them to serve me this year but the people say they cannot pay me for they have not made enough to feed their familys and to sue a man that is good for his contracts under those circumstances I cannot do it with the right kind of feeling."[34] Some creditors, in real need of money, preferred the softly-softly approach rather than the bailiffs. H. M. Bell reminded Virginia lawyer John McCue about a note for $211 but reassured him that "I of course do not wish & will not do anything to annoy you in reference to this note, but will hold it very much to suit your convenience, and hope you will be able to relieve me by from time to time paying in such amounts as you can conveniently do." Another of McCue's creditors told him, "I never was harder run for money than I am at this time" but rather than threaten court action he merely stated that swift payment of a $68 debt would "confer a great favor" on him.[35] In up-country South Carolina, court cases between individuals had a reputation for being "most unpleasant . . . unthankful, unpopular, and unprofitable" since the community would see it as "seeking undue advantages and taken advantages of the neighbors and grinding the poor." In middle Florida, try-ing to "coerce" payment of debts sometimes resulted in duels, such was the perceived insult to personal honor.[36]

Such reticence about using the court system did not exist everywhere and at all times. Thomas Chaplin experienced the humiliation of seeing slaves taken from his plantation to meet his debts: "I cannot express my feelings on seeing so many faithful Negroes going away from me forever, not for any fault of their own but for my extravagance. It is a dearly bought lesson, and I hope I will benefit by it."[37] Historians of antebellum America, regardless of section, agree that credit terms tended to be easier when the economic times were good and much tougher when times were hard. Virginian Joseph Waddell confided to his diary, "As to the 'hard times' I have never known anything like the present difficulty. So many persons are 'breaking' as to suggest the inquiry, upon meeting a friend, 'Any more failures since din-ner?' In the County Court 302 suits have been brought to the March term, besides many others in the Corporation Court."[38] Historians have also tended to agree that credit relationships between individuals tended to be-come less personal with time as the "market revolution" brought a capital-ist ideology to rural areas for the first time. Christopher Clark's study of western Massachusetts, for instance, demonstrated that there was a marked increase in debt recovery cases during the 1840s as western Massachusetts became more fully integrated into the regional economy.[39] Since market penetration has often been associated with modern transport links, and many parts of the South lacked access to railroads before the Civil War, one can legitimately question the degree to which southerners were oriented toward market values. Furthermore, long-distance trading did not necessarily mean that market ideology permeated other types of interpersonal relationships.[40]

The court records of Buncombe County clearly show that Patton, Smith, and Alexander were willing to seek repayment of debts: between 1825 and 1861 the three collectively launched 228 separate actions in the Court of Common Pleas to recover unpaid debts.[41] The existence of more than six hundred notes in the inventories of Patton, Smith, and Alexander where repayment had not been sought, however, is proof that the court system was not used indiscriminately against all debtors. Clearly Patton, Smith, and Alexander made individual decisions about each debtor and whether to pursue the repayment of a debt. In part this decision was a rational judgment about ability to pay: those pursued through the courts normally had a far greater ability to pay than those whose debts remained uncollected. In fact, of those taken to court for debt recovery by Patton, Smith, and Alexander more than half owned property valued at more than $1,000 in 1850. After all, there was little point in bringing cases against those with no property for the sheriff to sell. North Carolina's legal code exempted clothes, a bed, working tools, arms, and personal items to the value of $10 from seizure for payment of debts. This was extended in 1845 to exempt "one cow and calf, ten bushels of corn or wheat, fifty pounds of bacon, beef, or pork, or one barrel of fish, all the necessary farming tools for one labourer; one bed, bedstead and covering, for every two members of the family; two months' provision for the family; four hogs; and all necessary household and kitchen furniture, not to exceed fifty dollars in value," though homesteads themselves were not exempted from seizure in North Carolina until 1859.[42] Considering that a fifth of "desperate" debtors in 1850 owned no property according to the census, there was plainly nothing to gain by issuing proceedings against them. In fact, court proceedings could end up costing the plaintiff money. By 1822 the debtor's prison had been effectively abolished in North Carolina since debtors could swear an oath attesting to their poverty on their first appearance in court, without having to spend a certain qualifying period in jail.[43] William Smith took this route to avoid paying $20.83 to James Patton in 1841, though creditors could contest these declarations if they felt goods were being hidden from them. Furthermore, jailors were permitted to seek jail fees from creditors if debtors were unable to pay, and creditors were also liable for court fees if they wished to keep a case on the court docket. It was hardly surprising, therefore, that Patton, Smith, and Alexander dropped numerous cases after the sheriff reported that there were "no goods" to be seized.[44]

The protection offered to insolvent debtors was not unique to North Carolina; the list of exempt property in Mississippi was in fact more extensive than debtors in North Carolina could claim: 20 hogs, 150 bushels of corn, 20 bushels of wheat or rice, 800 pounds of pork or bacon, a yoke of oxen, a wagon, and a slave. Most states also had homestead exemptions several years before North Carolina in 1859. Legislators in Georgia had exempted a minimum of twenty acres per family from seizure as early as 1841 declaring, "It does not comport with the principles of justice, humanity or sound policy to deprive the family of an unfortunate debtor of a home and the means of an honest subsistence."[45] Only Virginia, Kentucky, and Missouri, of the slaveholding states, lacked a homestead law in 1860. Paul Goodman has pointed out that new states in the southwest advertised liberal homestead exemptions to encourage migration from the older eastern states, and indeed exempt acreages in Mississippi and Arkansas were the most generous in the South.[46]

The exemption of property by state legislatures often came in response to petitions from residents. Fifty-one citizens of Morgan County, Tennessee, informed the state governor that "the most ruinous consequences must follow if the people continue trying to collect debt off of each other[;] we believe that under existing circumstances thre[e] fourths of the community will be altogether ruined broke up and by the sacrifice of their property and their debts all remain unpaid." They requested that at least two years elapse before repayment was sought through the courts and further, a "mans property if sold by a collecting officer shall not be taken from him under two thirds its value."[47] In North Carolina the east coast residents of Perquimans County complained that "persons that is in debt is exposed to speculators and there [*sic*] property sold almost every day at a sacrifise" while those of Moore County in central North Carolina agreed that "the property of the poor is rapidly passing into the hands of the rich, for a mere trifle, consequently the rich are made richer and the poor poorer."[48] Although Patton, Smith, and Alexander did not take land or goods for themselves in settlement of debts, they were not above forcing the sale of lands or crops to third parties: Asa Brigman's 200 acres were sold for just $42 to meet a debt owed to James McConnell Smith.[49] The passage of the 1845 insolvent debtors law in North Carolina, however, did have a significant impact on the behavior of these three men, and indeed on all residents of Buncombe County. James W. Patton had placed twenty-four cases in the hands of the sheriff for execution in the five years before the passage of the 1845 act, but he initiated only a further five in the five years following. The total number of cases in the execution docket halved after 1845, from roughly 600 cases to roughly 300 cases per year. Of course, the increasing wealth of individuals such as Patton, Smith, and Alexander may have made them reluctant to pursue small debts, but the sudden and dramatic nature of the shift after 1845 strongly suggests that the insolvent debtors' law was partly responsible.

There is evidence that Patton, Smith, and Alexander did not use the courts simply to enforce the repayment of debts. Plaintiffs treated each case slightly differently—in some cases pursuing an individual relentlessly but on other occasions adopting a much softer line. Fewer than half of the 228 cases brought by Patton, Smith, and Alexander to the Court of Common Pleas ended with them receiving the amount owed in full. Indeed, the best way to get a debt paid was apparently to do nothing more than bring the case to court. More than a quarter of cases were settled immediately on the initiation of a suit, or shortly thereafter. In a further 10 percent of cases the plaintiff received his money in full after suspending the case, effectively giving the debtor more time to find the money without the threat of his goods and lands being sold. In these instances, merely bringing the case to court was a public statement by the plaintiff that he was determined to see his money returned, but the suspension showed that he also retained some faith in the debtor to meet his obligations. James W. Patton brought a suit against George Robeson for $242.10 in August 1833. Over the next eight years Patton was happy to leave the case suspended while Robeson paid off portions of his debt, finally clearing it in October 1841. The gentle approach adopted by Patton, Smith, and Alexander toward many debtors is perhaps because a more aggressive approach was clearly not more successful in securing repayments. In only five out of 228 cases was a debt repaid in full after the sheriff had seized and sold property. Indeed, it seems that creditors were more likely to receive at least part of the money they were owed by doing nothing than they were by seeking to seize the goods of their less wealthy neighbors.

What the court records do not explain is why certain individuals were pursued through the courts while others were not. Patton, Smith, and Alexander each had debts in their inventories dating back to the 1820s, 1830s, and 1840s, and as we have seen, the existence of these debts was not because of a reluctance to use the court system. While the 1845 insolvent debtor law might have deterred many new cases, it does not explain why James McConnell Smith never sought to recover the $10 he had loaned to Thomas J. Candler in 1834, or why James Mitchell Alexander failed to pursue Jonathan Roberts for the $8.50 borrowed in 1829. When cross-referenced with the federal census, however, data from the Court of Common Pleas does demonstrate that while credit was most frequently extended to those who lived in the vicinity of the lender, people pursued through the courts were more likely to reside in a different part of Buncombe County. None of those taken to court by James Alexander for debt recovery lived in the northerly townships of Reems Creek, Flat Creek, or Stocksville where Alexander's hotel was situated. Patton and Smith were more willing than Alexander to take their neighbors to court, but those from elsewhere in the county were still more likely than neighbors to have a sheriff's execution taken out against them. The disproportionate number of court suits brought against those living in a different neighborhood suggests that Patton, Smith, and Alexander found it more socially awkward to take court action against those whom they saw regularly. Indeed, to take such action risked community resentment from kinfolk.[50] It was far safer to pursue those not known in the locality, whose fate held little immediacy for local residents. Since all three men were more likely to lend money locally, these community ties effectively restrained their ability to recover the debts they were owed.

The full force of the law was rarely employed against those who had not repaid their debts, and large numbers were not pursued at all, and this strongly suggests that attitudes of creditors were not always dictated by financial considerations. In this sense James W. Patton had taken his father's advice to heart. James Patton Sr. had advised his son that those who would sell "the widow's cow or the poor man's land" for purely monetary reasons would lose respect among the community because "when the name of any man becomes conspicuous in the court docket the public are apt to form an unfavorable opinion of him." Thus "the rich man who lives only for himself, does not deserve the respect and esteem of his fellow-man . . . he shews by his conduct that he has in some measure separated himself from the rest of the world, and that he has no feelings connected with their interest and happiness."[51] By letting so many outstanding debts remain uncollected Smith, Patton, and Alexander demonstrated both their wealth (since men of lesser means would have been under greater financial pressures to ensure that debts were paid) and their personal benevolence. For those in desperate need the only other recourse was to approach the Wardens of the Poor, and while support from the wardens was forthcoming for the sick, elderly, and orphaned, the healthy men who got loans from Smith, Patton, and Alexander would not have been eligible for poor relief, however meager their situations, nor most likely would they have humbled themselves sufficiently to ask for it.[52]

Even though some rejected state help because of the "pauper" label, accepting a loan also placed them in a similar dependent position. The simple fact that the debt existed meant that the only thing standing between a debtor and a court appearance was the goodwill of the lender. Any perceived personal slight or insult might bring a swift end to the extension of credit, and the debt must therefore have acted to control the behavior of individuals to at least some degree. One might argue that unpaid debts effectively functioned as a form of charity when lenders had little intention of pursuing repayment through the courts, yet borrowed money was not charity and did not carry quite the same stigma. Indeed, the existence of the written record of the debt permitted those receiving the loan to believe that this was just another commercial arrangement, part of the normal, day-to-day, financial dealings that individuals had with one another. Yet what Patton, Smith, and Alexander were effectively doing was offering a private form of charitable help to some personally selected individuals without the associations of public dependency that welfare in rural communities usually entailed. Indeed, the small amounts of credit they made available to hundreds of Buncombe County residents helped to preserve their individual household independence. The overwhelming majority of the borrowers who can be traced were male heads of the household, and by extending credit to them, Alexander, Smith, and Patton reinforced the traditional dignity and responsibility of the male family head. In a society where the maintenance of personal independence and liberty held special significance, because of the existence of unfree forms of labor, marginal whites were elevated through their access to credit that was, so far as we can tell, unavailable to nonwhites.

The creditor/debtor relationship—in Buncombe County, North Carolina, at least—was fundamentally a personal one between two individuals. A significant amount has been written on the relationships between the elite and the non-elite in the antebellum South, much seeking to explain how the elite managed to unite white society when so much existed potentially to cause fissures. Besides racial solidarity, historians have stressed common evangelical culture, kinship bonds, and shared economic interests as factors that bound all whites together in complex ways.[53] In his study of antebellum western North Carolina, John Inscoe argued that the "Mountain Masters" effectively prevented divisions among whites by demonstrating their own ability to deliver economic progress for the region—for example, by establishing and maintaining lucrative markets for produce and providing "economic pump-priming" for tourism and outside investors. Furthermore, internal divisions among the elite over taxation, extension of the suffrage, and internal improvement also acted to defuse suggestions that they acted together at all times in support of their own interests. Perhaps most important, Inscoe suggests that the elites in western North Carolina were well integrated into their communities.[54] One of the most important ways they integrated themselves was through the provision of loans. Leading men in a community such as Patton, Smith, and Alexander were at the apex of a system that effectively provided adult white men with a small safety net, and one that was not available to free blacks. In this way the 85 percent of Buncombe County's artisans and yeoman farmers who did not own slaves were all given a stake in the status quo because it was the slaveholding system that provided the money that eventually trickled down in small amounts to them.

As abolitionist sentiment grew in the North and the sectional crisis worsened, the need for community cohesion in the South became more important. In fact, the leaders of Buncombe County, like their counterparts in the rest of western North Carolina, were very successful in welding together yeomen, tenants, and small farmers into active and ardent supporters of slavery. Pro-secession sentiment was so strong in Buncombe County that in April 1861, Captain William McDowell, Smith's son-in-law, organized the first company of troops recruited in North Carolina and marched at their head to Raleigh to join the war effort. Among those to serve in North Carolina's Confederate regiments were several who were indebted to either Patton, Smith, or Alexander. The small loans distributed by these three men perhaps functioned like grease to oil the wheels of society, acting to both ease personal financial distress and to create and cement personal bonds between the wealthy and the poor. Throughout the South personal benevolence that bound individuals together was perhaps the most socially significant of all charitable work.

5

Teaching Southern Poor Whites

THE OLD FIELD SCHOOL stood alone more than a mile from the nearest farm, "old, weather-beaten [and] windowless." Every once in a while a teacher would arrive for a three-month sojourn and local farmers would scrape together the fees to send their children to the dilapidated old building to learn how to read, write, and count. Attendance was best during the winter months when there was no crop to tend, but that was also when conditions were at their worst inside the school. The small stove near the teacher did little to warm the pupils, who had often walked several miles in the rain and snow to reach the school. If physical conditions inside the school were poor, the educational environment was little better. No talking was permitted inside the schoolroom, and boys and girls were not permitted to play together at break time. Those who broke the rules were beaten "terribly." The itinerant teachers willing to work for the meager wages on offer had a reputation for being "awfully severe," were rarely competent, and were often drunk. The teacher's "everlasting frown" was more likely to elicit "cringing fear" than respect, and most pupils left school knowing only marginally more than when they started.[1]

This stereotype of schooling in the antebellum South has more than a grain of truth in it. The spasmodic operation of these "field schools" did little to enhance literacy and numeracy among southern children. In spite of their existence the South had the highest illiteracy rates in the Union in 1840. Yet the stereotype tells only part of the story of antebellum southern education. Many southerners had long appreciated the social benefits of an educated public, having promoted free schools and parish schools from the second half of the eighteenth century; but they were slow to put in place the concrete measures that would have made free education available to all children. For most of the antebellum period southern legislatures frequently debated but rarely enacted, and even more sporadically funded, comprehensive school systems. From a slow start, however, came a real drive during the 1840s and 1850s toward providing education for all southern children. The reasons for this change will be explored in depth in this chapter, with specific attention paid to the role that state-funded education had in shaping the attitudes of the white poor toward the South. By 1861 several Confederate states had fully functioning systems of public education that were comparable to counterparts on the other side of the Mason-Dixon line. Understanding how and why lawmakers in the southern states changed their stance on public education, and especially the increased importance placed on free tuition for poor whites, is the main purpose of this chapter.

Historians of public education in antebellum America have long debated the tensions between the two prime motivators for those who promoted common schooling: reducing social disorder and liberating individual and collective potential. On the one hand, conservatives (mostly associated with the Federalists in the early nineteenth century) hoped that educating the masses would prevent the criminality, vice, and drunkenness that were perceived to be increasingly common, especially among new urban immigrants. In this sense popular education had a clear social purpose: to make society calmer, more peaceable, and much nicer to inhabit, especially for the semi-aristocratic elite who often constituted this conservative faction. Conversely there were those (often linked to Jeffersonian Republicanism) who believed that education was the only thing that could unlock the talents of individuals whose poverty and background condemned them to a life of manual labor. In effect, they saw education as enhancing social mobility. Moreover, these liberal-minded reformers believed that if the literacy and numeracy of the population were increased, society as a whole would benefit. The scientific and agricultural advances that might one day be made by these people would in effect be wealth-creating and be good for the advancement of the new American republic.[2] Of course these tensions between conservatives and liberals did not prevent common schooling from making significant advances in the early decades of the nineteenth century since the solution to the different problems as perceived by Federalists and Republicans was the same—more and better education being made available to the masses.

However, although education was seen as important by many of those in power, albeit for different reasons, literacy rates in New England and most of the mid-Atlantic states far outstripped those in the South. The reasons for this difference can be found in the approach often taken toward education during the colonial period. British colonists in the South had not been insensible to the importance of educational institutions for their children in the decades before the American Revolution, but there were numerous practical obstacles in the path of those promoting schools. Endowments from wealthy benefactors had enabled poor children to be educated at various parish schools in the Carolinas and, to a lesser extent, in Virginia. The free school of St. Helena's parish, South Carolina, for instance, received a £100 sterling legacy in the will of its late rector with the instruction that the interest on the capital be used to pay for the education of "poor children whose parents are not capable to pay for their schooling." The South Carolina legislature also made an annual appropriation toward the cost of teachers' salaries in each parish and was generally supportive of attempts to increase the number of schools in the colony, commenting that "nothing conduces more to the private advantage of every man, or the public benefit of a country in general, than a liberal education." But while many sizable southern settlements had schools before the American Revolution, education was by no means accessible to the majority of the southern population. The scattered nature of southern settlement patterns meant that many people simply lived too far from a school to allow their children to attend regularly. In the more densely settled areas, even when parish schools were built and were open to all, sometimes there was simply not enough space to accommodate all who wanted schooling, and on occasion there were insufficient teachers to teach them. Schools operated as completely independent units with no coordination or cooperation between them. The larger southern towns also had fee-paying schools for those who could afford to contribute toward their children's education and these schools often attracted the best teachers.[3]

Education was also not high on the list of priorities of southern state governments after the end of British rule, and most legislatures seemed content to allow the ad hoc systems of parish schools to remain undisturbed. Not until 1796 did a southern legislature attempt to establish a comprehensive system of education when Virginia legislators passed "An Act to establish

Public Schools." While far from a comprehensive public education system, since the act authorized only a limited amount of funding for the creation of school districts, the Virginia legislature was motivated to act on this matter from a belief that "however favourable republican government founded on the principles of equal liberty, justice and order, may be to human happiness, no real stability or lasting permanency thereof can be rationally hoped for, if the minds of the citizens be not rendered liberal and humane, and be not fully impressed with the importance of those principles from whence these blessings proceed."[4] Fifteen years later South Carolina passed its own public school act that provided $300 for each school and a mechanism for choosing local officials who would oversee the system. These "free schools" were to be free of charge to all children but, in a clause that would be debated at length in South Carolina in the later antebellum period, preference was given to "poor orphans and the children of indigent and necessitous parents."[5]

The glacial speed with which southern legislatures tackled the issue of public education contrasts starkly with the progress being made further north and provides ammunition to historians who have lauded the progress made in New England while decrying the slow pace of the South. Carl Kaestle believes that the typical southern state provided only "a modicum of state aid for the schooling of paupers, and the rest of education fell to independent institutions, principally the old field school and the academy," which he attributed to the opposition of elites toward "democratic" systems of education as well as the small and scattered rural population that made common schools unviable. Lee Soltow and Edward Stevens agreed with Kaestle that "school systems in the South did not provide the same level of access as in the North. . . . [W]ith so much invested in a system of private schools and academies, available resources for public schooling were minimal. . . . [I]t is evident that the South, under the prodding of self-righteous Yankees, began a new move toward publicly financed education after the war."[6] On a certain level these criticisms of the southern provision of education are correct: the average southern state could not begin to compare its system of public education with those of Massachusetts or Connecticut. Southerners were themselves acutely aware of the backwardness of their educational provision. Savannah-born Mary Telfair learned during a visit to New Haven, Connecticut, that "one hundred and 38 thousand dollars

[is] annually expended upon free schools…[and] there are not 5 children of 10 years of age in the state who cannot read." Georgia legislator William H. Stiles was ashamed that his state ranked twenty-third out of twenty-eight states with regard to literacy, and had to acknowledge that "the states most worthy of praise, or whose systems are most complete and efficient, are the New England states and New York."[7] Yet comparing the education systems of Massachusetts and Alabama, for instance, or New York and Georgia is hardly fair. In terms of history, social structure, makeup and density of population, economic orientation, and public ethos they could hardly have been more different. Perhaps a better comparison to use when judging the development of southern school systems is to see where most southern states were in the first decades of the nineteenth century and then see where most were in the 1850s. Only by seeing how far the southern states had come can one truly judge how important educational provision for all white children was held to be by those with the power and authority to make a difference.

The passage of the first school laws in Virginia and South Carolina suggests a growing interest in education in the South during in the first decades of the nineteenth century. In part this arose from concerns among political elites, and especially Jeffersonian Republicans who had pushed for a wider electoral franchise, that ignorance among voters made them vulnerable to demagogues. North Carolina governor James Turner argued in 1803 that "the most certain way of handing down to our latest posterity, our free republican government, is to enlighten the minds of the people"; his successor, Nathaniel Alexander, observed three years later "that in a government constituted as ours, where the people are everything, where they are the fountain of all power, it becomes infinitely important that they be sufficiently enlightened to realise their interests, and to comprehend the best means of advancing them."[8] With franchises in many southern states being open to all adult white males, the threat of hordes of uneducated voters being whipped up by persuasive oratory to vote in a particular way was clearly one that alarmed some in authority. One correspondent of the *Christian Monitor*, published in Richmond, Virginia, argued in 1815 that a comprehensive system of education would also help to foster patriotism: "The more extensive the system of education the better. For while it takes away those narrow feelings, and destroys those prejudices, which fit a people to be instruments of ambitious demagogues, it enlarges the circle of our attachments, and multiplies those associations, which as we have seen, lay the foundation for our warmest love of country."[9]

The proper instruction of southern youth was also attractive to those of a more conservative persuasion since it was widely thought to foster better behavior and greater morality among the ordinary people. Curbing the riotous excesses of youth would make society more stable and peaceable while reducing the general level of "sin" in the community. The correspondent of the *Christian Monitor* again had something to say on this:

> It is then of the utmost importance that the young be trained up in a course of virtuous conduct; and that moral principles should with the greatest care be emplanted in early life. Let parents remember their obligation to their country, and so instruct and discipline their children that they may be prepared for her service. And let the young men, of our land, remember that by yielding to the temptations to which they are exposed, that by a life of dissipation and intemperance, they are sinners against their country, as well as their God; and are gradually disqualifying themselves for the exercise of one of the noblest feelings of the human heart.[10]

Governor David Stone told the North Carolina legislature in 1809 "that letters and science, though useful as lights to enable a sound heart to shape a safe and beneficial course through the voyage of life, are mere delusions when not controlled and directed by correct moral principle, chastened and purified by the precepts of our holy Religion."[11]

While improving public morality might have motivated legislators, those actually managing common or free schools on a day-to-day basis were particularly impressed by the practical benefits for the children. The Free School Commissioners of Lexington District, South Carolina, wrote to the state legislature "expressing their entire approbation of the great advantages arising to this district in consequence of the publick aid given to schooling as we are induced to believe that there is a number of children who have been taught to read and write who never, in all probability had it not been for the liberal incouragement given by your honourable body in aiding the poor in schooling, would never [have] been taught the first rudiments of education."[12] Similarly in Cabell County, Virginia, Commissioners of the Free schools commented in 1832 that "there are a number of poor children in this county (who but for the application of this fund, would have remained in entire ignorance of the elementary branches of education) who have become enabled thereby to transact ordinary business, requiring reading, writing and common arithmetic with facility" while commissioners in Scott County were "of [the] opinion that the money appropriated for the purpose of educating the poor, has proved a great blessing to the poor inhabitants of the county" and were "highly pleased" with the results.[13]

Despite these positive reports from Cabell and Scott counties, the progress of popular education in most of Virginia was painfully slow. The "Public School Act" of 1796 did not result in large numbers of public schools being established throughout the state. Governor John Tyler criticized the Virginia legislature in 1809 for "its failure, by reason of a fatal apathy and parsimonious policy, to provide state schools," commenting wryly that "a stranger might think we had declared war against the arts and sciences."[14] Shamed into action, the Virginia legislature created a "Literary Fund" the following year with interest from the fund to be spent on establishing schools throughout the state. However the amount of money annually paid into the Literary Fund was relatively small, and consequently the income generated by the fund was also small, and certainly insufficient to establish a comprehensive system of schools throughout Virginia.[15] Not until 1816 was a large appropriation placed into the Literary Fund that would, so one correspondent of the Richmond *Enquirer* hoped, "diffuse . . . free schools in every county."[16] Yet within a couple of years this hope had been dashed as supporters of the University of Virginia managed to obtain part of the Literary Fund for their institution. Consequently, the amounts available for primary schools remained inadequate. In 1832 the school commissioners from Hampshire County informed the state authorities that "the sum allotted to this county, is totally inadequate to the education of the poor children in it" while those in Page County were "of [the] opinion that it will require a much larger sum than what has been allowed to educate all the poor children in the county."[17]

At least South Carolina and Virginia had actually tried to move toward a system of public education; most other southern states had not even taken these small steps, and poor children of indigent parents in most of the South were left without access to any forms of free education. In some places schools did exist, established either by legacy or other charitable fund, that were willing to admit the children of the poor, if not free then for nominal fees; however, two immediate problems arose: the abilities and qualifications of the teacher; and the amount of time any child spent in the classroom. The editor of Richmond's *Family Visitor* complained that too many local schools were run "by men of no religion, or morals; and as to their qualifications, they profess none. . . . [M]any of our teachers, if I may call them, cannot write five lines in common English, without making six or eight orthographical blunders. . . . Is this not a most deplorable situation? To have the ignorant and blind, the immoral, profane, lazy and profligate, as guides and instructors for our blessed and dear offspring?" Elliott Story recalled that his first teacher in Southampton County, Virginia, was "a very common teacher of reading, writing and arithmatick, in which branches he succeeded only tolerably well in teaching." Several of the schools he attended during his teens closed down as teachers got married, moved away, or died. At the age of seventeen Story started teaching at his own school without any formal qualifications whatsoever, and continued to do so until he was thirty-two when he determined on a mercantile career confessing that he found teaching "irksome." Indeed, a significant number of teachers were like this—only marginally more capable than the children they proposed to instruct. One educational reformer commented cynically, "How many do you find professing to teach, who had better be taught?"[18]

Even when a competent teacher could be found, the household and family claims on the labor of children often took precedence over schooling. In 1833 Elliott Story was attending a new school about two miles from his home but later noted in his diary: "I went but a small portion of the year, as I was obliged to stay at home and help my father in the crop, as he had a large family to support and no person to help him." John Dawson, free school commissioner in St. John's Berkeley Parish in low country South Carolina, also reported that "great difficulty has attended the collecting together the children of these scattered families for instruction. Many of them, are detained at home, to assist in the cultivation of the crops." South Carolina professors Stephen Elliot and J. H. Thornwell condemned "the carelessness of the poor about the education of their children, [and] the selfishness which leads them to prefer their labor to their improvement."[19]

A more worrying trend for supporters of public education was that even where free schools existed many poor people refused to send their children to places tainted with the tag of "charity." The governor of Virginia noted in 1820 that "to select fit objects of that charity as it is now dispensed an inquiry must necessarily be instituted which has not infrequently proved highly offensive to small cultivators who feel a just pride of independence for the certainty of being able to furnish abundant food and raiment although wholly unable to provide for the education of their children. Many of them feel unwilling to have their names placed in the list of paupers even for that important advantage." The reports of free school commissioners in Orange County a few years later confirmed his fears. They noted that "the high-minded Virginian, although poor, revolted at the idea of his children being taught in a charity school."[20] The same prejudices were apparent in other states. In Georgia the local justices of the peace were expected "to make out a list of all children in their respective districts, whose extreme indigence entitles them to a participation in the poor school fund," but the process of identifying these children necessarily entailed an acknowledgment from parents of their inability to pay school fees. Where such enquiries were required the school system, as legislator David Lewis observed, "can never reach a large number of children whose parents—too poor to pay—are too proud to take charity."[21] In South Carolina the Society for the Advancement of Learning commented in 1835 that "many poor persons possessing delicate feelings have absolutely refused to send their children to the poor schools. . . . [A] general feeling of contempt seems to exist, in the minds of the poor, for these schools. In short, no one in this country likes to be considered a pauper."[22] The Reverend C. B. Thrummel, reporting in 1840 on the state of free schools in All Saints Parish, South Carolina, said that the poor "will not profit by the free schools; but from pride, and delicacy of feeling, will rather keep their children at home altogether, than, by sending them to the free school, attach to them, as they think and feel, the stigma of being poor, and of receiving an education as paupers." Dr. E. Hazelius, reporting on Lexington District, found that "the poor but high-minded republican, supposes himself degraded, by accepting the gratuity which the state offers him."[23] C.G. Memminger told the South Carolina legislature that the failings of the state school system was their fault "because you have separated the poor and put them in schools by themselves—because you have required from them as a condition for admission that they shall make a confession of pauperism. . . . Say to the honest and frugal father, put aside your honourable desire of independence—confess yourself a pauper—accept the boon of the state, and your son may be admitted to receive his education with other paupers—and can any one fail to forsee the result?"[24]

If schemes of public instruction were ever to be established in the South this prejudice had to be overcome, or at least neutralized. Part of the problem was that the Democratic Party, powerful in most parts of the South, supported the idea of small government and the high level of intervention required to establish state educational systems was against their natural instincts. Educational reformers therefore had to make a strong case that government intervention was imperative. Archibald D. Murphey, a leading promoter of educational reform in North Carolina, believed that the state had a duty, even a right, to get involved in the education of the poor. In his 1816 report to the state governor he argued that "a republic is bottomed upon the virtue of her citizens; and that virtue consists in the faithful discharge of moral and social duties and in obedience to the laws. But it is knowledge only, that lights up the path of duty, unfolds the reasons of obedience and points out to man the purposes of his existence. In a government, therefore, which rests upon the public virtue, no efforts should be spared to diffuse public instruction; and the government which makes those efforts, finds a pillar of support in the heart of every citizen." A year later he went further claiming that "poor children are the peculiar property of the state, and by proper cultivation they will constitute a fund of intellectual and moral worth which will greatly subserve the public interest."[25] Other reformers tried to make education more attractive to legislators by painting it as essentially conservative. William Maxwell, speaking before the Literary and Philosophical Society of Hampden Sydney College, Virginia, in 1826, stated that while "education is necessary for all, I would take care to provide it especially in the first place, as soon as possible, for those whom we call the common people, (including the sons and daughters of the poorest in the land) because it is, . . . indispensable for them, to enable them to keep their proper station in society . . . it is that only thing also, which can properly qualify them to discharge the duties which they owe to the state, as good citizens." Without the state providing a basic level of education "our great danger really is, that our commons, or many of them, will be too ignorant and vicious, in spite of all we can do to enlighten and improve them, to maintain their rights, and do their duties as they ought. And so we must feel, most clearly, I think, that we should hasten, at once, to provide the necessary and proper education for them, and all of them, without delay."[26]

Only the state could deliver educational reform since parents were generally thought to be unable to see the benefits that would accrue from the education of their children. Philip Lindsley informed new graduates of the University of Tennessee that "the great mass of parents have shown themselves but sorry instructors and faithless guides to those who ought to be dearer to them than their own life. They are themselves, in general, too ignorant, to say no more, to do much. Hence, in our day, infant schools have been established in many places, to support this radical defect." An anonymous correspondent of the *Virginia Evangelical and Literary Magazine* thought it "extremely hazardous" to leave the instruction of the youth of the state to their parents.[27] Alonzo Church, speaking to the members of the Georgia Historical Society, believed he could detect that "the desire to acquire even the elements of knowledge is, with certain classes, diminishing—and the want of education is losing in the estimation of many, that reproach which heretofore has ever been attached to those in this condition. There may now be found, and especially at the polls, 'the esprit du corps' of ignorance."[28]

If the state was to play a significant part in providing education to every child, an organized and well-funded system had to be the answer. The first state to grasp the nettle was North Carolina in its Common School Act of 1839. North Carolina's governors, like those of many other states, had agitated for decades for more provision from the legislature for schooling. Governor Burton argued in 1826 that since the state "exacts and expects obedience from the citizens to its laws and institutions, it should give them the opportunity to appreciate their privileges and improve their condition." Four years later Governor Owen was ashamed that in all of North Carolina "there never has been established a single institution for gratuitous instruction."[29] Even the state's press were aware of the problem, the *Raleigh Star* commenting that "we are all duly sensible that the people of this state are greatly in the rear of the population of most states as it regards the facilities of intellectual improvement" and the *Western Carolinian* asking pointedly, "How long will North Carolina be careless of her most vital interests?"[30] Not everyone thought that common schooling was a good idea, however. "X" writing in the *Raleigh Register* complained of the potential cost of any comprehensive system fearing that it would raise taxes, and did not consider "it at all necessary, that *everybody* should be able to read, write and cipher. If one is to keep a store or a school, or to be [a] lawyer or physician, such branches may, *perhaps*, be taught him; though I do not look upon them as by any means indispensable: but if he is to be a plain farmer, or a mechanic, they are of no manner of use, but rather a detriment."[31]

The state legislature of 1838–1839 spent a great deal of time debating proposed school bills, aware that not only was there widespread support for such a measure among the people, but also that the Literary Fund of North Carolina, begun in 1825, now amounted to more than $2 million and would generate at least $100,000 in interest annually. The bill, passed in early 1839, ordered every county to hold a vote on whether they wished for a public school system to be established in their district, with two-thirds of the funding coming from the state, and one-third from the local taxpayers. Supporters of the proposal wasted no time in campaigning for a "yes" vote. Lawyer William D. Valentine noted in his diary after he had addressed the public at Bethel in Pitt County that "I had a goodly audience respectful and attentive. Common School is a popular theme in this neighbourhood. The people go for it no doubt."[32] Newspaper editorials urged voters to support the establishment of the new system when the time came to vote. The *Raleigh Register* thought that "the people of North Carolina will not withhold their assent to a measure, the benefits of which are to be the property and inheritance of their children." The *Rutherfordton Gazette* hoped "that the friends of Education, in every section of our state, will exert themselves in diffusing information among the people on this subject, previous to the elections in August, when the question will be submitted; let them see and correctly understand the principles upon which these schools are to be established, and there will not be a dissenting voice among those who properly appreciate the value of education."[33] When the votes started coming in from each county in August 1839 it was clear that the pro-school lobby had prevailed, with all but seven counties voting to adopt the new system and often by overwhelming majorities: only two people in Pasquotank County, for example, voted against the new system.[34]

Despite the initial optimism of newspaper editors that "in almost every place the people have manifested a desire to avail themselves of the benefit of the act of the last legislature," this enthusiasm waned rather quickly.[35] Asheville's *Highland Messenger* lamented the "ignorant, vicious, and lazy parents" who permitted their children to "grow up without even the cultivation of those habits of industry and those principles of moral honesty necessary to enable them to procure for themselves the necessaries of life."[36] "Cadmus," writing in 1846, criticized parents for "imagining they discharge their duty in relation to [their] children by giving them a few months tuition in the year, while the rest of the time is allowed up in physical labor and mental forgetfulness" but he also attributed the poor attendance of indigent children to "the incompetancy of the teachers." The real target for "Cadmus" was the lack of money forthcoming from counties to match state funding for common schools. If more money was available, his argument ran, the county would be able to attract better qualified teachers who would enthuse their pupils with the virtues of learning.[37] School commissioners in Craven County were confident that their own schools were doing well and "that a large majority of the children can now spell, read and write, and some have [been] made most . . . proficient in other branches of education." Yet even here the suitability of teachers was a concern. The county had an examining committee that vetted teachers for their moral and intellectual ability, though clearly moral character accounted for as much as, if not more than, intellect. One teacher was appointed who "is not qualified to teach any of the branches of education well. He might do to teach very small children. His moral character said to be very good" and another teacher, although acknowledged to be "intellectually qualified" was asked to resign for "inebriety." More worrying for the commissioners, however, "there appears to dwell an invincible prejudice in the limited comprehension, and biased minds of the *ignorant* wealthy, against the common school system hence, one not infrequently hears them regret that they supported it, or rejoice that they opposed it, or lament that it has been instituted and occasionally dubbed with the derisive epithet of the 'poor school.'" The commissioners echoed calls from other parts of the state for more money to support the system and increase the pay of teachers.[38]

Clearly what was required was a state official tasked with overseeing the proper implementation of the common school system, someone who would ensure that all teachers were capable of doing their jobs, and who would bring a degree of uniformity to the curriculum of North Carolina's schools. In 1846 the North Carolina legislature proposed "the selection of some citizen eminent for his talent and moral worth—one who enjoys the confi-

dence of the people, to whom shall be entrusted the general supervision of
the schools. One, who animated by a holy zeal for the public welfare, shall
travel over the state, stimulate the superintendents and committee-men to
the performance of the high duty entrusted to them—point out the happiness that springs from knowledge and the vice and degradation that are ever
the offspring of ignorance and folly." But it was not until 1852 that the first
state superintendent of education was appointed.[39] Calvin H. Wiley, the
Presbyterian minister who filled this post until 1866, must have quickly realized the immense nature of the task he had taken on. The first reports from
the school districts that he received made depressing reading and that from
Rowan County was fairly typical: "The people take but little interest in the
schools in this county. I can't prevail on the parents to take the interest they
should do. Men who are the most capable will not serve as committee men
and the consequence is the people elect men who are totally unfitted for
this office, some men have been elected who could neither read nor write.
The reason these men give me is that it's a troublesome office."[40]

Wiley immediately instituted several changes to overcome some of these
problems. To combat apathy Wiley set himself the task of personally visiting county seats, especially in remote parts of the state, and addressing the
public on the importance of education for all; to prevent the ignorance of
school commissioners Wiley had 13,000 copies of the school laws printed
and distributed to every clerk and commissioner throughout the state; and
to instill greater confidence in teachers he instituted annual examinations in
literacy and numeracy, and instructed school boards to employ only those
with a certificate that testified to their competency.[41] Finally he forcibly
reminded the state legislators, and others who read his widely circulated
report, that back in 1840, the first year of the common school system, North
Carolina's 632 common schools had taught roughly 14,000 pupils or about
10 percent of school-age children. In 1853 there were 2,131 common schools
with a collective enrollment of nearly 100,000 pupils or roughly 60 percent
of school-age children. In 1840 no more than a third of school-age children
received any form of tuition, but in 1853 Wiley estimated that all but 10,000
of the 165,000 school-age children in the state attended either public or private schools. It was this achievement of which Wiley was proudest, pointing
out that "the Common Schools of the German States, of Scotland and of
Massachusetts, in their present condition, are the result of the patient labor

of many years, and in some of the places named have been maturing for centuries. . . . It is, therefore, very absurd to compare ourselves with these States in their present condition, and thus to draw conclusions unfavorable to our ability to mature a good system of Public Schools. We are doing vastly better than the pioneer States did in the infancy of their progress."[42] Such was the rapid progress of North Carolina that by 1860 about two-thirds of the state's white children were being educated in common schools, almost exactly the same proportion that were being educated in the public schools of Massachusetts.[43]

The achievements of North Carolina did not go unnoticed by other southern states yet the progress of education in Virginia and South Carolina, states that were the first to legislate for common or free schools, continued to be slow. In South Carolina several different governors reminded the legislature that education was "the only sure basis of a free Government" and that schools were "the nurseries of free men" that would "imbue the minds of our youth with sound practical views, religious, moral and political." The state's free schools, in particular, were "capable of great improvement, and demand the paternal supervision of the legislature"; yet those with the power to do something about universal education often spoke about the usefulness of education in an abstract way while denying there was any fault in the existing system.[44] Representative Glover accepted that "whilst we are labouring to improve and perpetuate our political institutions, and to strengthen and secure the foundations of our government, we would be guilty of the grossest blindness, and overlook the surest method of ensuring these great ends, if we neglected the cause of popular education" but he denied the need for fundamental reform of the system, claiming only that it required better administration. Poor parents were told they needed to do more to ensure that their children attended school, yet nothing would be done to make the system more inclusive and less class-based. Indeed Glover argued that "the object of the state is not to expend money among the people: it is to improve and enlighten her poor children." Attitudes such as these meant that free schools would continue to be a ghetto for the poor while wealthier parents patronized institutions that charged tuition.[45] By the late 1840s the free school system was being attacked on all sides. Governor William Aiken decried the "very imperfect, and I might almost add, useless system, under which our free schools are at present conducted" while Governor John Hugh Means stated that he would "not hesitate to pronounce it an almost useless expenditure of the public fund."[46] Yet there were still those who argued that the system was the most appropriate for South Carolina's society. One author, in traditional Democratic Party style, opined that "the rich and poor are mutually necessary to each other's well being. The happiness of each depends upon his being in his true position." Over-educating the poor would only make them more aware of their lowly social status and therefore make them disgruntled. Furthermore, the independent and self-reliant nature of southern society was anathema to an overly centralized system of education overseen by bureaucrats.[47]

These views tended to be in a minority, however. More representative of the mainstream was Dr. James Henley Thornwell, Presbyterian minister and president of South Carolina College. He denied, in a report to Governor Manning, that the school system was ever intended to be solely for pauper children: "Throughout our statutes free schools mean public schools, or schools which are open to every citizen," and he advocated immediate action since "education is too complicated an interest, and touches the prosperity of the commonwealth in too many points, to be left, in reference to the most important class of its subjects, absolutely without responsibility to the government."[48] Governor James Adams agreed with Thornwell's diagnosis, stating "that what was intended to introduce gradually a general system of common schools has been perverted to the exclusive education of paupers." As a result the common school system in South Carolina required nothing less than a "thorough and entire reformation."[49] The lack of legislative progress was puzzling. The *Southern Quarterly Review* commented that South Carolina was not apathetic about education; rather "the subject has engaged her anxious attention; she has expended no little thought and reflection upon it." Yet nothing like the North Carolina system was created in South Carolina before the Civil War. It did not help the cause of fundamental reform that some leading politicians did not see flaws in the existing system. Rice planter Robert F. W. Allston, who served as governor of South Carolina between 1856 and 1858, believed that "the free schools are doing more good than they have been allowed credit for. Where ever educated gentlemen of the country have generously interested themselves in the subject, and with commendable zeal and public spirit have devoted a portion of their energies to the success of the schools, the law has operated well. As a basis for a practical system, regarding the character of our population and the geographic peculiarities of the state, I have not been able to arrange one more satisfactory."[50]

Allston's satisfaction with the operation of the free school system in South Carolina was supported by some of those who actually served as free school commissioners. Those in Fairfield District reported in 1857, "The board are gratified in being able to state that the Free School system has always operated well in Fairfield and is still doing all the good that can reasonably be desired," and counterparts in St. Helena's Parish believed that "the free school system has been of great benefit to the poor of this parish. . . . [I]f all the free schools are as well conducted and as beneficial in other parts of the state as in this parish the system is certainly a great public blessing."[51] And statistical compilations of the returns made by local free school commissioners confirmed that South Carolina was making some headway. The number of schools in South Carolina did not alter much between 1828 and 1860; if anything it fell slightly, but the number of pupils educated in those schools doubled over the same period, from 9,036 to 18,915. As a proportion of school-age children in the state, these figures represented a noticeable improvement, from 16.8 percent attending school in 1828 to 31.5 percent in 1860, but it remains obvious that one of the South's wealthiest states took far from a leading role in the cause of popular education.[52]

The greatest advances in South Carolina were made in Charleston, where a comprehensive system of common schools was established in 1856. The 900 pupils who attended the schools in their first year were principally drawn from "the poorer classes of society; but as soon as the influence of the school began to be felt, and the character of its training to be observed, it was appreciated by other portions of society, and the applications became more general." By 1860 the seven public schools in the city were educating 2,135 pupils. The school commissioners spent far more than their counterparts elsewhere in the state: in 1860 costs amounted to $28.74 per pupil, compared with an average of $6.69 elsewhere in the state. Charleston accounted for less than 10 percent of the white population of South Carolina as a whole, but the city expended fully half the money spent on free schools in the state in 1860. The vast majority of the cost of the public education system in Charleston did not come from the state treasury, however, but from city taxpayers: of $61,349 expended in 1860 only $12,000 came from the state. Charleston's free school commissioners explained the equity of a system that taxed wealthy property-owners to provide education for all by stating that "the government which protects, controls and taxes that property, is administered by voters, many of whom—nay, a majority of whom—may be ignorant, and uneducated. . . . Can any investment of part of their means be more judicious than to teach these rulers wisdom, and justice, and virtue?"[53] By pointing out the "direct interest" that the wealthy had in the education of the masses, Charleston's leaders were able to create a functioning and well-funded public school system on the eve of the Civil War.

Virginia was another southern state to dither over the introduction of a comprehensive system of public education. Old arguments, as a correspondent to the Richmond *Enquirer* pointed out, no longer carried the same weight after 1839 since "the sparseness of the population is . . . no reason why Virginia should go against the experience of the whole country . . . in failing to adopt a district organization, for even North Carolina has adopted such a system."[54] A more serious obstacle in the way of educational reformers was the view, common among many elite Virginians, that education was a private rather than a public concern. If elite members of the legislature were able to block a common school law, to some reformers it would mean that "with all our boasted republicanism we are in this matter more clearly ruled by an aristocracy than any country on earth, England excepted."[55] Agitators for a system of public schools in Albemarle County argued that "it is the interest of every member of a community that every other member should possess the elements of education"; however, "universal education, so useful to society, can be brought about only by the agency of public authority and of general taxation."[56] Governor James McDowell was firmly of the opinion that "education is a public as well as private concern . . . and further, that education is too sacred an element in the well-being and safety of a state, governed like ours, to be left to the hazards of unorganized, individual combination." According to his calculation in 1845 about 34,000 pupils attended a common school during the year, with a further 12,000 attending a fee-paying school, but more than 120,000 attended no school whatsoever. This situation was, in McDowell's words, "absolutely appalling" and he recommended that "the fostering hand of the government be extended" via the creation of a district school system that was essentially similar to the common schools of North Carolina. Voters in each district would vote to levy a local tax to support the new schools that would be open to all. Such a system would "at once destroy those designations of indigence and charity, which have kept so many thousands in ignorance."[57] The divisions within the Virginia legislature were epitomized by the Committee on Primary Schools that reported in 1845. The majority of the committee accepted that "the relation of parent and child is so sacred, that under a free government, no authoritative interference with the mode of the child's education should ever be contemplated" and found little fault with the existing system except for the level of funding, which it recommended should be increased. The minority on the committee, who felt so strongly about this issue that they wrote their own report, instead urged a wholesale revision of the system. In particular they criticized the existing system since "it creates a distinction between the rich and the poor" and instead recommended the creation of common schools open to all as "more conducive to that equality of feeling which is peculiarly appropriate to our republican institutions."[58]

The Second Auditor of the Literary Fund was doubtful of the efficacy of any new system, commenting that it would do little to overcome class prejudices among pupils: "The circumstances of poor youths entered by charity at a school attended by the sons and daughters of the wealthy, must necessarily be well known to their young neighbors and schoolmates, and will be as certainly noticed in a district school as in any other." Furthermore he observed "that until the poor shall be blessed with competence, the services of their children will be required to an extent that will deprive a great many of an opportunity of attending any school."[59] The reports from the counties were also mixed. School commissioners in Henry County stated "that the unfounded prejudice which formerly existed in the minds of the poorer classes, as to permitting their children to attend the schools when their tuition was paid from the fund, has altogether ceased. . . . The indigent children are becoming much more prompt and constant in their attendance, and consequently have made very decided improvement." In neighboring Patrick County, however, commissioners believed that the Literary Fund was being "frittered away to little purpose upon recipients whose parents esteem the privilege a boon of little or no value."[60]

Yet there was enough political pressure to ensure action. Those from the western parts of the state complained bitterly that part of the Literary Fund was appropriated to support the University of Virginia, "an institution whose tendencies are essentially for the very rich, while . . . primary schools are exclusively intended for the very poor"; as a result, "the men of small fortunes are left to their own means. . . . [T]he bone and muscle of the state, the men who pay the taxes are left out."[61] A number of residents of Richmond urged the legislature "to prepare the public mind to submit to the imposition of an education tax. The present income of the literary fund is inadequate, to the education even of the indigent children of the state, and we hope you will agree with us, that the instruction of all the children of the state, should be the object of any system that may be adopted. If the people will cheerfully pay the tax, their representatives will not hesitate to impose it. With sufficient funds a proper system can be speedily devised."[62] While these suggestions were not directly adopted, the passage of the District School Law of 1846 was intended to address some of the problems pointed out by Governor McDowell. Counties were permitted to hold a vote on whether to join the new scheme, but unlike North Carolina where the common school system had been approved by voters in most counties, the take-up was far lower in Virginia. By 1860 only eleven counties, mainly encompassing urban areas such as Norfolk, Portsmouth, and Fredericksburg, were operating the new district system, but those that adopted it generally believed it to be effective. Leroi Edward, president of the school commissioners in Norfolk, believed "that a public free-school system is cheaper than the old system in the aggregate . . . [and] that, by diffusing education more universally, it diffuses good morals and regularity of life, and makes society more peaceful and happy" while his counterpart in Portsmouth believed "the system is working efficiently with us" and that it constituted "the great fountain from which fertilizing streams already begin to flow and which shall truly enrich our community."[63] The difference that the district system could make is highlighted by the returns of Henry County to the Second Auditor of the Literary Fund. In 1844 the county had spent $382 educating 156 poor children, but five years later, with a new district school system in place, the county spent $4,000 (90 percent of which was raised locally through taxation) educating 1,391 children. Similar statistics can be obtained from Norfolk County, which educated 256 children at a cost of $700 in 1844, but 1,232 children at a cost of $8,000 in 1849. As in Henry County, more than 90 percent of the extra money came from local taxpayers.[64] In Jefferson County the "good substantial schoolhouses" reported by the commissioners in 1855 cost more than $4,000 a year to staff and maintain, but the commissioners also believed "the system is gradually accomplishing its object."[65]

The district system was not without its critics. A correspondent of the *Daily Southern Argus* criticized the new public schools since there would never be enough places for all local children. It was inevitable therefore that some well-off children would be taught while "little boys and girls of worthy widows and indigent fathers were deprived of the pleasure and benefit of instruction."[66] Elsewhere the old prejudices against universal education remained. The school commissioners in Charlotte County commented in 1853 that "where the rich and the poor do not mix freely together in the social relations of life, it is utter folly to attempt to get the children of the poor to attend the same schools with the children of the rich. Except in a very few cases, they will go a short time and then leave, because they imagine themselves abused and insulted because of their poverty." Furthermore, the cost of a district school system could not be denied. Those counties that voted for district schools ended up with higher local taxes. Henry County might have voted for the district system, but not everyone was happy with the decision. Several inhabitants petitioned the legislature complaining that "the power to vote direct tax upon property is given to the man who is utterly destitute . . . and the [school] commissioner's power to tax is unlimited."[67] In response to the objection "that it is unjust to require the wealthy to contribute to the education of the poor" Governor Joseph Johnson argued that "while the wealthy contribute the larger amount, they have the larger interest at stake." The cost was also addressed directly by memorialists from Halifax County to the legislature in 1854: "The next objection urged to the system of free schools, is the tax which it imposes on the community. This is opposed on the two grounds of its injustice and its enormity. . . . But where a great good is to be attained, which endures to the benefit of the whole community, and to which individuals are unequal, government has the right, and is bound by its responsibility and its duty to the public to give its aid. The education of the people fills perfectly all these conditions."[68]

Yet the cost issue continued to be a problem for some, and was partly behind the abolition of the district school system in Fredericksburg in December 1857. Evidently the $1,500 per year that the system cost was simply too much for the town council, and only one councilman voted to retain the system. The local press, however, were incensed by this decision, pointing out that when the vote on public schools had been taken in 1852 the result had been 378 to 27 in favor, and furthermore that the district school act made no provision for the abolition of the system by mere vote of the town council. Particularly embarrassing was that the actions of the council were picked up by the *Baltimore American*, which was scathing in its denunciation. Headlining its report "Advancing Backwards," the *American* could scarcely believe that the council "had the cheek to make such a movement . . . [when] the free school system of Fredericksburg was adopted by the citizens of that place, by a vote of nearly fifteen in favor to one against."[69]

The statistics collected by the state show that Virginia's common school system was making some progress, especially during the 1850s when the number of children at common schools rose by 58 percent while the school-age population rose by only 14 percent. However, even in 1860 only 12.7 percent of Virginia's school-age children were being educated in state-funded common or district schools. This was in stark contrast to neighboring North Carolina where two-thirds of all children were in common schools in 1860. Virginia even comes out poorly when compared to South Carolina where nearly a third of all children were in free schools in 1860. The school commissioners of Marion County laid the blame for this "miserable, rickety system of public education" firmly at the doors of the legislature and the "selfish, narrow-minded, impracticable bungling legislation that has been made on the subject." Thus, "while other states are becoming powerful by the liberal support they give public education, Virginia is impotent to everything that pertains to national greatness."[70] By virtually any measure Virginia's attempts to educate its children before the Civil War failed, and hundreds of thousands of children had minimal access to schools or teachers.

Elsewhere in the South the cause of popular education continued to make slow but steady progress. Tennessee established a school fund in 1817 that supported the education of the poor and by 1836 had a School Act that provided for a state superintendent and taxes for education. However it was not until 1854 that a system of common schools was comprehensively established throughout the state, and judging from the post-bellum views of many who attended rural schools the quality of the education imparted left a great deal to be desired. Nearly 90 percent of former pupils classified their experience as "poor," and only in Nashville, where the city-supported

Nashville English School (1821) and later the South Nashville Institute (1851) educated more than a thousand pupils in the 1850s, was free tuition widely available.[71] Florida created a fund for the education of poor children in 1839 mainly targeted at orphans, and by 1846 educational reformers were urging the legislature to formally organize a system of common schools in centers of population and itinerant teachers for the less well populated parts of the state.[72] By the early 1850s the appointment of a state superintendent of education gave added impetus to the cause of common schools. Superintendent Walker argued in 1854 that "under a free government nothing whatsoever can be of more vital importance than the general education of the people, since upon their intelligence and virtue depends the very existence of the government." Yet he also acknowledged "the apathy which has prevailed in the public mind on this all important subject. . . . Few persons anywhere seem to have given the subject much attention." By 1858, though, he was happy to report "the awakening interest of our people in our common schools. . . . [I]t seems that the time has almost arrived when all the children of Florida may and will be educated in her own institutions." In reality the statistics do not fully support his optimism. While there were twice as many children at school in 1860 as had been a decade earlier, fewer than half of all children in Florida attended school in 1860, placing the state ahead of Virginia and South Carolina but well behind North Carolina.[73]

Texas passed a variety of school laws in the 1850s and even followed North Carolina's example in appointing a state superintendent of education, but ultimately it did not create a universal system of public schools. Superintendent James Raymond commented bluntly in 1857 that "the annual school fund is too insignificant, when compared to the number of children to give hope or expectation of a system, affording general benefit, at all creditable to the state. Without a large increase of the fund, our efforts should be mainly directed to the education of such as are unable to pay tuition, and abandon the hope of a system of common schools, free to all—rich and poor—until we have the means to justify it."[74]

Mississippi appeared well on course to establish a common school system after the election of Albert Brown as governor in 1844. A main part of his campaign platform had been "the establishment of schools in which every poor white child in the country may secure, free of charge, the advantages of a liberal education," and he secured the passage of the 1846 school law authorizing the appointment of school commissioners and giving the local Board of Police the power to levy taxes to support new schools. However, pressure from various counties led to a succession of school laws and a fracturing of the system into confusing and disparate parts. Despite this, there were more children at school in Mississippi in the 1850s than ever before.[75] The *Mississippi Free Trader* noted in 1845 that a free school in Natchez had attracted 500 pupils during its first year of operation and had given a new impetus "to the natural desire of parents to secure the boon of a thorough mental and moral education for their children." As a result, "many respectable families have changed their residences and secured homes in the city, with the view of enabling the young amongst them to participate in its advantages."[76]

In Maryland, the mayor and city council of Baltimore were permitted to establish a public school system in 1825 but a detailed proposal that would have afforded free tuition to the children of all taxpayers (even those who only paid the $1 poll tax) was ultimately rejected on cost grounds.[77] Baltimore never created a system of common schools like the one in North Carolina; instead the city paid for the education of the indigent at public schools and the rest of the children who attended school paid fees. However, what is clear from the reports of the school commissioners is that the number of free places at these schools was increasing during the late 1850s. While the commissioners were pleased that "all classes of persons are availing themselves of the advantages of our schools," by 1862 they were alarmed at the increased expenditure on the education of the poor. In 1853 the city had paid for the education of just 271 children, but this figure had doubled by 1858 to 542 children and doubled again by 1862 to 1,037 children. The explanation, they believed, was that their own "visitors are not as careful as they ought to be in recommending beneficiaries."[78]

In Louisiana the greatest progress was made in the city of New Orleans where a public school system was established in the second municipality by northern-born residents in 1841. By 1850 the situation had changed from one where the schools were perceived to be "so worthless that no person having a proper solicitude for their offspring would send their children to them" to one where 3,500 children were regularly attending school. As elsewhere, about 90 percent of the cost of the system fell upon local taxpayers.[79] The city expressed "its great satisfaction upon the prosperous condition of its public schools, and upon the evident manifestation of their increasing popularity" and found it "delightful to perceive those of the more humble as well as those of the more favored citizens, seated side by side with each other and sharing all their advantages, and contending intellectually for superiority, the only distinction recognized among them."[80] Ever conscious of the need to justify the expense of a school system to taxpayers, the school commissioners argued that people moving to New Orleans to take advantage of the system would be able to afford higher rents to landlords, since they did not have to pay for schooling. Commissioners also repeated arguments from other states that "Republican institutions are founded on the principle that the people are qualified to govern themselves. It is, then, the duty of self-preservation on the part of the government, to provide the means that all the people be taught and trained in a knowledge of the duties incumbent on them as citizens; and it might be very easily shown that many would not be, without the institution of public schools."[81] By 1855 each municipality in New Orleans had a number of schools, including night schools for working teenagers, and their influence on the children of immigrants was thought to be particularly significant. Instead of these children being given "wrong ideas of liberty, regarding it, too often, as synonymous with unbridled licentiousness" they would now be taught "those things that will best qualify them for the proper performance of their duties as citizens of the great American republic." Such was the success of the New Orleans school system that it was also adopted by Vicksburg and Jackson in neighboring Mississippi.[82]

The progress in the rest of Louisiana, outside New Orleans, was far less encouraging. In 1849 the state superintendent for education reported that the state had 646 schools, educating 22,927 pupils (about 40 percent of those of school age); however, by 1856, although there were more schools, they were teaching only 7,949 pupils. It was hardly surprising therefore that the editor of *DeBow's Review* viewed the entire system in Louisiana as "burdensome, troublesome, expensive and void of practical benefit" and he scathingly pointed out that Tensas County was taxed $16,000 for a school system yet had no school operating.[83]

Like Virginia and South Carolina before it, Georgia created a $250,000 poor school fund in 1817 to pay for the education of indigent children, though they were supposed to be taught in the same schools as fee-paying students and not sent to dedicated "poor schools." This evidently did not happen everywhere and in many places the children of the poor were indeed marginalized in "poor schools." In 1837 the trustees of poor schools in thirty-two Georgia counties reported they had paid for the tuition of just 4,000 children during the past year, and perhaps in response to this the legislature passed a common school act in 1837 that supplemented the state support for education by merging the poor school fund with the academic fund. However, within three years the act had been repealed and the old system of paying for the education of pauper children alone was reinstated.[84] Since justices of the peace in each county had to make lists of indigent children who were entitled to have their tuition paid, it is hardly surprising that many parents rejected such a labeling. One teacher commented, "We have made the schools mere charities. We are living under the impression that the children of our state belong to two classes, one rich and the other poor. The poor schools of the state, by reason of the law that created them, are robbed of their influence for good which they might otherwise wield."[85] Under this system the progress made by the 1850s was limited. Only about half of school-age children were receiving some form of education, and the 1850 census counted more than 40,000 illiterate adults in the state. An 1849 report to the state legislature admitted that every attempt to introduce public education "has been ineffectual in realizing the hopes of patriotism, and securing to every citizen of Georgia that incalculable boon, the ability to read and write." It blamed this state of affairs on "false views of the duties of citizenship—a meagre sense of parental responsibility—a morbid pride (to be enlightened rather than censured)—a depreciated estimate of the benefits of knowledge compared with the products of manual labor—the debasement and stupefaction of a life of crime, extinguishing all noble aspirations—and the relentless demands of poverty upon the toil of parent and child."[86] Missing from this list was the shrinking amount of state funding available for education. The school fund, established in 1817 and added to on several occasions in the 1820s and 1830s to provide upwards of $40,000 a year for education, had, by 1843, shrunk to only $260,000, an amount that generated only $23,000 in interest that could be spent on schools. Between 1817 and 1843 the state had, in fact, regularly raided the capital of the school fund, at one point to assist in the construction of the Western & Atlantic Railroad between Chattanooga and Atlanta, and had never replaced the money. A similar story occurred at a local level with income for schooling in Macon, for instance, spent on reducing the city's debt.[87]

Yet there were many in the state who were not prepared to simply ignore the educational needs of children in Georgia. Contributors to the *Southern School Journal,* published by the Georgia State Teachers' Association, castigated the high rates of illiteracy and the low rates of school enrollment as "humiliating" and a "standing disgrace." One correspondent lamented the lack of public interest in the fact that 41,000 Georgians were illiterate: "An organ-grinder with his monkey traversing the state, would more fully catch the public eye than this fact, so full of reproach to Georgia patriotism and benevolence and statesmanship, seems to have done." The Reverend C. W. Lane, professor of natural philosophy and chemistry at Oglethorpe University, demanded, "Where is our patriotism, our state pride, our philanthropy? What necessity for a mighty agitation in behalf of general education? The public is asleep; editors are asleep; politicians, judges, legislators are asleep."[88]

However, not all those in government were asleep. Governor Howell Cobb told the state legislature in 1853 that "the honesty, purity and intelligence of the people, constitute the firm foundations of a Republican Government. To the extent of our ability, it is our duty to foster and nurture these elements of security and strength." One state legislator, urging a more comprehensive system of common schools in Georgia stressed the importance of having a state superintendent who would oversee its introduction rather than leaving this to "county officers, unqualified and unpaid." The appointment of this individual would be the first step, "and we can go on by degrees shaping the other parts, until the whole plan is completed, the whole system at length perfected."[89] While the appointment of a state superintendent of education in Georgia would not occur before the Civil War, a new common school law was passed in 1858 that used the dividends from the Western and Atlantic Railroad to boost the funds available for schooling by $100,000 a year, in effect repaying some of the money that the school fund had contributed toward the railroad's construction. The new law was widely welcomed: the Grand Jury of Lincoln County thought that it "may finally result in the establishment of such a system as will meet the wants of the country" while counterparts in Greene County hoped that "the day may not be far distant when a plain education free of charge will be secured to every son and daughter of Georgia."[90] The impact of this money was immediate. Bibb County had thirteen schools with 530 pupils in 1851, but thirty-four schools with 1,380 pupils in 1860. While not all counties experienced the same uplift—Upson County had 261 children in public schools in 1845 but only 160 in 1860—the vast majority reported that they had more schools and more pupils taking advantage of the opportunities offered by the state. This additional money meant that 89,945 (56 percent) of the 159,341 Georgia children between six and eighteen years of age were being taught in the state's public schools by 1860.[91] This rapid change in fortunes of the state educational system elevated Georgia from having one of the poorest rates of participation in public education in the South to having one of the best at the time of secession.

As in Louisiana and South Carolina the greatest progress toward a public education for all was taken in Georgia's largest city, Savannah. Aside from the Free School established by benevolent women in 1816, Savannah had a variety of fee-paying schools, some of which also took poor children on a scholarship basis. Gradually during the 1850s the city began to expand the amount of free education available to its white population. In 1851 the Inferior Court of Chatham County was permitted to set aside a common school fund invested mainly in railroad stocks, and in March 1855, when the fund had grown to $20,000, it opened the city's first public school. The school immediately attracted about 175 pupils, and the school commissioners could not hide their pleasure that "the success of this school far exceeds the expectations of its warmest friends." The large school fund generated more than $3,000 per year in interest and dividends, an amount that more than paid for schools not only in Savannah but also in outlying areas without the need for an annual tax appropriation.[92]

Simultaneously, the $5,000 legacy left to the city by Peter Massie in 1841 for educational purposes had been invested in stocks of the Central Rail Road and the Savannah Gas and Light Company, and by 1855 it was worth $14,000. The Massie School was opened in October 1855 with 225 pupils, only forty-five of whom paid fees. With the legacy exhausted, the city put aside about $3,000 per year from taxation to ensure the future operation of the school. As Mayor James P. Screven commented in 1857: "In cities of extended commerce, like Savannah, there must ever be a large number of citizens who cannot afford to educate their children out of the small earning of their labour. To keep these children from the evils incident to idleness, and to make them useful members of society in mature life, should be object of the rulers of the city, and no means are so well calculated to effect these objects as well regulated public schools." Not content to sit on their laurels, "from facts which have come to their knowledge," those administering the Massie School recommended that the city open new schools in the northeastern and northwestern parts of Savannah.[93] By 1858, only three years after the city had first made education a priority the mayor felt able to comment that "there is no good reason why, with us, any parent should permit a child or ward to grow up in idleness or ignorance. By our private and public institutions, we have a system of education suited to the wants and tastes of all classes of our people, and these many advantages prove the surest safeguard for the perpetuity of our free institutions." Alderman Richard Arnold, chairman of the board of commissioners of the Massie School, was particularly pleased with the "neatness and order which prevailed amongst the pupils.... Taken as they are, from all classes of society in our city, the absence of any external mark by which the richer could be distinguished from the poorer, all having the badge of a neat and clean personal appearance."[94]

By 1861 the city had inaugurated a new primary school system and had spent nearly $5,000 on education during the year. The increased importance placed on schooling cannot just be measured by numbers of pupils and financial statements; it can also be seen in the statements of public officials. Mayor Charles Colcock Jones reported to his tax-paying constituents that "advantages are thereby afforded to the poor of our city, for acquiring the elementary principles of a common school education, which would not be, in many instances, otherwise enjoyed. . . . Educational expenditures realize always an abundant harvest, in the increased intelligence and good order of the community."[95]

Of all the other southern states it was Alabama that actually came closest to mimicking North Carolina's achievement. While limited state funding had been available for education from the time of Alabama's accession to the Union, there was far from a comprehensive system of common schools as a result. Charles Lyell, visiting the state in 1846, commented that the region near Montgomery was one "where the schoolmaster has not been much abroad." Even Mobile, which had appointed school commissioners as early as 1826, chose to pay for the instruction of poor pupils at schools that charged tuition rather than create its own public school system free to all.[96] In 1845 Benjamin Porter asked the members of the Erosophic Society at the University of Alabama to "look at the youth of the land now awaiting the action of the state, providing for the universal education of her sons. Is it necessary, at this day, to remind you, or to enforce by argument, that the foundation of our government is virtue, that virtue springs from education, and that a state of ignorance is the worst of all states, a state successively of superstition, barbarity, despotism, crime? . . . Awake men of a meridian age, arouse statesmen and patriots! A young and noble generation stands ready to receive from you, the trusts of the past age."[97] Five years later John W. Pratt, also speaking at the University of Alabama, demanded, "How long shall the intellectual character of the state, remain as it is, at zero!" He went on to suggest that "we should use our influence to bring about a radical change in our preparatory school system."[98] Sentiments such as these clearly had an effect because in 1852 Mobile created a public school system that was intended to "educate the greatest number, in the best manner, and at the least expense." The physical embodiment of this was Barton Academy, an imposing classical-style building that emphasized in stone the willingness of the city to pay for the education of poor white children.[99] In 1854 the state created a system of free schools open to all children aged five to eighteen and backed by local school commissioners and a state superintendent. William F. Perry, the first state superintendent of education commented, "It is emphatically the people's system. It had its origin in their wants and wishes. Popular sentiment called it into being, and popular sentiment must be the vital breath of its existence."[100]

A year later Perry was pleased to report that there were a thousand new schools in the state; moreover,

> three-fourths of the youth of the state have hitherto either gone without instruction entirely, or have been crowded into miserable apologies for school-houses, without comfortable seats, without desks or black boards, often without the necessary text books, and still oftener without competent teachers. It would be the grossest arrogance to say that the adoption of the present system has supplied all these wants. It has certainly imparted a powerful impulse to the common school operations of the state. It has increased the attendances upon most of the schools previously kept up, and has led to the establishment of many, where none before existed.[101]

8. Barton Academy, opened in Mobile in 1846.

Reproduced from Edward King, *The Great South: A Record of Journeys in Louisiana, Texas, the Indian Territory, Missouri, Arkansas, Mississippi, Alabama, Georgia, Florida, South Carolina, North Carolina, Kentucky, Tennessee, Virginia, West Virginia, and Maryland* (Hartford, Conn.: American Publishing Company, 1875), 326.

As in North Carolina, the role of the superintendent was crucial. Perry and his successors journeyed throughout the state ensuring that the system was working, explaining to local officials what their responsibilities were, and providing them with the textbooks, teacher-training manuals, and legal instructions to help them do their job. By 1859 there were more than 2,500 free schools educating, as new superintendent Gabriel Duval estimated, about three-quarters of the school-age children in the state.[102]

By 1860 both North Carolina and Alabama had functioning public school systems providing free education to the majority of white children. Calvin Wiley was entirely correct to state, "Upon a calm review of the entire facts, it is neither immodest nor unjust to assert that North Carolina is clearly ahead of all the slave-holding states with her system of public instruction, while she compares favourably in several respects with some of the New England and Northwestern states."[103] Their successes showed that public education was certainly viable despite a relatively small population scattered over a relatively large area (when compared to some of the New England states). Moreover, the largely agrarian economy was not a bar to the establishment of public schools. North Carolina and Alabama were prime producers of cotton, and significant urban centers were few and far between. It was public support combined with political will that provided the finances and the structures that made these educational systems a success. Willis Clark, member of the Mobile school board and editor of the *Mobile Advertiser*, recalled that the public schools "attained so high a character, both with regard to discipline and thoroughness of instruction, that the rich soon sought them for their children in preference to sending them to the best private schools the city afforded."[104] Of course, the degree of public support for public education was always slightly fragile. William F. Perry commented in 1855 that "the people of the state, by an overwhelming majority, are favourable to the principle of public education, and are prepared to sustain the legislature in all judicious measures for giving additional efficiency to the system already in existence. It is not intended by this to convey the assertion that anything like general enthusiasm, or even general interest of the subject prevails. On the contrary, there is a degree of apathy and indifference greatly to be deplored. But sentiments of decided hostility to the law were rarely encountered."[105] It is perhaps more accurate to suggest that public toleration together with political will was the combination required to construct effective systems of public education.

The differences between southern attitudes toward public education in the early decades of the nineteenth century and those in the 1840s and especially in the 1850s are remarkable. Even in those states that had yet to put in place a proper publicly funded system of education, the increased interest in education was notable, and almost every state had more children in public schools in 1860 than in 1850. Calvin H. Wiley, probably the most notable educational reformer in the South, began to receive letters from other states enquiring about the system he was overseeing in North Carolina. W. J. Bennett wrote to Wiley from Charleston looking "for any advise [*sic*], information or other assistance it may be convenient to you to render us. . . . Our first effort has been to elevate the subject of popular education by annulling the practice of confining it to the indigent & in this transfer from free to common we have encountered severe opposition, as the tax payers are impressed with the idea that the school can never be rendered available to them. If you have any discussion or other papers upon this subject, we would be glad to have their aid, with your own suggestions." Similarly, when John Mallard of Liberty County sought "to promote the educational policy of Georgia" he wrote to Wiley stating that "a general system of common school education, and the establishment of a normal school, will, it is thought, be brought before the legislature of Ga. at its meeting in November next; and any information it may suit your convenience to give me, or any reports, you may send me to this place, bearing on the *plan, prospects, organization, present condition* etc of your common school system will be most thankfully received." Wiley's fame even spread outside of the South. When the superintendent of public schools of Sacramento, California, desired to obtain information as to the most effective system of public education that could be introduced in his state, Wiley was one of those he contacted.[106]

The state superintendents of education in North Carolina and Alabama both established journals of education that printed articles of interest for teachers and others involved with the local implementation of school laws. These journals, along with others such as the *Southern Teacher* and the *Southern School Journal*, also provided a forum for superintendents to expound on their philosophy of education more fully and for it to receive a wider audience since the circulation of these journals was not limited by state lines. Naturally many column inches were spent on promoting the usefulness of education and in trying to rebut those who criticized public schools. In answer to those who disliked the over-centralized nature of the system, the *Alabama Educational Journal* stated: "It is not the policy of the state, in the establishment of an educational system, to stifle individual effort, but to stimulate it," and the *North Carolina Journal of Education* went further claiming education was "necessary to the preservation of liberty. . . . [T]he most essential safeguard of a free state is the liberal education of her youth [especially] that broad and thorough culture which takes into its scope of instruction the whole faculties of the man, develops and directs them in such a manner as enamors him of liberty, constitutes him a devoted disciple, attaches him and all his powers to her service and makes him even more eager for the perpetuity of the state, than were his ancestors before him."[107]

Yet educational journals and letters written by individuals such as Wiley, while spreading good practice, are, on their own, insufficient to explain why there was such a sudden and dramatic increase of interest in popular education across the entire South during the 1850s. Why did educational reformers in every southern state try harder than ever before in the 1850s to get as many common white people in school as possible? Part of the answer can be found in an exploration of just who those reformers actually were. Far from being mainly New England transplants to the South, the vast majority of southern educational reformers were born and brought up in the South; only in New Orleans was the northern influence strongly felt.[108] William F. Perry, Alabama's first state educational superintendent, was a native Georgian; Calvin Wiley was born in Guildford County, North Carolina; James Thornwell was born in South Carolina in 1812. These men were deeply embedded in their communities, having served in local and state government and in many instances as university professors and school principals. As Jonathan Wells has shown, education reformers were also a key part of the nascent southern middle class. Largely absent from the private benevolent societies in southern towns, which were dominated by the very wealthy, middle-class reformers made the promotion of education their particular interest and they were not above approaching counterparts in the North for advice on how to advance their cause. But while they may have been in close contact with many northern reformers, these men could never be accused of trying to reform the South with a mainly northern agenda. Indeed the opposite is true. Even northern-born reformers in New Orleans were well aware when interviewing teachers "of the impropriety of engaging anyone entertaining objections to slavery." The goal of increasing the numbers and quality of schools was, to them, more important than any sectional prejudice.[109]

As the sectional divide between North and South deepened, and the verbal conflict over slavery became increasingly heated with both abolitionists and pro-slavery writers freely attacking the other side, promoters of popular education in the South entered the fray. Reformers had long been concerned that far too many elite citizens sent their children to Harvard, Yale, and Princeton instead of patronizing southern state universities. The Louisiana legislature argued in 1844 that "Louisiana should possess the means of educating her youths at home. Southern men should have southern heads and hearts, with sentiments untarnished by doctrines at war with our rights and liberties."[110] Another fear was that the "sacred office of the teacher has been profaned by being constituted the channel through which to instill into Southern minds, the execrable doctrines of Northern fanaticism." Of vital importance, to the State Superintendent for Education of Louisiana at least, was the creation of a cadre of southern teachers to end a reliance on "those hating us and our institutions."[111] Fears about northern educational influences had spread by the 1850s to embrace school textbooks. The Richmond *Daily Dispatch* recommended that textbooks printed in the North should be "thoroughly scrutinized" for abolitionism since "it is evident that no more powerful and insidious mode could be devised of disseminating the poison of abolition." One educational journal actually printed lists of "Books to be Rejected" as too "fanatical" including history and English textbooks.[112] In reality, the fear was out of all proportion to the problem. Few school textbooks printed in New England expounded at any length on the status of slaves; indeed, it was more common for them to depict slaves as "ignorant and degraded" people better off being looked after by their masters than in Africa.[113] This fact did not prevent several educational conventions in the South during the 1850s from urging Southern publishers to commission their own textbooks that imparted all the relevant knowledge to children but without any hint of abolitionism. However, few southern textbooks were actually published despite the sensitivities of educational reformers about using textbooks printed in Massachusetts or New York, and teachers were still calling for an end to "our former dependence for books . . . on those who now seek our subjection" in 1863.[114]

If southern textbooks mostly remained a dream rather than a reality, it was up to those superintending education to ensure that teachers imparted a true sense of sectional difference. The *Alabama Journal of Education* deplored the fact that "in the training of our youth we exhibit a perfect indifference to the relations which the youth is to sustain to his country. . . . These youths are to become me, to take our places, to be citizens of this great commonwealth. . . . This reckless, scornful indifference of ours to all public and political matters in our educational system is becoming a more prominent error."[115] William F. Perry, Alabama's superintendent of education, foresaw the looming conflict and the crucial role that proper education would play:

> Already clouds, dark and lowering, hang upon our horizon. No prophet's vision can foresee what the future has in store for us; what fierce trials await us; what great battles we may be called upon to fight. No human wisdom can now realize, what we may yet be made painfully to feel, how much of strength we have lost, through ignorance and vice, and how little of our strength we were able to spare. We want a population that is equal to any and every emergency; that is incapable alike of subjection and of anarchy: that, in the sunshine of peace, or in the storms of revolution, will make the eternal principles or *right* the rule of their actions,—a population such, that, though our present political system were ruthlessly torn asunder, and states were shot madly from their spheres like comets in space, each one, true to itself, true to the memories of the past, and true to posterity, would wheel into its own appropriate place, and revolve, in a new orbit, around the same grand center of constitutional freedom.[116]

In states, unlike Alabama, where the cause of popular education was far less advanced, the need to ensure proper southern teaching was even more acute. The commissioners of the free schools of Charleston, for instance, believed that the lack of a functioning school system would only help "to impart new causes of social mischief and political danger."[117]

No common schools in the South were open to free blacks, despite being funded by taxpayers, and tuition for free blacks remained a privately funded affair throughout the antebellum era. A free education paid for by the state was a privilege afforded only to whites, and this, for some, was the most positive feature of public education. As racially exclusive institutions, public schools could concentrate on molding the attitudes of white children toward slavery and the South. Calvin H. Wiley knew the importance of education in the coming struggle. Education was, in his words, "the South's best defense" since "the war of independence is not to be successfully carried on with powder and ball alone. . . . [N]othing is so important as the first training of the young intellect of the state; and what is more likely to influence this than the sources from which it imbibes its earliest knowledge? Impressed with these views, I have long labored to introduce into our schools a series of books designed to develop and foster a love of home and a spirit of independence and domestic enterprise . . . and to feed the young mind and heart of the state with food that will nourish a healthful and patriotic spirit." Wiley joined the chorus for new textbooks that would, in his opinion, help to purge schools "of all poisonous literature" from the North.[118] Wiley was well aware of the potential threat posed by abolition: "the peace of every social and political system depends on a just recognition of the mutual dependence of every on each other, and of the mutual obligation which this interest imposes. . . . There is as much danger of prejudice between the rich and poor, and between the different professions, as between master and slave. . . . [A]ll attempts to enhance this alienation and widen the breach between classes of citizens, is just as dangerous as efforts to excite slaves to insurrection." The true value of common schools, in such times, was that they acted to reduce class tensions.

> The common school system, though a common interest, is of special importance to those in moderate circumstances, and to mechanics and other honorable laborers who may be continually called from place to place; and no state institution is, therefore, so necessary to such as a system of schools which offers to them the means of educating their children wherever their interests may call them. Such an institution we have in our Common School system; and by guarding it with jealous care, and using all proper means to promote its efficiency, the great and good state of North Carolina says to all the vast variety of true men of every rank and class necessary to constitute a prosperous and powerful com-

monwealth, "you are welcome here, and your wants appreciated: behold the schools erected for your children by my provident care, in every part of my wide domain where you may choose to dwell in peace, under the authority of my equal laws."[119]

In the months between South Carolina's secession in December 1860 and North Carolina's in May 1861 Wiley had to defend the common school system from those who believed that money might be better spent on the war than on education. Dismantling the school system, he argued, would encourage many "worthy people in moderate circumstances" to emigrate with dangerous consequences for the state: "the non-slave-holders now among us, born and educated in the South, connected by ties of blood and affinity with the owners of slaves, or at all events familiar with the character of southern society, are, as a class, as conservative as any other; but if they should leave us, their places may be supplied by others raised under different systems, or educated with far different prejudices and sympathies. . . . It is just as essential to our safety to prevent a stampede of bone and muscle and skill and honest hearts from our borders as it is to import powder and ball and muskets." Therefore, "to apply the school funds entirely to other than their legitimate use at the very outset of our national & state difficulties, would be certainly very impolitic, it would represent us as deficient in resources. Or that we considered education a matter of small import & easily to be dispensed with."[120]

If the existence of common schools demonstrated to poor whites that their needs were taken seriously by the state, of equal importance was ensuring that children actually attended these schools to imbibe the teaching on offer. Spelling, reading, writing, and counting were all very well, but Wiley was also keen for children to learn about the society they inhabited and their own proper place in it:

> We all know what is the most dangerous element of society. . . . [W]e all agree it is found in the demoralised members of the ruling race, who sink from the level of its society to the associations of the colored community, bond and free. . . . [W]hite men whose tastes and character lead them to more intimate associations with the subject than with the ruling race, are not safe members of society in slaveholding communities. . . . We must preserve social distinctions between races whose political equality

cannot be permitted. . . . We must see that our part of the community preserves its relative position, and we must be constantly on the alert to prevent the sinking of any portion of the upper into the lower stratum of society to become a source of demoralization to the African element, a reflection on the progress of the whites, and a source of constant danger to the peace and order of the commonwealth. . . . [I]s it necessary to say more to convince us of the importance of our Common School system, and of the duty to prosecute its development with increased energy? The argument of the timid that the times are threatening or gloomy, is the most powerful reason for energetic action *now*, in favor of our domestic interests.[121]

Once the war had begun, supporters of common school education in North Carolina continued to press their case. A convention of teachers, organized by Wiley, issued a public *Address to the People of North Carolina* pointing out to those who demanded cuts to the common school budget that "the public funds devoted to educational purposes would be barely sufficient to keep two regiments in the field for a single year; as they are now used they are providing, fortifying, and drilling in the heart of society, an encampment of one hundred and fifty thousand souls for the honor and prosperity of the state."[122] If a starker contrast was needed for the relative importance placed on universal education in the various southern states, while Wiley argued to keep his budget, the Virginia convention of 1861 that determined on secession from the union, also appropriated the literary fund for military use, thus putting an end to any free schooling for inhabitants of the state for the duration of the war.[123]

While one might expect such sentiments from Calvin Wiley—almost certainly one of the most vocal supporters of popular education, and from North Carolina, which did more than any other state to create a working school system—he was not alone. Legislators across the South, after spending decades talking about education but doing little, began to realize that common schools had a vital role to play in molding white society into a unified whole. With the southern way of life under attack, respecting parental rights and keeping taxes low were not as important as the very survival of the South. The *Southern School Journal* argued that "there is no more charity in a state educating those who are to be her citizens, than there is an a father's educating his children. The state has, so to speak, a personal interest in the matter." Furthermore, if the poor man was unable to educate his children, "the public must help him, and he must be compelled to accept the proffered assistance."[124] As early as 1844 the *Southern Literary Messenger* was informing readers that "education is the cheapest defense of nations" and this military theme was picked by other advocates of public education who argued that the power of good teaching to mold and shape the minds of men meant that "schools are more valued than arsenals, scholars than soldiers."[125] Part of the reason the *Carolina Spartan* urged rapid reform of the free school system in South Carolina, so that all could benefit from free education, was because it would combat the influence of abolitionism since "an educated and intelligent people, cannot be enslaved" to ideologies contrary to their best interests. On a more practical level it was accepted that "large armies are composed of a majority of [the poor] class and [it] must be further admitted that the South will soon have to rely upon her own strength to defend her rights." The superintendent of Virginia's literary fund also thought that the common school system could mold the attitudes of the poor toward the South and slavery because it had "a good that no other system has, that the poor are watched over with parental care." In presenting a new free school bill to the South Carolina legislature in 1854, representative Joseph Tucker argued that any future conflict with the northern states would be resolved "not so much by the force of *Northern opinion,* as the existence or non-existence of an enlightened *Southern opinion.*"[126] Alonzo Church made exactly the same point to the members of the Georgia Historical Society in 1845: "Those peculiar domestic institutions, concerning which we are, at this time, with much propriety, peculiarly jealous, are in far greater danger from ignorance at home than from fanaticism abroad.... The jealousy and envy of a large, ignorant, and debased population, must be most dangerous, in such a government as ours, and to such a state of society as that to which I have just referred. Our only safety on this point, is in the general intelligence and virtue of our population." To do nothing would be an open invitation to social upheaval and political disaster: "If we have not our 'sans culottes,' we have those whose boastings are little less shameless, and whose ignorance and vice, if unchecked, must lead to scenes as those of Jacobin France during the darkest period of her revolution."[127]

In this sense, an effective system of common schools could help to overcome those internal divisions that all knew existed within white society. The *Mississippi Free Trader* argued in 1848 that common schools "beget harmony and a more intimate union among the citizens" while James Thornwell told the governor of South Carolina in 1853 that popular education was vital for "harmonizing and smoothing all the unevenness, harshness and inequalities of life" and as such it was "the cheap expedient for uniting us among ourselves, and rendering us terrible abroad." A central part of the strategy for the unification of white society involved dividing poor whites from the enslaved and free blacks. Most were well aware of the biracial interaction that occurred in a variety of clandestine environments, often involving the trading of homegrown or stolen produce in return for alcohol, tobacco, and other luxury items. Authorities in numerous southern towns and cities constantly tried to stamp out this trade by increasing the punishments for trading illegally, but with little effect.[128] By the 1850s, however, educational reformers began to listen to the complaints that white artisans had been making for decades about black competition, and adapted them to their own agenda. In 1856 the *Southern Quarterly Review* was urging slaveholding states to "pay particular attention to the education of their citizens" and illustrated this point by printing part of a speech given by William Henry Trescott. A native of South Carolina, Trescott told his audience at the Citadel in Charleston that "the white race must preserve its superiority by making its work mental as well as bodily. The state cannot with justice or safety allow the white man to come into competition with the black simply as a labourer. By the laws of the land, by our strongest instincts, by the very nature of things, there is an immense, an impassable gulf, between the lowest and humblest form of white labour and the highest development of black. And the only way to preserve this distinction, is to give to every workman in the state the education of a responsible citizen." If poor whites could not discern their proper role in a slave society it became the responsibility of the state "to afford that degree of education to every one of its white citizens which will enable him intelligently and actively to control and direct the slave labor of the state." [129]

William H. Stiles in Georgia agreed that a common school education should "mark more distinctively the difference which should exist in the two races among us. To elevate the indigent white among us, still further above the negro, and thus destroy whatever hostility there may exist between them. It is a fact . . . that our failure to educate the poor whites among us, and thus fit them for employments better suited to their caste, they have in certain cases been driven to similar occupations with slaves," leading to the impression "that the existence of the negro among us was injurious to them." Two years later Stiles argued that "it is of immense moment to us in the South that we so educate our youth that they may be able, amidst the unparalleled excitements by which they are surrounded, calmly and candidly to appreciate their condition . . . stand firm and erect amid the storm. . . . So educate them in short, that they may know as well what are the sacrifices of interest and feeling which for the preservation of the Union it may become necessary to make, as what are the obligations to right and honor, they should unhesitatingly maintain, even at the cost of a dissolution of this confederacy."[130]

While promoters of education in states from Virginia to Alabama stressed the need for popular education to foster a love of the South in the hearts and minds of the people, the school commissioners of Baltimore, in stark contrast, did not give their labors a specifically sectional importance. Education was intended simply, in their view, to elevate "youth up to such a point as will save them from poverty and vice, and prepare them for the adequate performance of their social and civil duties." If teaching young Marylanders had a wider political purpose it was not to defend the South's interest but indeed to reject the "sectional prejudice and the narrow spirit of party [that] are active for evil in every section of our land." J. N. Milton, treasurer of the board of commissioners of public schools in 1859, hoped that Baltimore's children would eventually "assist in cementing still firmer the bond that binds the states of our Union in a single happy confederacy" and as a result "sectional differences and divisions may disappear."[131] Of course there were many reasons for Maryland to remain in the Union instead of joining the Confederacy, but the views of those who managed Baltimore's public schools were clearly in accord with the wider population and not with fellow educationalists in other southern states.

The changes that took place in the attitudes of southern legislators and in wider government circles toward popular education during the 1850s were highly significant. In the end, the age-old argument about the need for education to control the behavior of the poor was reinvented by reformers to pertain to the attitudes of the poor toward the South itself. Faced with a large non-slaveholding white population amounting to three out of every four whites, southern elites suddenly had to think about the relationship between themselves and the white poor, as well as that between the white poor and the second largest social group in the South, the enslaved. Education was increasingly seen as the answer to this problem. The success of North Carolina demonstrated that the sparse and scattered population typical across much of the South was not an insurmountable obstacle to an effective system of publicly funded schools. If the children of the large number of non-slaveholding whites could receive an education that taught them about the southern way of life, and specifically about the "proper" relationship that should exist between whites and blacks, then the long-term future of society based on racial slavery would be secure. At the same time, teaching the children of the poor gratis was a graphic demonstration to their parents of the privileges that membership of the white, ruling, race accrued in the South.

Afterword

CHARITY, WELFARE, PHILANTHROPY, BENEVOLENCE, call it what you will, has a wider meaning in all communities. Rare indeed is the occasion when charity is freely given without any ensuing responsibilities, duties, or obligations being felt by or imposed on the recipients. In the antebellum South those dispensing relief to the poor were often motivated by humanitarianism as well as by religious sentiment to reform and improve the lives of the poor. In return for food, clothing, shelter, and education, the poor were supposed to become better people. Charitable work had an empowering role whereby the poor were cured, educated, and taught skills that would improve their future employability; it also was supposed to turn those who were a burden on society into more productive members of the community. An additional purpose of welfare was to prevent disorder and crime by taking beggars from the streets and housing them out of sight, and perhaps out of mind, in the poorhouse and removing children from the influence of drunken, violent parents. Society would, as a result, be calmer, quieter, and safer for all. Empowerment and control were by no means mutually exclusive and often worked in harmony to produce the same result. Those who ordered that orphan girls be taken to church every Sunday to receive moral and spiritual training, also provided them with literacy, numeracy, and training in skills such as sewing and domestic work that would provide them paid employment as adults. City and county authorities who built poorhouses and hospitals to house those who otherwise might have ended up begging on the streets also tried to send as many inmates back into the community as possible, having made them productive individuals either by curing them or renewing their work ethic. The poor were essentially being given the tools to prevent them from ever being a drain on public finances again. Newly learned Christian morals might control a drinking or gambling problem that had been the root cause of destitution, and improved skills might lead to a job that actually paid enough to live on. All those who supported or managed charity in the antebellum South therefore desired an improved society where both the poor, and society as a whole, were better off.

This book has argued that like the benevolent in the northern states—and for that matter, England—those involved with welfare and charity in the southern states conceived of their work in a broadly utilitarian manner. They believed that benevolence carried out a very useful social function in alleviating individual suffering and reintegrating some people back into the community. But a concurrent theme of all the chapters has been the political importance of charity and welfare in slaveholding communities that were increasingly aware of the dire situation of the white poor. The help offered to the indigent, the sick, the orphaned, and the widowed not only tells us a great deal about the humanitarian ethics of the antebellum South but is also suggestive of what the elite hoped to gain for their efforts and, in particular, what they expected from the poor in exchange. Naturally the benevolent elite wanted a society where most individuals were industrious and peaceable, but the evidence in the preceding chapters indicates that they also wanted one where all white people shared a common racial ideology of difference between themselves and enslaved African Americans, even if most whites would never actually own a slave. There were many things that promoted racial ties among whites, including intermarriage between the elite and the non-elite, an electoral franchise that gave the vote to most adult white men, attendance at the same churches, and economic interdependency. But charity brought a new group into the white "club"—the most marginalized and excluded whites. It was these white people who were most likely to trade, worship, compete, live, and sleep with African Americans, both slave and free, thereby undermining the racial solidarity of the South.[1] Therefore, it was crucially important that strategies were developed to reduce the potential for disaffection among indigent non-slaveholding whites.

By taxing themselves to support poorhouses that would shelter the indigent while also continuing outdoor relief programs for humanitarian reasons, the wealthy individuals who served as Commissioners of the Poor demonstrated that economy was not the most important factor in their work. Officials might have threatened on many occasions to deny help to those who refused to enter the poorhouse, but only occasionally was that threat carried out. Few Commissioners of the Poor were prepared to be sufficiently hard-hearted to refuse help to those who were plainly in need yet whose pride prevented them from accepting institutionalization. The vast sums provided by state legislatures to construct insane asylums and asylums for the blind, deaf, and dumb continued this fiscally liberal trend. Publicly funded buildings for the poor, built in the latest classical style with modern conveniences and landscaped grounds, became physical embodiments of the interest taken by the state in the needs of the most disadvantaged members of the white community. The more impressive the structure, the greater the impact this public statement had. When the elite organized themselves into private benevolent societies and invested considerable amounts of time, and often their own money, to ensure the success of their endeavors, the poor were given another demonstration of the elite's desire for a more inclusive society. The existence of such organizations told the white poor that the rest of white southern society was concerned about their welfare and would try to help them.

The *Mississippi Free Trader* summarized the prevailing attitude toward charitable giving in the antebellum South in 1849:

> As a general rule, no ... applications ought to be disregarded; better that contributions be made to ninety and nine unworthy applicants, than that one worthy one should meet with a rebuff. . . . [However] contributors should exercise prudential caution, before contributing their money for anything, of the utility, necessity and honesty of which they are not convinced; when satisfied on this point, they should give, give cheerfully, (the Lord loves a *cheerful* giver) not what others expect; not in proportion to what other men give; but what their own hearts dictate and their means will afford, in justice to themselves and their families. This is the charity which descends like the gentle dew of heaven; which blesseth both giver and receiver. This is the description of charity which layeth up for its dispenser "treasure in heaven."[2]

Southerners dispensed charity, both public and private, with what can perhaps best be described as purposeful generosity.

The message of social inclusivity that the elite were transmitting to the poor through their benevolent work was subtle. It was true that the white poor in the South had far greater access to public welfare and private charity than the black poor, but it is quite possible that some paupers were largely unaware of this for a large part of the early nineteenth century. Welfare was often provided unobtrusively with little explicit notice taken of just how much charity had effectively become a racial privilege. But by the 1850s, a more concerted effort was being made to ensure that the white poor knew that benevolence was something to which they had special access merely because of their skin color. Bigger and more impressive poorhouses, hospitals, and asylums were erected, costing even more money, and many private charitable organizations, especially those managed by men, were expanding their capacity to assist the indigent. Those managing charitable institutions justified this enhanced welfare provision by pointing out just how important it was for the white poor not to feel neglected or ignored. Increasingly the subtlety of any message about the position of the white poor in southern society gave way, for example, to the teaching of patriotic southern songs in the Charleston Orphan House and, by 1861, the veneration of the new Confederate flag by the boys at Bethesda. The message was being spelled out loud and clear—the southern elite were the only ones with the best interests of the white poor at heart.

This message achieved its greatest and most effective dissemination in the new public schools. During the 1850s many southern states made great strides toward making free education available to a majority of southern white children. The teaching offered to these children was never subtle, and from the 1840s on was often explicitly southern, intended to inculcate in the poor a deep love of their own state and with it a love of, or at least respect for, its domestic institutions—particularly slavery. A conference of teachers meeting in North Carolina in November 1861 asked the public to "wisely remember that the schools and the school literature of the State have been the great nurseries of the popular energy and patriotism which now enable her to take such a proud position in the struggle for Southern independence." Furthermore, these teachers believed that education had a vital role to play during the war: "The contest in which the Confederate States of America are engaged is not a war growing out of questions of commerce or political complications—it is a struggle for national existence and independence, and involving in the issue all that can affect the life of a civilized people. It requires, therefore, for its successful prosecution, the enlistment of the mind and heart of all ages, of both sexes, of every class of the people."[3] The common school systems established by 1860 in North Carolina, Alabama, Georgia, Tennessee, and the less well-organized systems of South Carolina, Virginia, and less-populated states had the capacity to shape the attitudes of the poor toward supporting the South and the Confederacy. Education was, as Georgia's *Southern School Journal* commented, "the lever by which the masses are moved."[4]

Historians can never be sure how far the white poor absorbed the messages the elite were giving them, though many former orphans did grow up to be hard-working, law-abiding members of society. It has also long been recognized that the majority of those fighting for the Confederacy during the Civil War were non-slaveholders. Rather than accepting the willingness of non-slaveholders to fight and die for a slave-based society as simply a historical enigma, this book has argued that the charitable webs formed first by elite southern women and later by elite southern men to complement and enhance the assistance provided by the state tied the elite and the non-elite together in crucial ways. Elites knew that their position at the pinnacle of southern society relied on the at least tacit acquiescence to the status quo of the non-slaveholding whites. Ensuring that non-slaveholders were content with the current social system involved a variety of stratagems, from promoting a shared gendered ideology of masterdom among males to turning a blind eye to the flouting of unpopular legislation. Benevolence furthered this aim by giving the poorest whites fewer reasons to feel disaffected with the status quo and by offering them education and training in the proper distinctions that should exist between black and white. Welfare and charity in the antebellum South were therefore important elements in the creation and maintenance of the "solid South."

Notes

Abbreviations used in the notes referring to the MSS minutes of each society.

BFBS	Beaufort Female Benevolent Society
CFOS	Columbia Female Orphan Society
FCSCN	Female Charitable Society of Charleston Neck
FSFS	Female Seaman's Friend Society
LBS	Ladies Benevolent Society, Charleston
LFS	Ladies Fuel Society, Charleston
NFOS	Norfolk Female Orphan Society
PBMA	Petersburg Benevolent Mechanics Association
POAS	Protestant Orphan Asylum Society, Mobile
SBA	Savannah Benevolent Association
SFA	Savannah Female Asylum
SFSS	Savannah Free School Society
SPHH	Savannah Poor House and Hospital
SPS	Savannah Port Society
SWS	Savannah Widow's Society

Introduction

1. Ravenscroft, *A Sermon Delivered*, 6, 7, 11, 13. The Reverend Dr. McPheeters also stressed that all were "descended from one common parent." *Raleigh Register*, August 3, 1821.

2. *Raleigh Register*, July 20, 1824.

3. See, for example, on the North: Alexander, *Render Them Submissive*; Boylan, *The Origins of Women's Activism*; Clement, *Welfare and the Poor*; Griffin, *Their Brothers' Keeper*; Griffin, *The Ferment of Reform*; Heale, "Patterns of Benevolence"; Kaestle, *The Evolution of an Urban School System*; Kaestle, *Pillars of the Republic*;

Melder, "Ladies Bountiful"; Reisner, *The Evolution of the Common School*; Rothman, *The Discovery of the Asylum*; Scott, *Natural Allies*; Soltow and Stevens, *The Rise of Literacy*. On the South, see Bellows, *Benevolence among Slaveholders*; Carrol and Coll, "The Baltimore Almshouse"; Clement, "Children and Charity"; Green, *This Business of Relief*; Johnson, "Poor Relief in Antebellum Mississippi"; Murray, "Charity within the Bonds of Race and Class"; Stacey, "The Political Culture of Slavery"; Klebaner, "Public Poor Relief in Charleston"; Klebaner, "Some Aspects of North Carolina Public Poor Relief."

4. See, for instance, Slack, *The English Poor Law*, and Oxley, *Poor Relief in England and Wales*.

5. Calo, "From Poor Relief to the Poorhouse," 393. Hartdagan, "The Anglican Vestry," 471; See Carr, "The Development of the Maryland Orphan's Court," 41–62 and Carr, "The Foundations of Social Order," 72–110.

6. Siler, "The Anglican Parish Vestry," 333; Nelson, *A Blessed Company*, 74–75; Watson, "Orphanage in Colonial North Carolina," 106.

7. Waterhouse, "The Responsible Gentry," 166–174; Bolton, *Southern Anglicanism*, 140–141.

8. Watson, "Public Poor Relief," 348; Bernhard, "Poverty and the Social Order," 149–153.

9. Allestree, *Whole Duty of Man*, 214–215.

10. Bacon, *A Sermon*, 6–7.

11. Henley, *A Sermon*, 2–6.

12. Lockley, "Rural Poor Relief," 969–972.

13. On Virginia parishes establishing workhouses, see Nelson, *Blessed Company*, 81–83. Rural parishes in South Carolina and North Carolina did not establish poorhouses before the Revolution.

14. St. Philip's Vestry Minutes, January 6, 1734.

15. Byrd, "White Poor and Poor Relief," 52, 71–72, 81. Stephen Wiberley's comparative study of poor relief in eighteenth-century Boston, New York, Philadelphia, and Charles-Town concluded that levels of relief were significantly higher in Charles-Town (over £5 sterling per pauper per year) than in the northern cities (£3–£4 per pauper per year). Wiberley, "Four Cities," 158.

16. Herndon, *Unwelcome Americans*, 2–22, citation on page 6.

17. Olivas, "God Helps Those Who Help Themselves," 279; Wulf, "Gender and the Political Economy of Poor Relief."

18. *Georgia Gazette*, November 8 and 22, 1764.

19. Easterby, *History of the St. Andrew's Society*, 30; *The Constitutional and Additional Rules of the South-Carolina Society*, preface; *The Rules of the Fellowship Society*, iv.

20. *The Constitutional and Additional Rules of the South-Carolina Society*, 43, 47; *The Rules of the Fellowship Society*, iii.

21. Fellowship Society Minutes, January 28, 1778; March 31, 1784.

22. Information about the orphans comes from "A Brief Account of the Rise, Progress and Present Situation of the Orphan House in Georgia" (1746), in White, *Historical Collections of Georgia*, 332–335, and Coulter and Saye, *A List of the Early Settlers*.

23. "A Continuation of Mr. Whitefield's Journal," July 11, 1738, Whitefield, *Journals*, 159–160.

24. "A Continuation of Mr. Whitefield's Journal," January 11, 1740, Whitefield, *Journals*, 395. The Union Society bought the Bethesda site in 1855 for similar reasons. Annual Report, April 23, 1855. *Minutes of the Union Society*, 140.

25. Gamble, *Bethesda*, 16.

26. "The Manner of the Children's Spending Their Time at the Orphan House in Georgia," *The General Magazine*, January 1741, in Haviland, "Of Franklin, Whitefield and the Orphans," 214–215.

27. Whitefield stated in a letter to the trustees that he was "very intent on filling his orphan house with all the children he could get." "Journal of the Earl of Egmont," Candler, *Colonial Records*, V, 319–320, dated March 10, 1740.

28. "Journal of William Stephens," *Colonial Records*, IV, 506, dated February 4, 1740.

29. Candler, *Colonial Records*, IV, 540–541; 596–597, dated March 25 and June 17, 1740; V, 330, dated April 2, 1740. See also Oglethorpe to the Trustees, dated April 2, 1740, ibid., XXII, Pt. 2, 339–341.

30. Candler, *Colonial Records*, V, 359–360, dated June 6, 1740. For the full regulations see ibid., XXIII, 109–111. The magistrates could also remove the children.

31. "Journal of the Earl of Egmont," Candler, *Colonial Records*, V, 359, dated, June 4, 1740.. Christopher Orton to the Trustees, March 4, 1741, ibid., XXIII, 229.

32. George Whitefield to Harmon Verlest, January 16, 1740. Egmont Papers vol. 14204, 301.

33. Ibid and Benjamin Martyn to James Oglethorpe, May 10, 1743. Candler, *Colonial Records*, XXX, 516.

34. Only forty-two orphans were admitted between 1739 and 1746. "A Brief Account of the Rise, Progress and Present Situation of the Orphan House in Georgia" (1746), in White, *Historical Collections Of Georgia*, 330.

35. For the later history of Bethesda see Gamble, *Bethesda, an Historical Sketch*.

36. See the history of the Union Society in the *Daily Morning News*, May 4, 1854. The Society was "composed chiefly of mechanics." *South Carolina Gazette*, November 15–22, 1760.

37. Ibid., 127. For examples of children whose education was paid for by the Union Society, see *Minutes of the Union Society*, 12, 13, and 17.

38. *Georgia Gazette*, November 15, 1764; *Georgia Gazette*, February 8, 1769. See also *History of the St. Andrew's Society of the City of Savannah*.

39. Act of Incorporation, May 21, 1757, *Rules of the Winyaw Indigo Society*, 3.

40. See, for instance, Minutes of the Camden Orphan Society 1786–1812 in

Foster, "A Documentary History," Vol. 12; the wills of James Winwright (1744) and James Innes (1759) in North Carolina in Coon, *Beginnings of Public Education*, 2–7; for Virginia, see Maddox, *Free School Idea*, 1–9.

41. Bacon, *A Sermon*, 19–20.

Chapter 1. The Safety Net

1. Petition of Henry Hoover, May 1826. Rowan County Records, Folder 1825–1829.

2. The 1778 South Carolina state constitution noted that the poor should be "supported" but made no mention of a system that would replace parish poor relief. The county courts assumed responsibility for the poor in some areas, but several vestries continued to make provision for the poor until about 1800. Constitution of 1778, Sec. 38; "An act authorizing the inhabitants of elective districts where county courts are not established to choose Commissioners of the Poor," passed February 19, 1791. Cooper and McCord, *Statutes at Large*, I, 145; V, 175–6. Salley, *Minutes of the Vestry*, February 4, 1800.

3. *Gazette of the State of Georgia*, March 15, 1787.

4. *The State Records of North Carolina*, Vol. 24, Laws 1777–1788, 93.

5. Boan, *A History of Poor Relief Legislation*, 21–23. Johnson, "Poor Relief in Antebellum Mississippi," 6. Ashcraft, *Public Care*, 6. Hutchins, *The History of Poor Law Legislation*, 52.

6. Effingham County, Inferior Court Minutes, 1832–1872; Chatham County, Inferior Court Minutes 1790–1805; 1855–1867; Buncombe County, Court of Common Pleas Minutes, 1792–1865.

7. *The Laws Now in Force*, 10–11.

8. "An act to set apart a fund for the support of the Poor in each county," *Acts Passed at the Fourth Annual Session*, 61.

9. Lancaster District, Minutes August 1, 1859.

10. Katherine Baker Hoskins, *Anderson County Historical Sketches*, available online http://www.Poorhousestory.com/TN_ANDERSON_History_p155_Sept 23_1976.htm (accessed June 2005). Chatham County (Georgia) Ordinary Inferior Court Minutes, May 26, 1790.

11. Buckingham, *The Slave States of America*, I, 114; in a sample of seventy counties in Virginia in 1840 0.56 percent of the population was receiving poor relief. In 1850 in a sample of thirty-seven counties the rate rose to 0.8 percent and remained at 0.7 percent in 1860. In a sample of twenty-one counties from North Carolina, South Carolina, and Georgia between 1820 and 1860, the average rate was 0.67 percent.

12. Auditor of Public Accounts, Overseers of the Poor Returns, Pittsylvania County, 1849 [hereafter APA, future references to these records will give only the

county name and the date]; Shenandoah County, Accounts, 1823; Pasquotank County, List of Paupers April 1830.

13. *The Code of the State of Georgia* , 41.

14. Lancaster District, Minutes August 1, 1853.

15. *The Code of the State of Georgia*, 141

16. Letter of Isaac Hughes to Wardens of the Poor, Letter of Washington Sandford to Wardens of the Poor, April 12, 1843. Craven County Wardens of the Poor Records, Folder 1843; Craven County, Minutes May 8, August 14, November 13, 1843.

17. Petition of Joseph Welman, February 26, 1826, Rowan County Records, Folder 1825–1829, and Minutes, February Term 1826. See also petitions of Nancy Blythe and Steven Chase, Lancaster District Minutes, February 19, 1855, and August 1, 1859.

18. Williamsburg District Minutes, March 1845.

19. APA, Dinwiddie County, 1834; APA, Shenandoah County, 1843.

20. Petition of Andrew Eller, February 1826. Rowan County Records, Folder 1825–1829.

21. APA, Middlesex Return, 1850.

22. Spotsylvania County, Minutes November 7, 1791.

23. Ashe County, Minutes November 27, 1849; 1850 census for Ashe County. For similar treatment in Georgia, see Gwinnett County, Inferior Court Minutes, 153–158; 281–282.

24. Gwinnett County, Inferior Court Minutes.

25. Williamsburg District, List of Paupers, August 6, 1860; Madison County Miscellaneous Records, Receipts 1859.

26. Archibald T. Smith papers, March 19, 1839.

27. Granville County, Accounts 1831–1834, February 8, 1833. See also Rowan County, Records, November 1844.

28. See, for example, Fluvanna County Minutes, June 1860: "It is ordered that the sum of $61.00 be paid by the sheriff of Fluvanna to the president of the board of the Overseers of the Poor for the county of Albemarle for maintenance and medical attention to J. W. Griffin who was migrating from this county to the west and had his leg broke by an accident in the county of Albemarle."

29. Klebaner, "Some Aspects," 489.

30. Sunley, *The Kentucky Poor Law*, 7–8; Vogt, "Poor relief," 185.

31. Anderson County, Petitions of George Tippen and John P. Benson et al., March 1850.

32. Rowan County, Minutes, February 1830. Klebaner, "Some Aspects," 481. Henry Barker was removed from the pauper list of Williamsburg District, South Carolina, after he reached the age of eighteen. Williamsburg District, Minutes, August 1831.

33. Chatham County, Inferior Court Minutes, July 23, 1856.

34. Orange County, Minutes, May 29, 1850. See also Pasquotank County, Minutes, November 30, 1850. Klebaner, "Some Aspects of Poor Relief," 481.

35. John Fitzgerald to Colonel Joseph Cathy, January 24, 1854. Cathy Papers.

36. Richmond County, Records, December 30, 1786.

37. Sampson County, Minutes, May 15, 1804; May 14, 1805; May 13, 1806.

38. Duplin County, Records, May 10 and July 10, 1805.

39. Rowan County, Minutes, February, May, and August 1827; May 1828; February 1830.

40. William Garland to Harriett Garland, May 4, 1841; Samuel Sweatt to William Garland, November 23, 1842, Garland Papers; Ball Family Papers, Plantation Account Book of John Ball, March 14, 1820. Account with Wm. C. Barton, April 1, 1854, Anonymous Carpenters Book 1853–1854.

41. APA, King William and King and Queen Counties, 1840; Johnson, "Poor Relief," 8–9.

42. See, for example, Montgomery County, Guardian's Records, January 8–9, 1832.

43. The Apprentice Act of 1715 empowered North Carolina parishes, later counties, to bind out orphans to those able to care for them. Johnson, *Antebellum North Carolina*, 703.

44. Buncombe County, Court Minutes [hereafter BCCM], April 1845. Wells had an estate valued at $200 in the 1850 census.

45. Ibid., October 1849.

46. An average of five to six children per year were indentured in Buncombe County, North Carolina, while two or three children in Lincoln County, Georgia, were indentured each year between 1805 and 1831. BCCM; Lincoln County, Apprenticeship Bonds, 1805–1831.

47. Goodwin was indentured in October 1822 and reached her majority on October 22, 1837. Ledbetter was indentured in February 1838 until he reached his majority on December 6, 1854. BCCM, October 1822 and February 1838.

48. Camden County, Inferior Court Minutes, June 4, 1799.

49. Thirty-three of the 126 boys offered anything got such training, most commonly blacksmithing (9). In contrast, orphans in colonial Edgecombe County were most likely to be trained as farmers. Watson, "Orphanage in Colonial North Carolina," 109.

50. Only eleven out of the fifty-two girls who received anything got a spinning wheel. Conversely, orphan girls in Cumberland County in 1800 were regularly ordered to be trained in "housewifery" and spinning. Johnson, *Antebellum North Carolina*, 705.

51. Free black children often received a larger cash payment from their guardian at the end of their term, almost in lieu of education. Leander Foster, for example,

was to receive $50 cash, as did Henry J. Hyatt. BCCM, October 1855 and June 1846.

52. For example, in October 1824, seven-year-old William Arrington and his four-year-old sister, Emily, were indentured to Peter Tredway, who promised to give them both two years of schooling. In 1850, however, Jonathan Cogdell was to receive three years of schooling, while his sister, Charlotte, was to receive only two. BCCM, October 1824. BCCM, October 1850.

53. Commissioners of the Poor, Williamsburg District, August 1831; Bellinger, *Compilation of Laws*, 54; Lincoln County, Inferior Court Minutes, May 1836, January 1837, February 1837; Greene County, Inferior Court Minutes, February 1852.

54. Watkinson, "Rogues, Vagabonds and Fit Objects," 18–19; Klebaner, "Public Poor Relief in America," 91–95. Despite the acts of the Georgia legislature, examination of numerous Inferior Court records from Georgia fails to produce any evidence of a poorhouse being supported or staffed out of county funds.

55. APA, Patrick County, 1833; APA, King and Queen County, 1850.

56. APA, Amelia County, 1829; APA, Essex County, 1843.

57. Person County, Minutes, July 1, 1831; APA, Isle of Wight County, 1850.

58. New Hanover County, Minutes, 1852.

59. Goochland County, 1847 Return.

60. Lincoln County, Minutes, October 1820, January 1821.

61. Cited in Klebaner, "Public Poor Relief in America," 106.

62. Halifax County, 1850 Return; New Hanover County, Minutes, September 8, 1851. Craven County, Minutes, 1845.

63. Cleveland County, Minutes, October 1850; see also April 29, 1848.

64. Dix, *A Review*, 15. The contract was dated November 1845.

65. Halifax County, 1850 Return.

66. Articles of Agreement with Wardens of the Poor and the Steward, December 30, 1825; Rowan County, Records, Folder 1825–1829.

67. Fluvanna County, Minutes, June 1, 1847.

68. Dix, *A Review*, 22; Dix, *Memorial Soliciting Enlarged and Improved Accommodations*, 26; Dix, *Memorial Soliciting a State Hospital*, 17, 20.

69. Orange County, Minutes, June 9, 1832; Pittsylvania County, 1850 Return; Nottoway County, 1840 Return; Lincoln County, Minutes, April 12, 1852.

70. Union County, Accounts October, 1838–1839. Anderson County, Report for 1859.

71. Pittsylvania County, 1850 Return.

72. Dix, *A Review*, 20; Dix, *Memorial Soliciting a State Hospital*, 17.

73. South Carolina Grand Jury Presentments, 1858, No. 7 Barnwell District.

74. Prince Edward County, 1850 Return.

75. Dix, *A Review*, 30.

76. Dix, *Memorial Soliciting a State Hospital*, 16; Petition of John Brown dated Poorhouse, November 19, 1829, Rowan County, Folder 1825–29.

77. Cited in Klebaner, "Public Poor Relief in America," 302.

78. Auditor of Public Accounts, Overseers of the Poor Returns for 1840.

79. Watkinson, "Rogues, Vagabonds and Fit Objects," 19. APA, Buckingham County, 1860.

80. APA, Frederick County and New Kent County, 1840.

81. Orange County, Minutes, September 3, 1850. Pasquotank County, Minutes, September 1853.

82. APA, Ohio County, 1830. Lincoln County, Minutes, October 18, 1820. APA, Buckingham County, 1860.

83. South Carolina Grand Jury Presentments, 1845, No. 8, Georgetown District. Petition of lawyers on behalf of Ephraim Pearce [1828], Craven County, Folder 1803–1829; Minutes, August 1828. Pasquotank County, Minutes, February 28, 1852.

84. Beaufort County, Minutes, September 7, 1840.

85. Wardens' order to John Mallory, Superintendent of the Poorhouse, May 18, 1835, Granville County, Accounts 1836–1839; U.S. Census Bureau, 1850, Granville, Orange, and Bertie counties, North Carolina.

86. South Carolina Grand Jury Presentments, 1845, No. 8, Georgetown District. Sumner County Archives, Loose Records: Misc: Poorhouse Occupants 1840–1849. Available online at this URL: http://www.rootsweb.com/~tnsumner/poorhous. htm (accessed September 2005); Stacey, "The Political Culture of Slavery," 133.

87. Murray, "Poverty and Its Relief," 317.

88. General Assembly, Annual Reports of the Comptroller General, Reports of the Transient Poor Fund, Reports for Charleston; *New Orleans Bee*, October 24, 1835.

89. "An act for the better relief and employment of the Poor of the parish of St. Philip's Charles Town," May 29, 1736. *Acts Passed by the General Assembly of South Carolina*, 32–39. The vestry of St. Philip's petitioned the assembly to assign a city lot for the construction of the Poorhouse. St. Philip's Vestry Minutes, January 6, 1734/5; Carrol and Coll, "The Baltimore Almshouse," 138.

90. Pease and Pease, *Web of Progress*, 103; Green, *This Business of Relief*, Appendix, Table 4.

91. *Acts Passed at the Third General Assembly of the Mississsippi Territory*, 9; Murray, "Poverty and Its Relief," 158.

92. Rothman, *The Discovery of the Asylum*, xiii.

93. Cited in Murray, "Poverty and Its Relief," 157.

94. Richmond City, Hustings Court, Minutes, June 5, 1820.

95. Charleston Poorhouse Minutes, May 30, 1822.

96. Cited in Klebaner, "Public Poor Relief in America," 23, 39.

97. *Report of the Trustees of the Alms-house for Baltimore City and County, 1827*, 5–6.

98. *By-laws of the Trustees and Rules for the Government of the Poor-house of Baltimore County*, 9. New Hanover County Minutes, September 8, 1851.

99. Richmond City, Hustings Court, Minutes, October 13, 1822.

100. Klebaner, "Public Poor Relief in America," 145, 147.

101. *Report of the Trustees of the Alms-house for Baltimore City and County, 1827*, Appendix D.

102. Charleston Poorhouse Minutes, November 14, 1821.

103. Richmond City, Hustings Court, Minutes, February 10, 1824.

104. See Montgomery City Council Minutes, 1820–1834; Murray "Poverty and Its Relief," 163–164.

105. Murray, "Poverty and Its Relief," 167.

106. New Hanover County, Minutes, September 12, 1853; March 13, 1854; March 15, 1859.

107. Montgomery City Council, Minutes, February 27, 1851; February 22, 1853. The salary of the hospital physician at $200 was the smallest salary of all public officials. The mayor was paid $900 while the keeper of powder magazine received $300. *Montgomery Weekly Advertiser and State Gazette*, December 23, 1854.

108. Klebaner, "Public Poor Relief in America," 95; Savannah, Board of Health, Minutes, June 11, 1851; see also June 2, 1824; January 25, 1851; August 10, 1858.

109. Richmond City, Hustings Court, Minutes, October 21, 1823.

110. Richmond City, Hustings Court, Minutes, June 9, 1828.

111. Green, *This Business of Relief*, Appendix, Table 2.

112. Klebaner, "Public Poor Relief in Charleston," 215; Murray, "Poverty and Its Relief," 165. Charleston Poorhouse Minutes, July 15, 1857.

113. Charleston Poorhouse, Commissioner's Letterbook, 1822–1853, July 9, 1840; Charleston Poorhouse Minutes, April 4, 1860, January 9, 1861.

114. Richmond City, Hustings Court, Minutes, April 1823.

115. Charleston Poorhouse Minutes, March 26 and August 4, 1852; June 15 and 29, 1859; September 19, 1860.

116. U.S. Census Bureau, 1860, Montgomery and Mobile counties, Alabama, and Richland County, South Carolina; Bellows, "Tempering the Wind," 198.

117. Charleston Poorhouse Minutes, November 9, 1842. The report was also published: *Report on the Free Colored Poor*.

118. *The Magnolia or Southern Apalachian* New Series 2, no. 2 (February 1843): 139.

119. Charleston Poorhouse Minutes, December 10, 1842.

120. Chatham County, Georgia, Inferior Court, Minutes, March 1791; July 4, 1793; August 6, 1793; February 28, 1794; October 1795; August 13, 1798.

121. Steffen, "Changes in the Organisation," 108, 115.

122. *Richmond Daily Dispatch*, September 12, 1856, cited in Bellows, "Tempering the Wind," 119.

123. Murray, "Poverty and Its Relief," 213–214.

124. Murray, "Fates of Orphans," 527. Murray, "Poverty and Its Relief," 224.

125. *By-laws of the Orphan House of Charleston*, 14, 20. Martineau, *Retrospect of Western Travel*, I, 234; Green, *Fit for America*, 181–215; Rotundo, "Body and Soul," 23–38; Whorton, *Crusaders for Fitness*, 270–304; Betts, "American Medical Thought," 139–152; Betts, "Mind and Body," 787–805.

126. *By-laws of the Orphan House of Charleston*, 23, 27; cited in Bellows, "Tempering the Wind," 134. Murray, "Literacy Acquisition," 172–195.

127. Murray, "Poverty and Its Relief," 216–217.

128. *Proceedings on the Sixty-Sixth Anniversary*, cited in Murray, "Poverty and Its Relief," 202; Bellows, "Tempering the Wind," 106, 110, 122; Murray and Herndon, "Markets for Children," 356–382. The proportion of children being indentured fell gradually from nearly 80 percent in the first decade of the nineteenth century to 40 percent in the 1850s; the proportion of children being returned to a parent rose from 10 percent to 40 percent over the same period. Though there is no immediate obvious explanation for this change it was clearly easier to return a child to a parent, especially if the parent specifically requested this, than go to the trouble of finding a suitable apprenticeship. Murray, "Fates of Orphans," 519–545. Murray, "Bound by Charity," 213–232. Murray "Poverty and Its Relief," 222–223; 234. As Bellows points out, some orphans were permitted to defy the wishes of the commissioners if the dispute was a matter of "honour." Bellows, "Tempering the Wind," 108.

129. *Proceedings on the Sixty-Sixth Anniversary*, 51–52.

130. *Richmond Daily Dispatch*, April 30, 1857.

131. Bellows, "Tempering the Wind," 108.

132. *By-laws of the Orphan House*, 36, 39;

133. Cited in Murray, "Poverty and Its Relief," 219; see also Bellows, "Tempering the Wind," 96.

134. Cited in Murray, "Poverty and Its Relief," 230. Bellows, "Tempering the Wind," 95 and 104.

135. Charleston Orphan House, Register of Visitors, January, April, and October 1860. On the landscape grounds, see *By Laws of the Orphan House*, 27. Address of the Reverend C. P. Gadsden at the Orphan House Anniversary, October, 1861, Charleston Orphan House Papers, Anniversary Celebrations.

136. Murray, "Poverty and Its relief," 239. Also, Murray, "Bound by Charity," 216.

137. Cited in Bellows, "Tempering the Wind," 102.

138. Cited in Bellows, "Tempering the Wind," 134; address of the Reverend C. P. Gadsden.

139. *Laws in Relation to the Overseers of the Poor*, 16.

140. Richmond City, Hustings Court, Minutes, June 18, 1819. Green, *This Business of Relief*, 32–35.

141. Pinckney, *An Address*, 15.

142. Oliver, "A Crumbling Fortress," 125; Weston, "The Evolution of Mental Health in Antebellum Louisiana," 310. Dates for the founding of insane asylums in each state are listed in Dix, *Memorial Soliciting Enlarged and Improved Accommodations*, 6–7.

143. *Reports of the Board of Directors*, 6. Mellown, "The Construction of the Alabama Insane Hospital," 85; Weaver, "Establishment and Organisation of the Alabama Insane Hospital," 222.

144. McCandless, "Curative Asylum," 181; Oliver, "A Crumbling Fortress," 132; Dix, *Memorial Soliciting a State Hospital*, 40; Dain, *Disordered Minds*, 29.

145. *Third Annual Report of the Trustees of the Georgia Academy for the Blind*, 3; Weaver, "Establishment and Organisation of the Alabama Insane Hospital," 220.

146. McCandless, "Curative Asylum," 179; Dain, *Disordered Minds*, 45; Oliver, "A Crumbling Fortress," 134.

147. Weston, "The Evolution of Mental Health," 310, 318; *Reports of the Board of Directors and Superintendent of the Asylum for the Insane of North-Carolina*, 22; *First Published Annual Report of the Resident Physician*, 24; Mellown, "The Construction of the Alabama Insane Hospital," 91.

148. *Seventh Annual Report*, 4; *Sixth Annual Report of the Commissioners*, 17; *Report of the Trustees, Superintendent and Resident Physician*, 20.

149. *Weekly Raleigh Register*, March 20, April 3, 1861.

150. Mellown, "The Construction of the Alabama Insane Hospital," 91–93.

151. McCandless, *Moonlight, Magnolias and Madness*, 76; McCandless, "Curative Asylum," 178–181; Oliver, "A Crumbling Fortress," 130. Like South Carolina, Louisiana's insane asylum admitted only a very small number of blacks. Gordon, "The Development of Louisiana's Public Mental Institutions," 57, 103.

152. Dain, *Disordered Minds*, 19.

Chapter 2. Southern Women Assume the Charitable Role

1. The *Bulletin's* editorial was reprinted in the Savannah *Republican*, September 11, 1858.

2. Amos, "City Belles," 3–6; Lebsock, *The Free Women of Petersburg*, 148–153; *Services and Addresses at the Opening of the Church Home*, 18.

3. *St. Louis Enquirer*, February 16, 1824; *Missouri Republican*, January 26, 1824; *Savannah Morning News*, March 18, 1854.

4. Boylan, *Origins of Women's Activism*, 7.

5. Varon, *We Mean to Be Counted*, 12; *Fortieth Annual and First Printed Report*, 3; Bend, *An Address*, 7.

6. Rules of the Charitable Association for the Relief of the Sick Poor of Charleston Neck, adopted July 21, 1824, FCSCN Minutes.

7. *A Brief Account*, 3–4; *An Account of the Origin*, 3; Second Annual Report,

Columbian Museum, January 7, 1819. For a similar claim to be "rescuing" poor children from their parents, see the Fourth Annual Report, *Daily Georgian*, January 10, 1821.

8. Murray, "Poverty and Its Relief," 226; *Raleigh Register*, July 4, 1822; *Revised Constitution and By-Laws*, Report 1822. POAS December 21, 1848; *Constitution and By-Laws of the Female Humane Association*, 4.

9. Bend, *An Address*, 7; *Annual Report of the Managers of the Ladies' Benevolent Society*, 3; *Rules and Regulations of the Richmond Female Humane Society*; *Constitution of the Ladies Benevolent Society*, 9; LFS Minutes, September 6, 1832; *Charleston Observer*, December 21, 1833.

10. *Daily Morning News*, May 11, 1854.

11. *Religious Herald*, April 4, 1828; *Georgian,* January 28, 1823.

12. *Constitution and By-Laws of the Society for the Relief of the Indigent Sick*, 10; CFOS Constitution, Art. 8. The Female Humane Association in Baltimore reported collections from Presbyterian, Baptist, Lutheran, Methodist, Calvinist, and Catholic churches in 1802. *A Brief Account*, 23.

13. Boylan, *Origins of Women's Activism*, 219–226.

14. Alexander, *Render Them Submissive*, 133–135. Boylan, *Origins of Women's Activism*, 18.

15. *A Brief Account*, 3

16. *An Account of the Rise*, 3. The relevant issues of the *Boston Gazette* are apparently no longer extant.

17. Holcombe, *The First Fruits*, 77; The account Holcombe read was probably *The Institution of the Boston Female Asylum*.

18. *A Brief Account*, 3

19. *Georgia Analytical Repository*, 1 (1802): 68–69; *Daily Georgian*, April 22, 1828.

20. Constitution of the BFBS.

21. Bend, *An Address*, 7; *Georgia Analytical Repository*, 1 (1802): 73; M. M. Wilman to William Duncan, September 19, 1860, William Duncan Papers; *First Annual Report of the Orphan Asylum and Female Free School of Alexandria*, 4.

22. Bend, *An Address*, 10–11.

23. Boylan, *Origins of Women's Activism*, 213. *Second Annual Report of the Dorcas Benevolent Society*, 4. The Dorcas Society in Savannah was assisting around a hundred persons with food and clothing as early as 1817. *Savannah Gazette*, January 25, 1817; *Savannah Republican*, January 23, 1819.

24. *Friend to the Family*, January 22, 1851; *Daily Georgian* January 19, 1854; *Daily Morning News*, May 12, 1854; February 12, 1858; "Fragment Society."

25. *Savannah Gazette*, January 25, 1817; *Charleston Observer*, December 21, 1833; Tuscaloosa FBS, January 7, 1861; *Friend to the Family*, January 22, 1851.

26. "Juvenile Female Benevolent Society of Columbia." The mothers of the First

Directress and Secretary of this society were themselves members of the Columbia Female Benevolent Society. *Columbia Telescope*, April 19, 1816.

27. LBS June 15, 1825; see also December 15, 1824; BFBS, May 13, 1818; CFOS, January 23, 1843.

28. Records of the LBS Visiting Committee, June 15, 1825.

29. *The Second Annual Report of the Rector*, 5.

30. LFS, 1835; *Georgian*, January 28, 1823; *Revised Constitution and By-Laws*, Report 1823.

31. *Revised Constitution and By-Laws*, 1; *Annual Report of the Managers of the Ladies' Benevolent Society*, 3–4. See also the formation of the Benevolent Society in Savannah in 1829 that sought to augment the funds of the Savannah Female Asylum while also "furnishing employment to the industrious poor, offer[ing] to receive needlework, put it out, and superintend its execution." *Daily Georgian*, January 10, 1829.

32. *Revised Constitution and By-Laws*, Report 1823; *Richmond Whig*, November 22, 1845; *Annual Report of the Managers of the Ladies' Benevolent Society*, 5.

33. *Annual Report of the Managers of the Ladies' Benevolent Society*, 5–6; *Louisiana Advertiser*, October 14, 1826; *Daily Morning News*, May 23, 1856. See also *Daily Georgian*, March 7, 1849; *A Friend to the Family*, March 22, 1849; *Daily Morning News*, March 18, 1854; and Lockley, "Spheres of Influence," 114–115.

34. *Annual Report of the Managers of the Ladies' Benevolent Society*, 4; *Savannah Morning News*, May 3, 1857.

35. *Daily Georgian*, March 7, 1849 and March 8, 1850; *Savannah Morning News*, February 24, 1851; February 24, 1855; March 5, 1857. *Savannah Republican*, March 2, 1858. For a similar complaint about poor workmanship, see *Richmond Whig*, November 22, 1845.

36. Buckingham, *The Slave States of America*, I, 124.

37. *Georgia Analytical Repository* 1 (1802): 69–71; *The Institution of the Boston Female Asylum*, 7–8.

38. CFOS Rule No 13.

39. *Revised Constitution and By-Laws*, Report 1822. Boylan, *Origins of Women's Activism*, 137–145.

40. Varon, *We Mean to Be Counted*, 12.

41. An act of Incorporation of the Savannah Free School Society, December 19, 1818. For similar acts, see An act to encourage the Female Asylum of Savannah, December 13, 1809, and An act to incorporate the Female Asylum of Savannah, December 15, 1810. Acts of Georgia.

42. An act incorporating a society for the maintenance and education of poor Female children, by the name of the Female Humane Association Charity School, December 31, 1801, *A Brief Account*, 9.

43. An act for incorporating a society to educate and maintain poor orphan

and other destitute Female children by the name of the Orphaline Charity School, January 20, 1808. An act to incorporate the Humane Impartial Society of the City of Baltimore, December 27, 1811. Available online at http://www.mdarchives.state. md.us/megafile/msa/speccol/sc2900/sc2908/html/. Bend, *An Address*, 3–4; *A History of the Orphan House*, 1.

44. Petition of the Protestant Orphan Asylum Society of Mobile (1840), POAS.

45. Ibid.

46. Varon, *We Mean to Be Counted*, 18–20.

47. SFSS, November 3, 1817.

48. An act of incorporation of the Savannah Free School Society, December 19, 1818. Acts of Georgia.

49. The school petitioned originally in 1817 without success, but was granted a site in 1818. For reports of the petitions, see Savannah City Council Minutes, June 6, 1817; February 23, April 4, May 4, June 8, 1818.

50. CFOS, February 1841, March 1842.

51. *First Annual Report of the Orphan Asylum and Female Free School of Alexandria*, 2.

52. Fiske Manuscripts, Folder 6, March 24, 1824; Bend, *An Address*, 8.

53. For example, fifty-one of 189 directresses of female benevolent societies in Savannah in the 1850s belonged to more than one society, with five belonging to four different organizations.

54. In Columbia, the families of benevolent women owned on average $83,000 of property and thirty-seven slaves; other property holders owned an average of $33,000 of property and twenty-seven slaves. When non-property holders are included, average wealth drops to just $10,000 and five slaves. In Beaufort the figures are $62,000 and sixty slaves for benevolent women, compared to $29,000 and thirty-six slaves for other property holders and $23,000 and twenty-four slaves for the entire community. Quist, *Restless Visionaries*, 88–89.

55. A list of donors is contained in *An Account of the Origin*, 17. Information about marriages was gleaned from *Marriages in Chatham County*, Vol. 1. Moses Cleland, husband of Mary Cleland; Sheldon Dunning, husband of Mary Dunning; and William Taylor, husband of Mary C. Taylor each contributed $50 to the $1,395 total.

56. POAS, December 9, 1839. The results were not immediately impressive; two female members persuaded their husbands to join the society and only a further three managed to convince their husbands to donate funds. Harriet Amos has shown that the governing elite of Mobile were generally Episcopalian, and so, in theory, the managers of the POAS should have had ready access to them. Amos, *Cotton City*, 67. Lists of members and donors can be found in *Constitution and First Annual Report*, 6–7.

57. CFOS Accounts, 1839 and 1852. Data about SFSS subscribers are taken from three lists drawn up before 1820. While about 300 names appear on all three lists, a

further sixty-six appear on just one or two, confirming that the composition of the subscribers fluctuated annually. See "An act of Incorporation of the Savannah Free School Society," *Acts of the General Assembly of the State of Georgia* (1818), 104–109; *An Account of the Origin*, 18; SFSS, List of Subscribers, 1820; SFSS, November 1847. Anne Boylan describes precisely the same decline in subscribers over time for most female benevolent societies in New York and Boston. Boylan, *Origins of Women's Activism*, 177.

58. *An Appeal in Behalf of the Ladies Fuel Society*, 3

59. LBS, September 15, 1851.

60. *Journal of the Proceedings of the 33rd Annual Convention*, 34, 44.

61. *At a meeting of the Female Humane Association*; SFSS, Fifth Annual Report, *Daily Georgian*, January 15, 1822.

62. LBS, September 15, 1840.

63. *Mobile Register*, December 26, 1838. NFOS, January 26, 1816; Montgomery *Daily Post*, April 14, 1860; for a similar case, see BFBS, November 1, 1825.

64. *Mobile Register*, December 11 and 21, 1848. See also CFOS, May 1843, and Accounts 1854–1855; *Raleigh Register*, July 4, 1822.

65. *Columbian Museum*, January 21, 1803.

66. *Savannah Republican*, January 22, 1803. Such criticisms, while not frequent, were more common in the North. Boylan, *Origins of Women's Activism*, 20–21.

67. POAS, November 1846. *Account of the Origin*; *Savannah Republican*, January 6, 1814; and SFA, April 13, 1840.

68. NFOS, January 2, 1817; POAS, May 2, 1840. Amounts raised for the SFA were $469 in 1807, $733 in 1810, $655 in 1811, $700 in 1812, $872 in 1814, $770 in 1815, $1,250 in 1816, $1,195 in 1819, $421 in 1826. The SFSS raised $929 in 1819 and a further $589 in 1821. *Columbian Museum*, January 7, 1811, and February 17, 1812; SFA Minutes, May 6, 1812; May 21, 1820; *Savannah Republican*, May 7, 1808; December 27, 1814; December 23, 1815; December 31, 1816; February 2, 1820. *Georgian*, February 23, 1827. SFSS, March 5, 1821. *Savannah Republican*, January 21, February 17 and 24, 1819. Nathan Fiske was told that a single sermon at the Independent Presbyterian Church for the Savannah Female Asylum had raised $1,500. Fiske Manuscripts, Folder 6, March 24, 1824.

69. For example, in 1816, sermons raised $638 at the Independent Presbyterian Church (IPC) and $470 at Christchurch, but only $90 at First Baptist and $52 at the Methodist chapel. SFA, May 2, 1816. In 1819, the congregation of the IPC could raise $1,155 ($690 for the Savannah Female Asylum and a further $465 for the SFSS). The congregation of Christchurch raised a respectable $649 ($332 for the SFA and a further $317 for the SFSS). The members of the First Baptist Church could raise only $165 ($87 for the SFA, $76 for the SFSS), while the Methodist congregation raised just $157 ($86 for the SFA and $71 for the SFSS). *Savannah Republican*, January 21, February 7, 17 and 24, 1819.

70. CFOS, May 6, 1840; NFOS, January 2, 1845.

71. *Daily Georgian*, November 9, 1829.

72. *Raleigh Register*, April 18, 1849.

73. *Alabama Journal*, December 10, 1830 (quote relating to a fair for the Montgomery Female Benevolent Society); *Daily Georgian*, December 16, 1829; *Mobile Register*, December 23, 1858; *United States Catholic Miscellany*, December 10, 1859. *Georgian*, January 19, 1829. See also the $1,340 raised for the Ladies Seamen's Friend Society in Charleston in 1833 (*Charleston Observer*, March 2, 1833) and the ball held by the German Ladies Society in Savannah (*Daily Morning News*, October 10 and 19, 1853).

74. *Mobile Register*, January 1, 1844; December 31, 1846.

75. *A Friend to the Family*, March 1, 1849.

76. POAS, May 2, 1840; Accounts for 1858–1859, and 1859–1860, Treasurer's Account book of the CFOS.

77. *Fortieth Annual and First Printed Report*, 3–5, 7.

78. *Savannah Republican*, January 6, 1814; December 27, 1814; December 23, 1815; December 31, 1816; February 13, 1819; February 7, 1820. Little financial data exist for this society beyond this date, though one set of accounts in 1827 has no record of income from shares. *Georgian*, February 23, 1827. SWS, Account Book, 1859–1863; $1,089 out of $2,264 came from dividends in 1860; LBS, 275; $1,273 out of $2,893 came from dividends in 1860. For examples of other societies purchasing stocks and shares, see BFBS, January 8, 1830; *At a Meeting of the Female Humane Association*, 2; *Revised Constitution and By-Laws of the Raleigh Female Benevolent Society*, 7

79. Bend, *An Address*, 6. LBS, 275, 205.

80. BFBS, January 8, 1830; June 1832.

81. LBS, 28, 56, 65.

82. NFOS, November 26, 1821. BFBS, July 31, August 15, September 3, 10, 1822; May 12, 1827. The Records of the Distribution of Destitute Orphans for New Orleans from 1852 to 1892 are available online at http://nutrias.org/~nopl/inv/orphanstranscriptions.htm (accessed Apr. 2005). Wheeler and Neblett, *Chosen Exile*, 117. The Richmond Female Humane Society received $300 annually from the Richmond Common Council. *Constitution and By-Laws of the Female Humane Association*, 3. New Orleans city council contributed $1,600 per year to the Poydras Asylum from 1824, while the state of Louisiana had provided $2,000 as early as 1819. Wisner, *Public Welfare Administration*, 28. The Natchez Female Charitable Society was granted $500 from the taxes on slave auctions in Adams County. An act to change the name and style of the Female Charitable Society, and for other purposes, February 3, 1825, *Laws of the State of Mississippi*, 87–88.

83. *Charleston Observer*, July 13, 1833.

84. BFBS, October 17, 1816; September 20, 1818; January 8, 1830; CFOS, Accounts 1840, 1843, 1844.

85. Louisiana *Advertiser*, January 21, 1828; *Mobile Advertiser*, December 9, 1851. For similar payments, see *Mobile Register*, December 21, 1848.

86. An act to vest the Poor School Fund in the county of Chatham in the Savannah Free School Society. SFSS, November 1, 1824, December 20, 1824, July 4, 1825, January 20 and February 4, 1827.

87. *Mobile Register*, December 19, 1850.

88. *Fortieth Annual and First Printed Report*, 1857; *Savannah Republican*, February 17, 1812; *Augusta Chronicle*, May 14, 1823.

89. *Revised Constitution and By-Laws*, Report 1823; *Annual Report of the Managers of the Ladies' Benevolent Society*, 7.

90. Data about slaveholdings was taken from the slave schedule of the 1860 census.

91. *Fortieth Annual and First Printed Report*, 5.

92. SFA. May 6, 1813, August 12, 1813.

93. FSFS, January 1846.

94. NFOS, October 2, 1837.

95. The Sisters of Charity arrived in Mobile on December 16, 1841. McGill, *The Golden Jubilee*, 19–20.

96. The date of the *Mobile Tribune* is in doubt since an extant dated copy has not been found. The ladies pasted two clippings from the paper in the back of one of their minute books but did not date them. There is mention in the minutes from September 1861 about this case, and it is likely that this is roughly the date of the newspaper articles.

97. BFBS, September 11, 1827; January 9, November 7, December 6, 1828.

98. NFOS, October 7, 1816; July 1, 1822; April 1, 1820; January 2, 1821.

99. SFSS, December 4, 1832. In this case the teacher might have been aware that in 1820 the former teacher was paid $800 a year and that the salary had steadily decreased during the 1820s to $500 a year by 1830. BFBS, March 24, June 3, 1823.

100. NFOS, July 1, 1827. For a similar reaction to long-staying guests see BFBS, April 1842.

101. POAS, February 14, 1860.

102. BFBS, November 1841, October 1855, November 1856.

103. CFOS, March 1842, July 22, 1842.

104. McGill, *The Golden Jubilee*, 13, 20.

105. SWS, March 1851.

106. SFA, February 7, 1839.

107. *Georgia Analytical Repository* 1, no. 2 (July–August 1802): 70; Fiske Notes, Folder 6, March 24, 1824; NFOS, April. 1, May 10, August 5, 1846 (Quote); March 5, July 15 and 25, 1847.

108. *Richmond Daily Dispatch*, January 3, 1860. Natchez Female Benevolent Society, Constitution, Art. 6.

109. History of the Widow's Row, in Frances Beverley Papers.

110. "2nd Annual Report"; FCSCN, July 21, 1825; *Richmond Whig*, November 22, 1845.

111. *Richmond Whig*, November 22, 1845.

112. SWS, February 1849.

113. *Annual Report of the Managers*, 4; *The Columbia Telescope*, April 9, 1816, cited in Mobley, *The Ladies Benevolent Society of Columbia*, 21.

114. FCSCN, July 28, 1826; July 21, 1827.

115. "Annual Report."

116. *Revised Constitution and By-Laws*, Annual Report 1823.

117. LBS Minutes, September 15, 1843; September 19, 1844.

118. *Second Annual Report of the Dorcas Benevolent Society*, 4. NPOA, March 3, 1851; SFA, May 1, 1834.

119. CFOS, March 28, 1844; POAS, February 2, 1841, May 14, 1844; BFBS, January 1829, September 25, 1832.

120. SFA, May 20, 1818; SWS, February 1849.

121. Poydras Orphan Asylum Papers, Box 3, Letter, August 19, 1852, cited in Murray, "Poverty and Its Relief," 229; BFBS, September 17, 1816; SWS, February 1849; Mobile Female Benevolent Society, May 7, 1860.

122. SFA, August 19, 1817; October 1, 1818; BFBS, September 17, 1816; May 20, 1820; September 9 1823; SFA, December 1, 1840; September 2, 1841; Tuscaloosa FBS, January 5 1860; BFBS, May 1836.

123. SWS, October 1860.

124. Constitution of the CFOS, Art 9. *A Brief Account*, 3.

125. *A Brief Account*, 8.

126. SFA, September 15, 1833. See also February 6, June 4, 1840 (quote), July 21, 1841; BFBS, January 17, 1817; July 1851. Savannah *Daily Morning News*, May 11, 1854; August 12, 1823. For similar regulations in Nashville, see Wheeler, *Chosen Exile*, 110. *Natchez Gazette*, March 18, 1826.

127. NFOS, February 1, 1816; POAS, January 2, 1861.

128. SFA, April 7, 1825. See also December 4, 1817; December 6, 1821; April 4, 1822; November 14, 1822; June 1, 1826.

129. POAS, March 2, 1847; SFA, May 6, 1825.

130. SFA, July 29, 1811; August 7, 1811.

131. BFBS, August 26, 1834; August 18, 1835.

132. POAS, Admissions Record Book, 1850–1886.

133. SFA, March 6, 1828; POAS, October 3, 1854.

134. *Sermon and Reports at the Fifth Anniversary*, 9.

135. *Fortieth Annual and First Printed Report*, 15.

136. *Alexandria Orphan Asylum*, 3; *Fortieth Annual and First Printed Report*, 5.

137. *Fortieth Annual and First Printed Report*, 14–15. SFA Rule 5, April 5, 1838. *Constitution and First Annual Report*, 3.

138. *Constitution and By-Laws of the Female Humane Association*, 11; SFA, Rule 2; CFOS, Rule 10; BFBS, February 1843; *Mobile Register*, December 31, 1840. Albert Pickett specifically noticed that the inhabitants of the Camp Street Asylum in New Orleans were "clean and well dressed." Pickett, *Eight Days in New-Orleans*, 24.

139. BFBS, September 27, 1833; see also Poydras, Rule 13, *Fortieth Annual and First Printed Report*, 14. SFA, April 13, 1840.

140. *Mississippi Free Trader*, May 3, 1851.

141. *Constitution and By-Laws of the Female Humane Association*, 11.

142. BFBS, September 27, 1833.

143. Lockley, "Spheres of Influence," 102–104; U.S. Census Bureau, Beaufort County, South Carolina.

144. *Rules and Orders of the Baltimore Benevolent Society*, 11.

145. BFBS, July 23, 1820; August 22, 1820; September 10, 1822; March 24, 1823.

146. NFOS, January 2, 1819; POAS, May 2, 1840.

147. POAS, April 2, 1844.

148. BFBS, March 30 and June 2, 1827.

149. POAS, April 5, 1859.

150. Nashville POA, January 6, 1851, cited in Murray, "Poverty and Its Relief," 233.

151. SFA, April 24, 1818; December 13, 1819. NFOS, April 18, 1820.

152. NFOS, March 2, 1821. For similar cases see NFOS, January 1821, and SFA, January 2, 1824.

153. NFOS, January 2, 1830 (see also July 1 and August 12, 1822). SFA, July 1, 1813. The Beaufort Female Benevolent Society was among those that would accept children back after they had been bound out. BFBS, January 9 and March 12, 1828.

154. SFA, December 1, 1825.

155. Murray, "Poverty and Its Relief," 212.

156. SFA, August 5, 1818.

157. BFBS, April 20 and May 12, 1827.

158. SFA, October 7, 1812; August 3, 1815; April 6, 1820.

159. POAS, May 4, 1858; see also BFBS, July 4, 1858.

160. SFA, July 3, 1834; February 5, 1835; February 4, 1836; December 4, 1828; April 2, 1829; October 1831.

161. Murray, "Poverty and Its Relief," 219; Clement, "Children and Charity," 351.

162. *Daily Morning News*, May 11, 1854.

163. Lockley, "Moulding the Poor Children of Antebellum Savannah."

164. M. M. Wilman to William Duncan, September 19, 1860, William Duncan Papers.

165. Information about the girls is taken from the minutes of the SFA and the BFBS, Marriage and Deaths in the Savannah Records; also the 1860 census for Chatham County and Beaufort District.

166. Cited in Downs and Sherraden, "The Orphan Asylum," 272.

167. Phillips, *Freedom's Port*, 15, 170–171; Bell, *Revolution*, 123–127; Gehman, *Free People of Color*, 67–76; Johansen, "Intelligence, though Overlooked," 452–458.

168. LBS, Charleston, 36–37.

169. Boylan, *The Origins of Women's Activism*, 222. FCSCN, October 21, 1824; May 1857; LBS Charleston, 117–118, 274, 281.

Chapter 3. The Male Response

1. Gongaware, *The History of the German Friendly Society*, 64–63; Linn, *The History of the German Friendly Society*, 30, 37.

2. *Constitution and By-laws of the St. Andrew's Society of Baltimore*, 14.

3. *Handbook of Philanthropic and Social Service Agencies*, 30. *Act of Incorporation and By-laws of the Hibernian Society of Baltimore*, 5, 14.

4. "An act to incorporate the Hibernian Society of the City of Savannah," passed December 10, 1812. Acts of Georgia; Shoemaker, "Strangers and Citizens," 178. Hibernian Society Minutes, March 14, 1846.

5. An act to incorporate the Savannah Association of Mechanics, December 16, 1793. *Acts of the General Assembly of the State of Georgia* (1794), 18.

6. *The Constitution of the Charleston Mechanic Society*, 3; *Rules of the Charleston Carpenters Society*, Preamble.

7. *Charter, Constitution and By-Laws of the Petersburg Benevolent Mechanic Association*; PBMA, April 13, July 12, October 11, 1825; January 8, 1827.

8. Watkinson, "Reluctant Scholars," 432, 436–437, 440–441, 444.

9. *Rules and Regulations of the Brown Fellowship Society*, 11. Johnson and Roark, *Black Masters*, 212–222; Johnson and Roark, "A Middle Ground."

10. *Savannah Republican*, January 8, 1814

11. An act to incorporate the Savannah Poor House and Hospital Society, December 10, 1808. Acts of Georgia; *Savannah Republican*, November 5, 1805.

12. For admissions data broken down by nativity, see *Columbian Museum*, January 7, 1811; *Savannah Republican*, January 8, 1814, and January 7, 1815; January 3, 1817.

13. Agreement between United States Government and the Savannah Poor House and Hospital, 1811, Mackay-Stiles Papers, Series A, Folder 15. SPHH, March 14, 1838.

14. A. S. Bullock to William H. Crawford, February 1, March 20, and July 11, 1821. A. S. Bullock Letterbook, Savannah Port Papers.

15. *Georgian*, April 12, 1822.

16. *Georgian*, April 17, 20, 1822

17. *Georgian*, March 21 and 25, 1823.

18. *Georgian*, May 3, 1823; Savannah City Council Minutes, April 14, 1825; July 5, 1827.

19. *Georgian*, February 11, 1832.

20. SPHH, February 8, 1842; February 19, 1850; October 17, 1858 (Tipton Case); February 6, 1860.

21. *Columbian Museum*, January 7, 1811; SPHH, February 6, 1841, February 2, 1857, February 7, 1858. *Report of Thomas M. Turner*, 16.

22. Catherine E. McGolrick to Doctor Grimes, June 4, 1811. Mackay-Stiles Papers, Series A, Folder 15.

23. SPHH, February 8, 1842; February 15, 1843; August 6, 1842.

24. *Rules and By-Laws of the Savannah Poor-House and Hospital Society*, 24; SPHH, February 6, 1841; September 17, 1839; June 27, 1851.

25. Habersham, "Savannah Hospital," 89.

26. SPHH, November 28, 1851; February 7, 1858.

27. Minutes of the Trustees of Roper Hospital, July 2 and October 1849. Medical Society of South Carolina Minutes, October 2, 1854.

28. Can't Get Away Club Typescript History. Mobile *Weekly Advertiser*, August 30, 1855. For the arrival in Savannah of two doctors, three assistants, and two nurses paid for by the Can't Get Away Club see *Savannah Morning News*, September 25, 1854. The infirmary they established treated seventy-three patients before it closed in mid-October; fifty-nine of these survived the epidemic; *Savannah Morning News*, October 14, 1854. Both Savannah and Charleston sent similar help to Norfolk in 1855. *Report of the President of the Howard Association*, 3; SBA, August 20, 1855.

29. Montgomery *Advertiser and State Gazette*, October 31, 1854.

30. *Report of the President of the Howard Association*, 3, 5; *Constitution and By-laws of the Howard Association*, 10.

31. *Savannah Morning News*, September 23 (city census and mayor passing over money) and October 2, 1854 (total given during September). See also *Report of the President of the Howard Association*, 7

32. SBA, *Savannah Benevolent Association*, 14–15. *Savannah Morning News*, October 2, 1854.

33. SBA, March 12, 1855; September 30, December 6, 1858; June 6, 1859. *Savannah Benevolent Association*, 33–34.

34. *A Warning to the Citizens of Baltimore*, 14–15.

35. *The Fundamental Rules and Regulations of the Lancastrian Institution*, 4.

36. *Christian Monitor*, October 21 and November 11, 1815. *Rules and Regulations for the Government of the Richmond Lancasterian School*, 5.

37. Minutes of the Chatham Academy, May 3, 1813; February 15, 1820; and June 4, 1854, Edward Clifford Anderson Papers. *Rules and Regulations for the Government of the Richmond Lancasterian School*, 3, 15.

38. *Daily Georgian*, January 29, 1823; *Mobile Register*, December 23, 1858.

39. Powers, *Black Charlestonians*, 51–54; Bell, *Revolution*, 124.

40. See Bellows, "My Children, Gentlemen, Are My Own," and Murray, "Fates of Orphans."

41. An ordinance to regulate the terms on which children are to be schooled

on the funds of the Union Society. *Minutes of the Union Society*, 28–29, April 23, 1795.

42. *Minutes of the Union Society*, 156, April 26, 1856.

43. *Minutes of the Union Society*, 70.

44. For example, Joseph Eppinger was first bound to merchant Petit De Villiers, but later to carpenter J. H. Ash. John Trevoyer was moved from cabinetmaker Dougald Ferguson to carriage-maker William Warner, and Alexander Wilson was moved from printer J. M. Cooper to blacksmith L. S. Bennett.

45. *Daily Morning News*, May 11, 1854.

46. Minutes of the Winyaw Indigo Society 1853–1884 in Foster, "A Documentary History of Education in South Carolina," Vol. 10., April 7 and December 1, 1854.

47. Minutes of the Fellowship Society, September 12, 1804; March 12, 1828; March 12, 1856.

48. Minutes of the Fellowship Society, July 18, 1827; May 14, 1828; September 16, 1829.

49. LBS, 90.

50. *Virginia Evangelical and Literary Magazine* 5 (1822): 278–279.

51. SPS, Constitution, June 3, 1844.

52. SPS, January 14, January 21, February 4, November 4, November 11, 1845; January 12, April 8, 1846; January 10, 1848.

53. SPS, March 5, 1851; May 4, 1852.

54. SPS, March 21, 1860; Female Seaman's Friend Society Minutes.

55. *Twelfth Annual Report of the Board of Managers*, 9; Yates, *An Historical Sketch*, 12, 29, 31.

56. For examples of children whose education was paid for by the Union Society, see *Minutes of the Union Society*, 12, 13, and 17: Minutes, July 1, 1793; September 2, 1793; April 23, 1794.

57. *Report and Proceedings on the Subject of a House of Refuge*, 2, 4, 10.

58. *Charleston Observer*, March 22, 1828.

59. Petition of the Charleston Benevolent Society, General Assembly Papers, ND 02100; *Charleston Observer*, March 22, 1828.

60. *Louisville Public Advertiser*, May 16, 1827; *Charleston Observer*, March 22, 1828.

61. Pinckney, *An Address*, 15.

62. Tripp, *Yankee Town*, 33.

63. *Services and Addresses at the Opening of the Church Home*, (1851), 6, 18.

64. *Sermon and Reports at the Second Anniversary*, 3; *Sermon and Reports at the Fourth Anniversary*, 9; *Sermon and Reports at the Eighth Anniversary*, 6.

65. *Sermon and Reports at the Seventh Anniversary*, 12; *Sermon and Reports at the Sixth Anniversary*, 13; *Sermon and Reports at the Fifth Anniversary*, 9.

66. *Sermon and Reports at the Eighth Anniversary*, 4–5.

67. *Richmond Whig*, November 22, 1845; November 28, 1846.

68. *Richmond Daily Whig*, February 7, 1846.

69. Richmond Male Orphan Society Papers, Constitution Art. 5, "The object of the society," Sec. 3 and 4.

70. Jane Taylor Dieke, *History of the Richmond Home for Boys*, 4–5, Male Orphan Society Papers.

71. Ibid., 6–8.

72. *Fourth Report of the Baltimore Manual Labor School*, 5.

73. *Tenth Report of the Directors of the Baltimore Manual Labor School*, 8.

74. *Baltimore American*, November 9, 1849.

75. Ibid., November 21, 1849.

76. Address to the Public, 1850; Visitors Manual, 1850; both cited in Culver, "A History," 16, 17, 28, 30.

77. *Friend to the Family*, January 21, 1851; SFA, September 5, 1816; April 8, 1841.

78. Report of Bishop England to the Cardinal Prefect of Propaganda, *American Catholic Historical Society* 8 (1897): 323, cited in Kelly, "Charleston's Bishop John England and American Slavery," 51.

79. "The Society of the Sisters of Charity." Not to be confused with the Catholic Sisters of Charity who operated orphanages in Baltimore, Mobile, and New Orleans, the Charleston Sisters of Charity were associated with St. Michael's Episcopal Church.

80. SFSS, November 1845.

81. Details about these men have been taken from the 1860 federal census manuscript returns for Mobile County, Alabama, and Richmond City, Virginia.

82. *Proceedings of the 108th Anniversary of the Union Society*, 11; *Proceedings of the 109th Anniversary of the Union Society*, 7; *Savannah Republican*, April 25, 1861. SFSS, January 1848, March 1853, February 1855.

83. *Minutes of the Union Society*, 135, 140–143; *Savannah Morning News*, April 25, 1860.

84. Lists of members with dates of admission are in *Minutes of the Union Society*, Appendix, 6–18.

85. For example, thirty-three girls were housed in the SFA in 1850, but only twenty-eight in 1860.

86. Church, *A Discourse*, 4–5.

87. Georgia Infirmary Papers.

88. *Gospel Messenger*, 29 (October 1852), 200.

89. *Gospel Messenger*, 1 (December 1824), 376; Tripp, *Yankee Town*, 33.

90. *Savannah Republican*, April 25, 1861.

91. *Minutes of the Union Society*, 162–164. A list of those from Savannah who served with Confederate forces can be found in Lee and Agnew, *Historical Record*, 119–128. The speeches given by boys at the Charleston Orphan House were

clearly credited as being authored by others. Charleston Orphan House Papers, Anniversary Celebrations, 1804–1861.

Chapter 4. The Personal Touch

1. Mary Anna Claiborne Account Book; Brevard, cited in McCurry, *Masters of Small Worlds*, 110. In 1860 Brevard owned 209 slaves and her personal property was valued at $170,000.

2. *Liberty Weekly Tribune*, November 9, 1855 (Missouri). Available online at http://newspapers.umsystem.edu (accessed December 2006).

3. *Tallahassee Star of Florida*, January 17, 1845, cited in Baptist, *Creating an Old South*, 121; Rosengarten, *Tombee*, 135, 398, 487, 529.

4. Hahn, *Roots*, 54. Charles Derby to James Winchester, June 13, 1822, James Winchester Papers.

5. Hahn, *Roots*, 55.

6. Chesnut, *A Diary from Dixie*, 401.

7. McCurry, *Masters of Small Worlds*, 127; Bellows, *Benevolence among Slaveholders*, 165–166.

8. Atherton, *The Southern Country Store*, 14, 52, 106. Murdoch, "Letters and Papers of Dr. Daniel Turner," 481. Beeman, "Trade and Travel in Post-Revolutionary Virginia," 179; Ball, *Slavery in the United States*, 191.

9. Muldrew, *Economy of Obligation*, 96, 303–304.

10. Finn, *The Character of Credit*, 3.

11. Mann, *Republic of Debtors*, 3, 17, 47, 134.

12. Bolton, *Poor Whites*, 102; Patton, *Biography*, 16.

13. Patton, *Biography*, 20, 23, 25.

14. Buncombe County's population of 13,425 in 1850 occupied 1,105 sq. miles. In 1851, Madison County was created out of the northern portion of Buncombe County so by 1860 Buncombe's population had fallen slightly to 12,654 and its area to 656 sq. miles. In 1850, 81 percent of those listed with an occupation were farmers. Occupational data come from the original manuscript census returns, while census statistics come from http://fisher.lib.virginia.edu/collections/stats/histcensus.

15. Sondley, *A History of Buncombe County*, II, 828.

16. Inscoe, *Mountain Masters*, 31. In 1860, Asheville was home to eight of the ten physicians in the county, and all but one of the cabinetmakers.

17. In 1850 Patton's estate was worth $35,000, Smith's $30,000, and Alexander's $15,000. All three owned more than fifty slaves. In 1860, Patton's real estate was valued at $67,267 and his personal estate at $193,390, much of which can be accounted for by the seventy-eight slaves he owned. Inventories for the estates of Daniel Blake, John E. Patton, and Nicholas Woodfin, the other wealthiest citizens of Asheville in

1850, have not been located since there are no inventories extant between 1868 and 1899.

18. Buncombe County, Court of Common Pleas, Minutes [BCCPM], July 1847.

19. Patton also donated $1,000 toward the Ravenscroft School. N. W. Woodfin Papers, Box 1, Folder 4, dated November 29, 1854.

20. Harris, *Plain Folk*, 98; Hahn, *Roots*, 70. Buncombe County, Record of Inventories 1822–1929—fourteen out of twenty-two inventories contained notes.

21. The share of total county wealth held by those owning ten or more slaves was 27.8 percent in 1850 and 39 percent in 1860.

22. All the inventory information comes from Buncombe County, Record of Inventories 1822–1929. Out of 763 "desperate" debts in the inventories of elite citizens, Smith, Patton, and Alexander account for 457.

23. Harris, *Plain Folk*, 97.

24. Both cases cited in Harris, *Plain Folk*, 96.

25. Harris, *Plain Folk*, 98; Sarah Wadley Diary, August 2, 1861.

26. James W. Patton to William A. Patton, February 25, 1861, James W. Patton Papers.

27. Easterby, *South Carolina Rice Plantation*, 152, 156.

28. These figures are taken from the 1850 and 1860 federal censuses for Buncombe County.

29. Sondley, *History of Buncombe County*, II, 746.

30. Harris, *Plain Folk*, 97, 99.

31. Tripp, *Yankee Town*, 28–29.

32. Interestingly, James Patton did bring a suit against Joshua Heron in January 1859 for $125.52. Buncombe County, Execution Docket. Heron repaid $10.80 in April 1860, but there is no further record as to the outcome of this case.

33. Diary of Joseph Addison Waddell, February 11, 1856. Online at the Valley of the Shadow: http://valley.vcdh.virginia.edu/.

34. Cited in Harris, *Plain Folk*, 96–97.

35. H. M. Bell to John McCue, January 11, 1860; Robert Cowan to John H. McCue, November 18, 1857. Available online at http://etext.lib.virginia.edu/etcbin/civwarlett-browse?id=A8050 and http://etext.lib.virginia.edu/etcbin/civwarlett-browse?id=A8513 (accessed January 2006).

36. Ford, *Origins*, 67; Baptist, *Creating an Old South*, 225.

37. Rosengarten, *Tombee*, 348.

38. Harris, *Plain Folk*, 100; Clark, "The Consequences of the Market Revolution," 30; Diary of Joseph Addison Waddell, February 11, 1856.

39. Clark, *The Roots of Rural Capitalism*, 37–38, 199–200. The impact of the panic of 1837 was particularly important in breaking down these community bonds. See also Sellers, *The Market Revolution*. For an excellent summary of the contours

of the historiographic debate, see Stokes and Conway, *The Market Revolution in America*, 1–20.

40. This point is made in Watson, "Slavery and Development," 48.

41. Buncombe County, Execution Docket.

42. *Revised Statutes of the State of North Carolina*, 322; "An act in favour of poor debtors," *Laws of the State of North Carolina*, 46. Goodman, "The Emergence of Homestead Exemption," 472.

43. Coleman, *Debtors and Creditors*, 224.

44. Buncombe County, Execution Docket, April Term 1833 and July Term 1834. BCCPM, October Term 1841. Case of A. S. Watson vs. A. B. Rowan, April 14, 1860, in Buncombe County, Miscellaneous Records, 1786–1946, Folder: Insolvent Debtors; *Revised Statutes*, 324.

45. Goodman, "The Emergence of Homestead Exemption," 470; Bolton, *Poor whites*, 102–103.

46. Goodman, "The Emergence of Homestead Exemption," 472, 477.

47. Petition of Citizens of Morgan County, Governor James Jones Papers, Box 1, Folder 3. May 23, 1842.

48. North Carolina General Assembly Session Records, November 1840–January 1841, Box 4, Folder: Petitions (Perquimans); November 1842– January 1843, Box 6, Folder: Petitions (Moore).

49. In this instance the purchaser, John Brigman, was most likely a relation of the debtor. Execution Docket, April 1830.

50. Bolton, *Poor Whites*, 128–129.

51. Patton, *Biography*, 18, 21, 25.

52. *Asheville News*, January 13, 1859. The poor relief available to Buncombe residents is explored more fully in Lockley, "The Purpose of Public Poor Relief."

53. The most important contributors to this debate are Hahn, *The Roots of Southern Populism*; Harris, *Plain Folk*; Ford, *The Origins of Southern Radicalism*; McCurry, *Masters of Small Worlds*.

54. Inscoe, *Mountain Masters*, 263, 112–113. Inscoe and McKinney, *The Heart of Confederate Appalachia*, 16–20.

Chapter 5. Teaching Southern Poor Whites

1. This account is based on the diary of William Valentine, April 27 and May 3, 1854, on the 1841 rules of a school in the Elijah Timmerman Papers, and an account in the *Natchez Courier*, May 23, 1848.

2. These tensions are neatly summarized in Curti, *Human Nature*, 181–182. For historians emphasizing the social control argument, see Kaestle, *The Evolution of an Urban School System*, 112–137; Kaestle, *Pillars of the Republic*, 207; Matthews, *Toward a New Society*, 147–148; Soltow and Stevens, *The Rise of Literacy*, 11. For

those stressing the individual potential argument, see Walters, *American Reformers*, 213; Hunt, "Home, Domesticity, and School Reform," 266–267.

3. Salley, *Minutes of the Vestry*, June 22, 1748; "An act for the founding and erecting of a free school in Charlestown, for the use of the inhabitants of this province of South Carolina," passed December 12, 1712, Sec. 21 and 22; "An act for founding and erecting, governing, ordering and visiting a free school in the town of Dorchester," Cooper and McCord, *Statutes at Large*, II, 395, III, 378. On Virginia, see Beverley, *History of Virginia*, 240; "Education in Colonial Virginia: Part III: Free Schools," 71–85; Nelson, *Blessed Company*, 220.

4. Knight, *Documentary History*, II, 153.

5. Ibid., 156.

6. Kaestle, *Pillars of the Republic*, 198; Soltow and Stevens, *The Rise of Literacy*, 120.

7. Mary Telfair to Mary Few, undated, William Few Papers, Folder 11, Item 154. *Speech of Mr. Stiles*, 13.

8. Coon, *The Beginnings of Public Education*, I, 43, 54.

9. "On Patriotism," 181.

10. Ibid.

11. Coon, *The Beginnings of Public Education*, I, 60.

12. Counterparts in Lancaster District commented that free schools were "more generally embraced by the inhabitants." General Assembly Records, Free School Reports, Lexington District 1814, Lancaster District 1816.

13. Knight, *Documentary History*, V, 48, 74

14. Maddox, *The Free School Idea*, 47.

15. Ibid., 48–52.

16. *Richmond Enquirer*, March 9, 1816.

17. Knight, *Documentary History*, V, 56, 69.

18. *Family Visitor*, May 31, 1823. Story Diary, 1830, February 5, 1838, June 1853. Cobb, *Educational Wants of Georgia*, 6.

19. Story Diary, 1833. *Reports on the Free School System*, 70, 5.

20. Maddox, *The Free School Idea*, 80, 85.

21. *Columbus Enquirer*, August 30, 1834; *Report on Public Education*, 36.

22. *The South Carolina Society for the Advancement of Learning*, 10.

23. *Reports on the Free School System*, 11, 44.

24. *Report on Public Education*, 60.

25. Coon, *The Beginnings of Public Education*, I, 105, 144.

26. Maxwell, *An Oration*, 11–12.

27. Lindsley, *The Cause of Education in Tennessee*, 12; *Virginia Evangelical and Literary Magazine*, 6 (1823), 175.

28. Church, *A Discourse*, 8.

29. Coon, *The Beginnings of Public Education*, I, 295, 459.

30. *Raleigh Star*, January 22, 1835. Extract from *Western Carolinian*, reprinted in the *Raleigh Register*, November 19, 1838.

31. *Raleigh Register*, November 9, 1829.

32. Valentine Papers, Diary, Vol. 3, August 1, 1839.

33. *Raleigh Register*, January 14, 1839; *Rutherfordton Gazette*, reprinted in the *Raleigh Register*, April 6, 1839.

34. For details of the votes, see *Raleigh Register*, August 10, 17, and 24, 1839.

35. *Highland Messenger*, June 5, 1840.

36. *Highland Messenger*, April 21, 1843.

37. *Highland Messenger*, May 22, 1846.

38. Report of Examining Committee November 20, 1852; Letter of Wilson Owens, June 2, 1852; Summons of the Board of Superintendents of Common School, February 5, 1853; Report of the Teacher in No. 10 district, R. Lewis, dated October 1, 1847; Report of the Present State of Common School in District No. Nine, December 1847. Craven County, Miscellaneous School Records, Box: Names of Children and Teacher Applications; Folder: Teacher Applications. Folder: Common School Reports and Settlements, 1841–1849.

39. Knight, *Documentary History*, V, 117, 130–135.

40. Rowan County Report, Wiley Papers (NCSA), Box 16, Common School Reports, 1854.

41. *First Annual Report of the General Superintendent of Common Schools*, 4–8.

42. Ibid., 30–34, 29.

43. *Report of the General Superintendent of Common Schools for the year 1860*, 3; Vinovskis, "Trends in Massachusetts Education," 512.

44. *Governor Hayne's Message*, 11; *Governor McDuffie's Message*, 2.

45. *Reports on the Free School System*, 3, 7.

46. *Message No. 1 of His Excellency William Aiken*, 5; *Message No. 1 of His Excellency Governor Means*, 3.

47. "Free School System in South Carolina," (1849), 35, 47–48.

48. Thornwell, *Letter to Governor Manning*, 37, 42.

49. *Message of Governor James Adams*, 9.

50. "The Free School System of South Carolina" (1856), 126; *Message No. 1 of His Excellency R. F. W. Allston*, 7.

51. General Assembly Records, Free School Reports, Fairfield District, 1857; St. Helena Parish, 1859.

52. Meriwether, *History of Higher Education in South Carolina*, 115.

53. *Report of the Board of Commissioners of Free Schools*, 3–4; "Free Schools of Charleston," 485. Figures regarding expenditures come from General Assembly, Free School Reports, Oversize 1860–1861; 1860 Synopsis.

54. *Richmond Enquirer*, November 26, 1841.

55. *Richmond Enquirer*, January 23, 1843.

56. *Facts and Hints relative to Free Schools*, 3, 15.

57. Governor's Message, *Journal of the House of Delegates of Virginia (1845)*, 9–10.

58. Education Convention Reports, *Journal of the House of Delegates of Virginia (1845)*, Doc. 16, 8–9.

59. Second Auditor's Report of the Literary Fund, *Journal of the House of Delegates of Virginia* (1846), Doc. 4, 5–6.

60. Ibid., 29, 34.

61. Maddox, *Free School Idea*, 138.

62. Broadside on Education.

63. Conway, *Free Schools in Virginia*, 10; Maddox, *Free School Idea*, 165.

64. *Journal of the House of Delegates of Virginia*, 1845, Document 4, 20–21; *Governor's Message and Annual Reports of the Public Officers of the State*, Doc. 4, 23, 61.

65. Maddox, *Free School Idea*, 165.

66. *Daily Southern Argus*, September 27, 1858, cited in Turnbull, "Early Public Schools in Norfolk," 7.

67. Maddox, *Free School Idea*, 157.

68. *Governor's Message and Annual Reports of the Public Officers of the State* (1855), xvii. *The Memorial of Sundry Citizens*, 11.

69. *Fredericksburg Weekly Advertiser*, January 9, February 6, 1858.

70. Maddox, *Free School Idea*, 160.

71. Pippin, "Common School Movement," 177–178; Bailey, *Class and Tennessee's Confederate Generation*, 46–47; Bailey, "Tennessee's Antebellum Society from the Bottom Up," 264; Nagy, "Wanted: A Teacher for the Nashville English School," 171–185; Nagy, "The South Nashville Institute," 180–196.

72. Knight, *Documentary History*, V, 89–90; 110–115.

73. Pyburn, *The History of the Development*, 63; Cochran, *History of Public Schools*, 23–26.

74. Knight, *Documentary History*, V, 187.

75. Mayes, *History of Education in Mississippi*, 278–282.

76. *Mississippi Free Trader and Natchez Gazette*, November 11, 1845.

77. Sheller, "The Origins of Public Education."

78. *Ordinances of the City of Baltimore*, 14; *Annual Report of the School Commissioners of Baltimore County*, supplement; *12th Annual Report of the School Commissioners of Baltimore County*, 4, 8.

79. Reinders, "New England Influences," 182, 190.

80. "System of Common Schools," 470–471, 473.

81. Ibid., 474.

82. *Annual Report of Superintendent of Public Schools, Fourth District*, 7–8; "System of Common Schools," 480.

83. *DeBow's Review*, (August 1850): 240; (April 1857): 445; (September 1859): 278.

84. Jones, *Education in Georgia*, 25–26; Georgia House Journals, 1837, Appendix, 35–37.

85. Cited in Bowden, *Two Hundred Years of Education*, 213.

86. *Report on Public Education*, 12.

87. *Report on Public Education*, 31; Jenkins, "Ante-bellum Macon and Bibb County," 343.

88. *Southern School Journal* 2 (1854): 143–144, 171; 3 (1855): 25.

89. *Speech of Mr. Stiles of Chatham*, 9, 16, 19. *Report on Public Education*, 92.

90. Lincoln County Grand Jury Presentment, April 1859, Lincoln County Poor School Minutes 1852–1870; Statement of Greene County Grand Jury, March 1859, Greene County School Commissioner Minutes, 1856–1869.

91. Mathews, "The Politics of Education," 181–206; *Report on Public Education*, 169–189.

92. Chatham County, Inferior Court, Minutes, November 29, 1855; February 25, 1856; Report of Free School Commissioners December 31, 1855; February 10 1857.

93. Bowden, *Two Hundred Years of Education*, 229–230; *Report of Edward C. Anderson*, 4–5. *Report of James P. Screven*, 14, 32–33.

94. *Report of Thomas M. Turner*, 11, 27.

95. *Report of Charles C. Jones*, 21.

96. The sixteenth section of each township was donated by the legislature for school use. Rogers et al., *Alabama*, 117; Charles Lyell, cited in Roche, "An Englishman's Impressions," 224; Amos, *Cotton City*, 180–183.

97. Porter, *The Past and the Present*, 35.

98. Pratt, *An Address*, 17.

99. Pyburn, "Mobile Public Schools," 177.

100. Amos, *Cotton City*, 188; *The Free School Law*, 5.

101. *Report of the Superintendent of Education of the State of Alabama*, 15.

102. Knight, *Documentary History*, V, 166–174; Report of Gabriel B. Duval, *Superintendent of Education of the State of Alabama*, 3, 5.

103. *North Carolina Journal of Education* (February 1858): 63.

104. Amos, *Cotton City*, 191.

105. *Report of the Superintendent of Education of the State of Alabama*, 15.

106. Letter of W. J. Bennett, October 22, 1856; Letter of N. Slater, November 30, 1858, Wiley Papers (NCSA); Letter of Jno. B. Mallard, July 28, 1857, Wiley Papers (SHC).

107. *Alabama Educational Journal* (October 1, 1857), 74; *North Carolina Journal of Education* (March 3, 1858): 80.

108. Kathryn Pippin identified fifty-six key educational reformers in the South who wrote/spoke widely on education, held some kind of educational post either in government or as a teacher, and were recognized by others as being a reformer. Only five of these men were born in New England. Pippin, "The Common School Movement," 52, 292–303; Reinders, "New England Influences."

109. Reinders, "New England Influences," 184. On the links between middle-class northern and southern educational reformers, see Wells, *The Origins of the Southern Middle Class*, 132–150.

110. Knight, *Documentary History*, V, 285.

111. *The Educational Repository and Family Monthly* (March 1860): 167; Reinders, "New England Influences," 193.

112. Richmond *Daily Dispatch*, December 14, 1853. Cobb, *Educational Wants of Georgia*, 7; *The Educational Repository and Family Monthly* (May 1860): 259.

113. Reinders, "New England Influences," 187–188.

114. John Hardin Best has incorrectly claimed that no school textbooks were published in the South. Examples include the *First Class Southern School Book* by B. F. Griffin of Macon (cited in *Georgia Telegraph*, January 28, 1830); *The Southern Reader or Child's Second Reading Book*, published in Charleston in 1841 and re-printed in 1845; and the *North Carolina Reader* published in the 1850s containing a history of the state. Best, "Education in the Forming of the American South," 46.

115. *Alabama Educational Journal* (April 1859): 210.

116. *Annual Report of Wm. F. Perry*, 26.

117. *Report of the Board of Commissioners of Free Schools*, 15.

118. *North Carolina Journal of Education* (February 1860): 57.

119. *Report of the General Superintendent of Common Schools for the year 1859*, 37–39.

120. *Report of the General Superintendent of Common Schools for the year 1860*, 11. Letter of M. W. Cuthbertson, May 15, 1861, Wiley Papers (SHC).

121. *Report of the General Superintendent of Common Schools for the year 1860*, Pt. II, March 1861, 13–15.

122. *Address to the People of North Carolina*, 3, 10, 14.

123. Maddox, *Free School Idea*, 168–169.

124. *Southern School Journal* 2 (1854): 153; 3 (1855): 64.

125. *Southern Literary Messenger* 10 (February 1844): 65; 19 (1853): 298.

126. *Carolina Spartan*, June 28, October 11, 1849, cited in Eelman, "An Educated and Intelligent People Cannot Be Enslaved," Paras. 1, 22, and 36. Maddox, *Free School Idea*, 134.

127. Church, *A Discourse*, 8–9.

128. For more on interracial trading, see Lockley, *Lines in the Sand*, 57–97; Lockley, "Trading Encounters between Non-Elite Whites and African Americans," 25–48. Forret, "Slaves, Poor Whites," 783–824.

129. *Mississippi Free Trader and Natchez Gazette*, July 11, 1848; Thornwell, *Letter to Governor Manning*, 42, 49; "The Free School System in South Carolina" (1856), 155; Trescott, "The States' Duties," 148.

130. *Speech of Mr. Stiles of Chatham*, 8; Stiles, *An Address*, 26.

131. *Report of the School Commissioners*, 18; *31st Annual Report of the Board of Commissioners*, 165.

Afterword

1. These interracial relationships in low county Georgia are described in full in Lockley, *Lines in the Sand*. For the Carolinas, see Forret, *Race Relations at the Margins*.

2. *Mississippi Free Trader*, December 19, 1849.

3. *Address to the People*, 2, 10.

4. *Southern School Journal*, March 1855, 30.

Bibliography

Manuscript Sources

Acts of Georgia. Records of the States of the United States. Cambridge University Library.

Anderson County, Petitions to the Commissioners of the Poor, 1850–1853. South Carolina Archives, Columbia.

Anderson, Edward Clifford. Papers. Southern Historical Collection, University of North Carolina at Chapel Hill.

Anonymous Carpenters Book, 1853–1854. Georgia Historical Society, Savannah.

Ashe County, Minutes of the Wardens of the Poor, 1832–1855. North Carolina State Archives, Raleigh.

Auditor of Public Accounts, Overseers of the Poor Returns. Library of Virginia, Richmond.

Ball Family Papers. South Carolina Historical Society, Charleston.

Beaufort College Minutes, 1795–1860. South Caroliniana Library, Columbia.

Beaufort County, Minutes of the Wardens of the Poor, 1839–1868. North Carolina State Archives, Raleigh.

Beaufort Female Benevolent Society Minutes, 1814–1860. South Caroliniana Library, Columbia.

Beverly, Frances. Papers. University of South Alabama, Mobile.

Broadside on Education, 1845. Virginia Historical Society.

Buncombe County, Court of Common Pleas Minutes, 1792–1865. North Carolina State Archives, Raleigh.

Buncombe County, Court of Pleas and Quarter Sessions, Execution Docket, 1825–1861. North Carolina State Archives, Raleigh.

Buncombe County, Miscellaneous Records, 1786–1946. North Carolina State Archives, Raleigh.

Buncombe County, Record of Inventories, 1822–1929. North Carolina State Archives, Raleigh.

Can't Get Away Club, Typescript History. Historic Mobile Preservation Society Archives, Mobile.

Cathy, Joseph. Papers. North Carolina State Archives, Raleigh.

Charleston Orphan House Papers. Charleston County Public Library, Charleston.

Charleston Poor House Papers. Charleston County Public Library, Charleston.

Chatham County, Inferior Court Minutes, 1790–1805, 1855–1867. Georgia Archives, Morrow.

Claiborne, Mary Anna. Account Book. Virginia Historical Society, Richmond.

Cleveland County, Minutes of the Wardens of the Poor, 1847–1868. North Carolina State Archives, Raleigh.

Craven County, School Records. North Carolina State Archives, Raleigh.

Craven County, Wardens of the Poor Minutes, 1837–1871. North Carolina State Archives, Raleigh.

Craven County, Wardens of the Poor Records, 1803–1861. North Carolina State Archives, Raleigh.

Cuyler, Telamon. Collection. Hargrett Rare Books and Manuscripts Library, University of Georgia, Athens.

Duncan, William. Papers. Georgia Historical Society, Savannah.

Duplin County, St. Gabriel's Parish, Wardens' Records, 1799–1817. North Carolina State Archives, Raleigh.

Effingham County, Inferior Court Minutes, 1832–1872. Georgia Archives, Morrow.

Egmont Papers. Hargrett Rare Books and Manuscripts Library, University of Georgia, Athens.

Fellowship Society Minutes, 1762–1858. South Caroliniana Library, Columbia.

Female Charitable Society of Charleston Neck Minutes, 1824–1860. South Carolina Historical Society, Charleston.

Female Seamen's Friend Society Minutes, in Mrs. Valerie Burroughs Papers, Special Collections, Duke University Library, Durham.

Few, William. Collection. Georgia Archives, Morrow.

Fiske, Nathan W., Manuscripts. Newberry Library, Chicago.

Fluvanna County, Overseers of the Poor Minutes, 1844–1914. Library of Virginia, Richmond.

Garland, William Harris. Papers. Southern Historical Collection, University of North Carolina at Chapel Hill.

General Assembly. Annual Reports of the Comptroller General. Reports of the Transient Poor Fund. South Carolina Archives, Columbia.

General Assembly Papers. Governor's Messages. South Carolina Archives, Columbia.

General Assembly Records. Free School Reports. South Carolina Archives, Columbia.

Georgia House of Representatives Journals, Georgia Archives.

Georgia Infirmary Minutes, 1833–1865. Georgia Historical Society, Savannah.

German Friendly Society Records (Charleston). South Caroliniana Library, Columbia.

Granville County, Records of the Wardens of the Poor, 1787–1868. North Carolina State Archives, Raleigh.

Greene County, Inferior Court Minutes, 1852. Georgia Archives, Morrow.

Greene County, School Commissioners Minutes, 1856–1869. Georgia Archives, Morrow.

Gwinnett County, Inferior Court Minutes, 1820–1832. Georgia Archives, Morrow.

Hebrew Orphan Society Minutes (Charleston). South Caroliniana Library, Columbia.

Hibernian Society Minutes (Charleston). South Caroliniana Library, Columbia.

Jones, Governor James. Papers. North Carolina State Archives, Raleigh.

Ladies Benevolent Society Minutes. South Caroliniana Library, Columbia.

Ladies Fuel Society Minutes, 1832–1860. South Carolina Historical Society, Charleston.

Lancaster District, Minutes of the Commissioners of the Poor, 1853–1868. South Carolina Archives, Columbia.

Lincoln County, Apprenticeship Bonds, 1805–1831. Georgia Archives, Morrow.

Lincoln County, Inferior Court Minutes, 1835–1867. Georgia Archives, Morrow.

Lincoln County, Poor School Minutes, 1852–1870. Georgia Archives, Morrow.

Lincoln County, Wardens of the Poor Records, 1820–1868. North Carolina State Archives, Raleigh.

Mackay-Stiles Papers. Southern Historical Collection, University of North Carolina at Chapel Hill.

Madison County, Miscellaneous Records, 1851–1932, Box 4 Folder: Wardens of the Poor Records 1859–1861. North Carolina State Archives, Raleigh.

Medical Society of South Carolina Minutes. Waring Library, Medical University of South Carolina, Charleston.

Mobile Female Benevolent Society Records. University of South Alabama, Mobile.

Mobile Protestant Orphanage Asylum Society Admission Rolls. Baptist Children's Home, Mobile.

Mobile Protestant Orphanage Asylum Society Minutes, 1839–1966. Historic Mobile Preservation Society Archives, Mobile.

Montgomery City Council Minutes. Alabama Department of Archives and History, Montgomery.

Montgomery County, Guardian's Records. Alabama Department of Archives and History, Montgomery.

Natchez Female Benevolent Society Papers. Center for American History, University of Texas at Austin.

New England Society Papers. South Carolina Historical Society, Charleston.

New Hanover County, Wardens of the Poor Minutes, 1850–1868. North Carolina State Archives, Raleigh.

Norfolk Female Orphan Society Minutes, 1816–1853. University of Virginia Library, Charlottesville.

North Carolina General Assembly Session Records. North Carolina State Archives, Raleigh.

Orange County, Minutes of the Wardens of the Poor, 1832–1856. North Carolina State Archives, Raleigh.

Pasquotank County, Minutes of the Wardens of the Poor, 1807–1831. North Carolina State Archives, Raleigh.

Patton, James W. Papers. Southern Historical Collection, University of North Carolina at Chapel Hill.

Petersburg Benevolent Mechanics Association Records. Virginia Historical Society, Richmond.

Richmond Amicable Society Minutes, 1788–1816. Virginia Historical Society, Richmond.

Richmond City, Hustings Court, Minutes of the Overseers of the Poor, 1817–1828. Library of Virginia, Richmond.

Richmond County, Virginia, Overseers of the Poor Records, 1786–1842. Library of Virginia, Richmond.

Richmond Female Humane Association Papers. Virginia Historical Society, Richmond.

Richmond Male Orphan Society Papers. Virginia Historical Society, Richmond.

Roper Hospital, Minutes of the Trustees. Waring Library, Medical University of South Carolina, Charleston.

Rowan County, North Carolina, Records of the Wardens of the Poor, 1771–1871. North Carolina State Archives, Raleigh.

St. David's Society Minutes. South Caroliniana Library, Columbia.

St. George's Society Records. South Carolina Historical Society, Charleston.

St. Philip's Episcopal Church, Vestry Minutes. South Carolina Archives, Columbia.

Sampson County, Minutes of the Vestry—Wardens of the Poor, 1785–1824. North Carolina State Archives, Raleigh.

Savannah Benevolent Association Minutes, 1854–1928. Georgia Historical Society, Savannah.

Savannah Board of Health Minutes. Georgia Historical Society, Savannah.

Savannah City Council Minutes. Georgia Historical Society, Savannah.

Savannah Female Asylum Minutes, 1810–1843. Georgia Historical Society, Savannah.

Savannah Free School Society Minutes, 1816–1856. Georgia Historical Society, Savannah.

Savannah Poorhouse and Hospital Minutes, 1836–1876. Georgia Archives, Morrow.

Savannah Port Papers. Special Collections, Duke University Library, Durham.

Savannah Port Society Minutes, 1843–1860. Georgia Historical Society, Savannah.

Shenandoah County, Virginia, Overseers of the Poor Account Books. Southern Historical Collection, University of North Carolina at Chapel Hill.

Smith, Archibald T. Papers. Southern Historical Collection, University of North Carolina at Chapel Hill.

Society for the Orphan and Destitute Female Children of Columbia Minutes, 1839–1865. South Caroliniana Library, Columbia.

Society for the Relief of the Widows and Orphans of the Clergy of the Church of England in the Province of South Carolina Papers, 1762–1813. South Carolina Historical Society, Charleston.

South Carolina Grand Jury Presentments. South Carolina Archives, Columbia.

Spotsylvania County, Minutes of the Overseers of the Poor, 1791. Library of Virginia, Richmond.

Story, Elliott Lemuel. Diary. Virginia Historical Society, Richmond.

Timmerman, Elijah. Papers. South Caroliniana Library, Columbia.

Tuscaloosa Female Benevolent Society Minutes, 1853–1869. Hoole Special Collections, University of Alabama Library, Tuscaloosa.

U.S. Census Bureau. Microfilm copies of each state's surviving manuscript returns are respectively in the Library of Virginia, the North Carolina State Archives, the South Carolina Archives, the Georgia Archives and the Alabama Department of Archives and History. Also available online at http://www.census.gov.

Valentine, William D. Papers. Southern Historical Collection, University of North Carolina at Chapel Hill.

Wadley, Sarah Lois. Diary. Southern Historical Collection, University of North Carolina at Chapel Hill.

Widow's Society Records. Georgia Historical Society, Savannah.

Wiley, Calvin H. Papers. North Carolina State Archives, Raleigh.

Wiley, Calvin H. Papers. Southern Historical Collection, University of North Carolina at Chapel Hill.

Williamsburg District, Minutes of the Commissioners of the Poor, 1831–1868. South Caroliniana Library, Columbia.

Woodfin, N. W. Papers. Southern Historical Collection, University of North Carolina at Chapel Hill.

Printed Sources

An Account of the Origin and Progress of the Savannah Free School Society. New York: Day and Turner, 1819.

An Account of the Rise, Progress and Present State of the Boston Female Asylum. Boston: Russel and Cutler, 1803.

Act of Incorporation and By-laws of the Hibernian Society of Baltimore. Baltimore: E. John Schmitz, 1960.

Acts of the General Assembly of the State of Georgia. Augusta: Alexander M'Millan, 1794.

Acts of the General Assembly of the State of Georgia. Milledgeville: S. and F. Grantland, 1818.

Acts Passed at the Fourth Annual Session of the General Assembly of the State of Alabama. Cahawba: Wm. B. Allen, 1823.

Acts Passed at the Third General Assembly of the Mississippi Territory. Natchez: T. and S. Terrell, 1805.

Acts Passed by the General Assembly of South Carolina. Charles-Town: Peter Timothy, 1736.

Address to the People of North Carolina: Conference of Teachers and Friends of Education. Raleigh: n.p., 1861.

Alexander, John K. *Render Them Submissive: Responses to Poverty in Philadelphia, 1760–1800.* Amherst: University of Massachusetts Press, 1980.

Allestree, Richard. *The Whole Duty of Man.* Williamsburg: W. Parks, 1746.

Amos, Harriet. "'City Belles': Images and Realities of the Lives of White Women in Antebellum Mobile." *The Alabama Review* 34, no. 1 (January 1981): 3–19.

———. *Cotton City: Urban Development in Antebellum Mobile.* Tuscaloosa: University of Alabama Press, 1985.

Annual Report of the Board of Administrators of the Charity Hospital. New Orleans: The Board, 1839.

Annual Report of the Board of Visitors of the Natchez Institute. Natchez: The Institute, 1854.

Annual Report of the Managers of the Ladies' Benevolent Society. New Orleans: Sherman, Wharton, 1855.

Annual Report of the School Commissioners of Baltimore County. Baltimore: James Lucas, 1854.

"Annual Report," *Southern Evangelical Intelligencer* 2, no. 31 (October 28, 1820): 244–247.

Annual Report of Superintendent of Public Schools, Fourth District, New Orleans, May 15, 1855. New Orleans: Carson and Armstrong, 1855.

Annual Report of Wm. F. Perry, Superintendent of Education of the State of Alabama. Montgomery: N. B. Cloud, 1858.

An Appeal in Behalf of the Ladies Fuel Society of Charleston SC. Charleston: Walker, Evans, 1860.

Ashcraft, Virginia. *Public Care: A History of Public Welfare Legislation in Tennessee.* Knoxville: University of Tennessee Record, 1947.

At a Meeting of the Female Humane Association, February 5th, 1816. Richmond: Ritchie, Trueheart and Duval, 1816.

Atherton, Lewis E. "Mercantile Education in the Antebellum South." *Mississippi Valley Historical Review* 39, no. 4 (March 1953): 623–640.

———. *The Southern Country Store, 1800–1860.* Baton Rouge: Louisiana State University Press, 1949.

Bacon, Thomas. *A Sermon Preached at the Parish Church of St. Peter's in Talbot County, Maryland on Sunday the 14th of October 1750, for the Benefit of a Charity Working School to Be Set Up in the Said Parish for the Maintenance and Education of Orphans and Other Poor Children and Negroes.* London: J. Oliver, 1751.

Bailey, Fred Arthur. *Class and Tennessee's Confederate Generation.* Chapel Hill: University of North Carolina Press, 1987.

———. "Tennessee's Antebellum Society from the Bottom Up." *Southern Studies* 22, no. 3 (Fall 1983): 260–273.

Ball, Charles. *Slavery in the United States: A Narrative of the Life and Adventures of Charles Ball, a Black Man.* New York: J. S. Taylor, 1837.

Baptist, Edward E. *Creating an Old South: Middle Florida's Plantation Frontier before the Civil War.* Chapel Hill: University of North Carolina Press, 2002.

Beeman, Richard R., ed. "Trade and Travel in Post-Revolutionary Virginia: A Diary of an Itinerant Peddler, 1807–1808." *Virginia Magazine of History and Biography* 84, no. 2 (April 1976): 174–188.

Bell, Caryn Cossé. *Revolution, Romanticism and the Afro-Creole Protest Tradition in Louisiana, 1718–1968.* Baton Rouge: Louisiana State University Press, 1997.

Bellinger, E. *Compilation of Laws relating to the Powers and Duties of Commissioners of the Poor in South Carolina.* Columbia: R. W. Gibbes, 1859.

Bellows, Barbara L. *Benevolence among Slaveholders: Assisting the Poor in Charleston, 1670–1860.* Baton Rouge and London: Louisiana State University Press, 1993.

———. "'My Children, Gentlemen, Are My Own': Poor Women, the Urban Elite, and the Bonds of Obligation in Antebellum Charleston." In *The Web of Southern Social Relations: Women Family and Education*, edited by Walter J. Fraser, Jr., R. Frank Saunders, Jr., and Jon L. Wakelyn, 52–71. Athens: University of Georgia Press, 1985.

———. "Tempering the Wind: The Southern Response to Urban Poverty, 1850–1865." Ph.D. diss. University of South Carolina, 1983.

Bend, Joseph G. L. *An Address to the Members of the Protestant Episcopal Church.* Baltimore: Joseph Robinson, 1811.

Bernhard, Virginia. "Poverty and the Social Order in Seventeenth-Century Virginia." *Virginia Magazine of History and Biography* 85, no. 2 (April 1977): 141–155.

Best, John Hardin. "Education in the Forming of the American South." *History of Education Quarterly* 36, no. 1 (Spring 1996): 39–51.

Betts, John Rickards. "American Medical Thought on Exercise as the Road to Health, 1820–1860." *Bulletin of the History of Medicine* 45, no. 2 (March-April 1971): 139–152.

———. "Mind and Body in Early American Thought." *Journal of American History* 54, no. 4 (March 1968): 787–805.

Beverley, Robert. *The History of Virginia.* London: B. and S. Tooke, F. Fayram and J. Clarke, and T. Bickerton, 1722.

Boan, Fern. *A History of Poor Relief Legislation and Administration in Missouri.* Chicago: University of Chicago Press, 1941.

Bolton, Charles. *Poor Whites of the Antebellum South: Tenants and Laborers in Central North Carolina and Northeast Mississippi.* Durham, N.C.: Duke University Press, 1994.

Bolton, S. Charles. *Southern Anglicanism: The Church of England in Colonial South Carolina.* Westport, Conn.: Greenwood Press, 1982.

Bowden, Haygood S. *Two Hundred Years of Education*. Richmond: Dietz Printing, 1932.

Boylan, Anne M. *The Origins of Women's Activism: New York and Boston, 1797–1840*. Chapel Hill: University of North Carolina Press, 2002.

A Brief Account of the Female Humane Association. Baltimore: Warner and Hanna, 1803.

Brown, Roy M. *Public Poor Relief in North Carolina*. Chapel Hill: University of North Carolina Press, 1928.

Buckingham, James Silk. *The Slave States of America*. London: Fisher and Son, 1843.

By-Laws of the Orphan House of Charleston, South Carolina. Revised and Adopted by the Board of Commissioners, 4th April, 1861. Charleston: Evans and Cogswell, 1861.

By-Laws of the Trustees and Rules for the Government of the Poor-house of Baltimore County. Baltimore: P. and R. W. Edes, 1818.

Byrd, Michael Dane. "White Poor and Poor Relief in Charles Town, 1725–1775: A Prosopography." Ph.D. diss. University of South Carolina, 2005.

Calo, Zachary Ryan. "From Poor Relief to the Poorhouse: The Response to Poverty in Prince George's County, Maryland, 1710–1770." *Maryland Historical Magazine* 93, no. 4 (Winter 1998): 393–427.

Candler, Allen D., ed. *The Colonial Records of the State of Georgia*. New York: AMS Press, 1970.

Carr, Lois Green. "The Development of the Maryland Orphan's Court." In *Law, Society and Politics in Early Maryland*, edited by Aubrey C. Land, Lois Green Carr and Papefuse, 41–56. Baltimore: John Hopkins University Press, 1977.

———. "The Foundations of Social Order: Local Government in Colonial Maryland." In *Town and County: Essays on the Structure of Local Government in the American Colonies*, edited by Bruce C. Daniels, 72–110. Middletown, Conn.: Wesleyan University Press, 1978.

Carrol, Douglas G., Jr., and Blanche D. Coll. "The Baltimore Almshouse, an Early History." *Maryland Historical Magazine* 66, no. 2 (Summer 1971): 135–152.

Charter, Constitution and By-Laws of the Petersburg Benevolent Mechanic Association: Origin, January 4, 1825. Petersburg: n.p., 1826.

Chesnut, Mary Boykin. *A Diary from Dixie*. New York: D. Appleton, 1905.

Church, Alonzo. *A Discourse Delivered before the Georgia Historical Society on the Occasion of Its Sixth Anniversary on Wednesday, 12th February 1845*. Savannah: The Society, 1845.

Clark, Christopher. "The Consequences of the Market Revolution in the American North." In *The Market Revolution in America: Social, Political and Religious Expressions*, edited by Melvyn Stokes and Stephen Conway, 23–42. Charlottesville: University of Virginia Press, 1996.

———. *The Roots of Rural Capitalism: Western Massachusetts, 1780–1860*. Ithaca: Cornell University Press, 1990.

Clement, Priscilla Ferguson, "Children and Charity: Orphanages in New Orleans, 1817–1914." *Louisiana History* 27, no. 4 (Fall 1986): 337–352.

———. *Welfare and the Poor in the Nineteenth Century City: Philadelphia 1800–1854.* Toronto: Associated University Presses, 1985.

Cobb, Thomas R. R. *Educational Wants of Georgia: An Address Delivered before the Society of the Alumni of Franklin College.* Athens: Reynolds and Bro., 1857.

Cochran, Thomas Everette. *History of Public Schools in Florida.* Lancaster, Penn.: New Era Printing, 1921.

The Code of the State of Georgia. Atlanta: John H. Seals, 1861.

Constitution and By-Laws of the Female Humane Association of the City of Richmond. Richmond: Shephard and Colin, 1843.

Constitution and By-laws of the Howard Association of Charleston. Charleston: Walker and Evans, 1855.

The Constitution and By-Laws of the St. Andrew's Society of Baltimore. Baltimore: Wm. Woody, 1825.

Constitution and By-Laws of the Society for the Relief of the Indigent Sick. Baltimore: J. F. Wiley, 1869.

Constitution of the Charleston Mechanic Society. Charleston: James and Williams, 1858.

Constitution and First Annual Report for the Protestant Orphan Asylum Society of Mobile. Mobile: Farrow and Dennet, 1860.

Constitution of the Ladies Benevolent Society of Charleston and Regulations for the Visiting Committee. Charleston: A. E. Miller, 1852.

The Constitutional and Additional Rules of the South-Carolina Society. Charles-Town: Peter Timothy, 1770.

Conway, Moncure Daniel. *Free Schools in Virginia: A Plan of Education, Virtue and Thrift vs. Ignorance, Vice and Poverty.* Fredericksburg: Recorder Print, 1850.

Coon, Charles L. *The Beginnings of Public Education in North Carolina: A Documentary History, 1790–1840.* Raleigh: Edwards and Broughton, 1908.

Cooper, Thomas, and David McCord, eds. *The Statutes at Large of South Carolina.* 10 vols. Columbia: n.p., 1836–1841.

Coulter, E. Merton, and Albert B. Saye, *A List of the Early Settlers of Georgia.* Athens: University of Georgia Press, 1949.

Culver, L. Margaretta. "A History of the Baltimore Association for the Improvement of the Condition of the Poor." M.A. diss. Johns Hopkins University, 1923.

Curti, Merle. *Human Nature in American Thought: A History.* Madison: University of Wisconsin Press, 1980.

Dain, Norman. *Disordered Minds: The First Century of Eastern State Hospital in Williamsburg, Virginia, 1766–1866.* Williamsburg: Colonial Williamsburg Foundation, 1971.

Dix, Dorothea L. *Memorial Soliciting a State Hospital for the Protection and Cure of the Insane.* Raleigh: Seaton Gales, 1848.

————. *Memorial Soliciting Enlarged and Improved Accommodations for the Insane of the State of Tennessee*. Nashville: B. R. M'Kennie, 1847.

————. *A Review of the Present Condition of the State Penitentiary of Kentucky*. Frankfort, Ky.: A. G. Hodges, 1846.

Downs, Susan Whitelaw, and Michael W. Sherraden. "The Orphan Asylum in the Nineteenth Century." *Social Service Review* 57, no. 2 (June 1983): 272–290.

Easterby, J. H. *History of the St. Andrew's Society of Charleston, South Carolina*. Charleston: The Society, 1929.

————. *The South Carolina Rice Plantation as Revealed in the Papers of Robert F. W. Allston*. 2nd ed. Columbia: University of South Carolina Press, 2004.

Eelman, Bruce W. "'An Educated and Intelligent People Cannot Be Enslaved': The Struggle for Common Schools in Antebellum Spartanburg, South Carolina." *History of Education Quarterly* 44, no. 2 (Summer 2004): 250–270.

Facts and Hints Relative to Free Schools Addressed Particularly to the People of Albemarle. Charlottesville: James Alexander, 1849.

Finn, Margot C. *The Character of Credit: Personal Debt in English Culture, 1740–1914*. Cambridge: Cambridge University Press, 2003.

First Annual Report of the General Superintendent of Common Schools. Raleigh: W. W. Holden, Printer to the State, 1854.

First Annual Report of the Orphan Asylum and Female Free School of Alexandria. Washington: U.S. House of Representatives Documents, No. 65, January 25, 1833.

First Published Annual Report of the Resident Physician of the Lunatic, Idiot and Epileptic Asylum of the State of Georgia. Milledgeville: n.p., 1845.

Ford, Lacy K., Jr. *The Origins of Southern Radicalism: The South Carolina Upcountry, 1800–1860*. New York: Oxford University Press, 1988.

Forret, Jeff. "Slaves, Poor Whites, and the Underground Economy of the Rural Carolinas." *Journal of Southern History* 70, no. 4 (November 2004): 783–824.

————. *Race Relations at the Margins: Slaves and Poor Whites in the Antebellum Southern Countryside*. Baton Rouge: Louisiana State University Press, 2006.

Fortieth Annual and First Printed Report of the Poydras Female Asylum, together with the Medical Report of B. Stille, M.D. New Orleans: Clark and Brisbin, 1857.

Foster, Gertrude. "A Documentary History of Education in South Carolina." Ph.D. diss. University of South Carolina, 1932.

Fourth Report of the Baltimore Manual Labor School for Indigent Boys. Baltimore: John D. Toy, 1849.

"Fragment Society." *Southern Evangelical Intelligencer*, 2, no. 31 (October 28, 1820): 206.

The Free School Law of the State of Alabama also a Circular of the Superintendent. Montgomery: Advertiser and Gazette Job Office, 1854.

"Free Schools of Charleston." *De Bow's Review* 27, no. 4 (October 1859): 485.

"Free School System in South Carolina." *Southern Quarterly Review* 16, no. 31 (October 1849): 31–53.

"The Free School System of South Carolina." *Southern Quarterly Review* 2, no. 1 (November 1856): 125–160.

The Fundamental Rules and Regulations of the Lancastrian Institution within This City. Richmond: Ritchie, Trueheart and Du-val, 1817.

Gamble, Thomas. *Bethesda, an Historical Sketch.* Savannah: News Print Press, 1902.

Gehman, Mary. *The Free People of Color of New Orleans: An Introduction.* New Orleans: Margaret Media, 1994.

Ginzberg, Lori D. *Women and the Work of Benevolence: Morality, Politics and Class in the Nineteenth Century United States.* New Haven: Yale University Press, 1990.

Gongaware, G. V. *The History of the German Friendly Society of Charleston, South Carolina.* Richmond: Garrett and Massie, 1935.

Goodman, Paul. "The Emergence of Homestead Exemption in the United States: Accommodation and Resistance to the Market Revolution, 1840–1880." *Journal of American History* 80, no. 2 (September 1993): 470–498.

Gordon, Richard Lawrence. "The Development of Louisiana's Public Mental Institutions, 1735–1940." Ph.D. diss. Louisiana State University, 1979.

Governor Hayne's Message. Columbia: A. S. Johnston, 1833.

Governor McDuffie's Message Number 1. n.p.[Columbia] 1836.

Governor's Message and Annual Reports of the Public Officers of the State. Richmond: William F. Ritchie, 1850.

Governor's Message and Annual Reports of the Public Officers of the State. Richmond: William F. Ritchie, 1854.

Governor's Message and Annual Reports of the Public Officers of the State. Richmond: William F. Ritchie, 1855.

Green, Elna C. *This Business of Relief: Confronting Poverty in a Southern City, 1740–1940.* Athens: University of Georgia Press, 2003.

Green, Harvey. *Fit for America: Health, Fitness, Sport and American Society.* New York: Pantheon Books, 1986.

Griffin, C. S. *The Ferment of Reform, 1830–1860.* London: Routledge and Kegan Paul, 1969.

———. *Their Brothers' Keeper: Moral Stewardship in the United States, 1800–1865.* New Brunswick: Rutgers University Press, 1960.

Habersham, J. C. "Savannah Hospital: Clinical Report." *Savannah Journal of Medicine* 2, no. 2 (July 1859): 89–92.

Hahn, Steven, *The Roots of Southern Populism: Yeoman Farmers and the Transformation of the Georgia Upcountry, 1850–1890.* Oxford: Oxford University Press, 1983.

Handbook of Philanthropic and Social Service Agencies in Savannah and Chatham County, Georgia, February 1, 1913. Savannah: Associated Charities, 1913.

Harris, J. William. *Plain Folk and Gentry in a Slave Society: White Liberty and Black Slavery in Augusta's Hinterlands*. Middletown, Conn.: Wesleyan University Press 1985.

Hartdagan, Gerald E. "The Anglican Vestry in Colonial Maryland: A Study in Corporate Responsibility." *Historical Magazine of the Protestant Episcopal Church* 40, nos. 3 and 4 (September and December 1971): 315–335; 461–479.

Haviland, Thomas P. "Of Franklin, Whitefield and the Orphans." *Georgia Historical Quarterly* 29, no. 4 (December 1945): 214–215.

Heale, M. J. "Patterns of Benevolence: Associated Philanthropy in the Cities of New York, 1830–1860." *New York History* 57, no. 1 (January 1976): 53–79.

Henley, S. *A Sermon Preached at Williamsburg, May 5, 1771*. Williamsburg: Mess. Payne, Davies, Elmsley, and Pearch in London, 1771.

Herndon, Ruth Wallis. *Unwelcome Americans: Living on the Margin in Early New England*. Philadelphia: University of Pennsylvania Press, 2001.

A History of the Orphan House and Episcopal Free School Society of All Saints' Church, Fredericktown, Maryland, 1838–1915. n.p., n.d.

History of the St. Andrew's Society of the City of Savannah. Savannah: Kennickell, 1950.

Holcombe, Henry. *The First Fruits in a Series of Letters*. Philadelphia: A. Cochran, 1812.

Hunt, Robert E. "Home, Domesticity and School Reform in Antebellum Alabama." *The Alabama Review* 49, no. 4 (October 1996): 253–275.

Hutchins, Myldred Flanigan. *The History of Poor Law Legislation in Georgia, 1733–1919*. Atlanta: Cherokee, 1985.

Inscoe, John C. *Mountain Masters: Slavery and the Sectional Crises in Western North Carolina*. Knoxville: University of Tennessee Press, 1989.

Inscoe, John C., and Gordon B. McKinney. *The Heart of Confederate Appalachia: Western North Carolina in the Civil War*. Chapel Hill: University of North Carolina Press, 2000.

The Institution of the Boston Female Asylum, Organized September 26, 1800. Boston: Russel and Cutler, 1801.

Jenkins, William Thomas. "Ante-bellum Macon and Bibb County, Georgia." Ph.D. diss. University of Georgia, 1966.

Johansen, Mary Caroll. "'Intelligence, Though Overlooked': Education for Black Women in the Upper South, 1800–1840." *Maryland Historical Magazine* 93, no. 4 (Winter 1998): 443–465.

Johnson, Christopher S. "Poor Relief in Antebellum Mississippi." *Journal of Mississippi History* 49, no. 1 (February 1987): 1–21.

Johnson, Guion Griffis. *Antebellum North Carolina: A Social History*. Chapel Hill: University of North Carolina Press, 1937.

Johnson, Michael P., and James L. Roark. *Black Masters: A Free Family of Color in the Old South*. New York: Norton, 1984.

———. "'A Middle Ground': Free Mulattoes and the Friendly Moralist Society of Antebellum Charleston." *Southern Studies* 21, no. 3 (Fall, 1983): 246–265.

Jones, Charles Edgeworth. *Education in Georgia.* Washington: Government Printing Office, 1889.

Journal of the House of Delegates of Virginia. Richmond: Samuel Shepherd, 1845.

Journal of the House of Delegates of Virginia. Richmond: Samuel Shepherd, 1846.

Journal of the Proceedings of the 33rd Annual Convention of the Protestant Episcopal Church in the Diocese of Georgia. Macon, Ga.: Benjamin F. Green, 1855.

"Juvenile Female Benevolent Society of Columbia." *Southern Evangelical Intelligencer* 1, no. 13 (June 19, 1819): 98–99.

Kaestle, Carl F. *The Evolution of an Urban School System: New York City, 1750–1850.* Cambridge, Mass.: Harvard University Press, 1973.

———. *Pillars of the Republic: Common Schools and American Society, 1780–1860.* New York: Hill and Wang, 1983.

Kelly, Joseph. "Charleston's Bishop John England and American Slavery." *New Hibernia Review* 5, no. 4 (Winter 2001): 48–56.

Klebaner, B. J. "Public Poor Relief in America, 1790–1860." Ph.D. diss. Columbia University, 1952.

———. "Public Poor Relief in Charleston, 1800–1860." *South Carolina Historical Magazine* 45, no. 4 (December 1954): 210–220.

———. "Some Aspects of North Carolina Public Poor Relief, 1700–1860." *North Carolina Historical Review* 31, no. 4 (October 1954): 449–492.

Knight, Edgar W. *A Documentary History of Education in the South before 1860.* Chapel Hill: University of North Carolina Press, 1950.

The Laws Now in Force Which Relate to the Duties of the Overseers of the Poor. Richmond: Samuel Shepherd, 1832.

Laws in Relation to the Overseers of the Poor. Richmond: Enquirer Print, 1860.

Laws of the State of Mississippi. Jackson: Silas Brown, State Printer, 1825.

Laws of the State of North Carolina. Raleigh: Thomas J. Lemay, 1845.

Lebsock, Suzanne. *The Free Women of Petersburg: Status and Culture in a Southern Town.* New York and London: Norton, 1984.

Lee, F. D., and J. L. Agnew. *Historical Record of the City of Savannah.* Savannah: J. H. Estill, 1869.

Lindsley, Philip. *The Cause of Education in Tennessee: An Address Delivered to the Young Gentlemen Admitted to the Degree of Bachelor of Arts at the First Commencement of the University of Nashville, October 4, 1826.* Nashville: Hunt, Tardiff, 1833.

Linn, Rev. C. A. *The History of the German Friendly Society of Savannah, Georgia, 1837–1937.* Savannah: The Society, 1937.

Lockley, Timothy James. *Lines in the Sand: Race and Class in Lowcountry Georgia, 1750–1860.* Athens: University of Georgia Press, 2001.

———. "Moulding the Poor Children of Antebellum Savannah." In *Bound to*

Labor: Varieties of Apprenticeship in Early America, edited by John E. Murray and Ruth Wallis Herndon. Forthcoming, Ithaca: Cornell University Press.

———. "The Purpose of Public Poor Relief in Buncombe County, North Carolina, 1792–1860." *North Carolina Historical Review* 80, no. 1 (January 2003): 28–51.

———. "Rural Poor Relief in Colonial South Carolina." *The Historical Journal* 48, no. 4 (December 2005): 955–976.

———. "Spheres of Influence: Working Black and White Women in Antebellum Savannah." In *Neither Lady nor Slave: Working Women of the Old South*, edited by Susanna Delfino and Michele Gillespie, 102–120. Chapel Hill: University of North Carolina Press, 2002.

———. "Trading Encounters between Non-Elite Whites and African Americans in Savannah, 1790–1860." *Journal of Southern History* 66, no. 1 (February, 2000): 25–48.

Maddox, William A. *The Free School Idea in Virginia before the Civil War*. New York: Teachers College, 1918.

Mann, Bruce. *Republic of Debtors: Bankruptcy in the Age of American Independence*. Cambridge, Mass.: Harvard University Press, 2002.

Marriages of Chatham County, Georgia. Vol. 1, 1748–1852; Vol. 2, 1852–1877. Savannah: Georgia Historical Society, 1993.

Martineau, Harriet. *Retrospect of Western Travel*. New York: Harper and Brothers, 1838.

Mathews, Forrest David. "The Politics of Education in the Deep South: Georgia and Alabama, 1830–1860." Ph.D. diss. Columbia University, 1965.

Matthews, Jean V. *Toward a New Society: American Thought and Culture, 1800–1830*. Boston: Twayne, 1991.

Maxwell, William. *An Oration on the Improvement of the People Spoken before the Literary and Philosophical Society of Hampden Sydney College*. Norfolk: Thomas G. Broughton, 1826.

Mayes, Edward. *History of Education in Mississippi*. Washington: Government Printing Office, 1899.

McCandless, Peter. "Curative Asylum, Custodial Hospital: The South Carolina Lunatic Asylum and State Hospital, 1828–1920." In *The Confinement of the Insane: International Perspectives, 1800–1965*, edited by Roy Porter and David Wright, 173–192. Cambridge: Cambridge University Press, 2003.

———. *Moonlight, Magnolias and Madness: Insanity in South Carolina from the Colonial Period to the Progressive Era*. Chapel Hill: University of North Carolina Press, 1996.

McCurry, Stephanie. *Masters of Small Worlds: Yeoman Households, Gender Relations and the Political Culture of the Antebellum South Carolina Low Country*. New York: Oxford University Press, 1995.

McGill, M. A. *The Golden Jubilee of the Catholic Orphans of Mobile, Ala.* Mobile: Graham and Delchamps, 1891.

Melder, Keith. "Ladies Bountiful: Organised Women's Benevolence in Early Nineteenth Century America." *New York History* 48, no. 3 (July 1967): 231–254.

Mellown, Robert O. "The Construction of the Alabama Insane Hospital, 1852–1861." *Alabama Review* 38, no. 2 (April 1985): 83–104.

The Memorial of Sundry Citizens of the County of Halifax to the Virginia Legislature Praying for the Establishment of Free Schools in the State. Richmond: Macfarlane and Fergusson, 1854.

Meriwether, Colyer. *History of Higher Education in South Carolina.* Washington: Government Printing Office, 1889.

Message of His Excellency James H. Adams. Columbia: E. H. Britton, 1855.

Message No. 1 of His Excellency Governor Means. Columbia: Johnson and Cavis, 1852.

Message No. 1 of His Excellency R. F. W. Allston. Columbia: T. S. Piggot, 1857.

Message No. 1 of His Excellency William Aiken. Columbia: A S. Johnson, 1846.

Minutes of the Union Society, Being an Abstract of Existing Records from 1750 to 1858. Savannah: John M. Cooper, 1860.

Mobley, Johnson Bland, Jr. *The Ladies Benevolent Society of Columbia, South Carolina.* Columbia: Piedmont Printmakers, 1993.

Muldrew, Craig. *The Economy of Obligation: The Culture of Credit and Social Relations in Early Modern England.* New York: St. Martin's Press, 1998.

Murdoch, Richard K. "Letters and Papers of Dr. Daniel Turner: A Rhode Islander in South Georgia." *Georgia Historical Quarterly* 53, nos. 3 and 4 (Fall and Winter 1969): 341–393, 476–509; 54, nos. 1 and 2 (Spring and Summer 1970): 91–122, 244–282.

Murray, Gail S. "Charity within the Bonds of Race and Class: Female Benevolence in the Old South." *South Carolina Historical Magazine* 96, no. 1 (January 1995): 54–70.

———. "Poverty and Its Relief in the Antebellum South. Perceptions and Realities in Three Selected Cities: Charleston, Nashville, and New Orleans." Ph.D. diss. Memphis State University, 1991.

Murray, John E. "Bound by Charity: The Abandoned Children of Late Eighteenth Century Charleston." In *Down and Out in Early America*, edited by Billy G. Smith, 213–232. University Park: Pennsylvania State University Press, 2004.

———. "Fates of Orphans: Poor Children in Antebellum Charleston." *Journal of Interdisciplinary History* 33, no. 4 (Spring 2003), 519–545.

———. "Literacy Acquisition in an Orphanage: A Historical-Longitudinal Case Study." *American Journal of Education* 110, no. 1 (February 2004): 172–195.

Murray, Gail S., and Ruth Wallis Herndon. "Markets for Children in Early America: A Political Economy of Pauper Apprenticeship." *The Journal of Economic History* 62, no. 2 (June 2002): 356–382.

Nagy, J. Emerick. "The South Nashville Institute." *Tennessee Historical Quarterly* 36, no. 2 (Summer 1977): 180–196.

———. "Wanted: A Teacher for the Nashville English School." *Tennessee Historical Quarterly* 21, no. 2 (Summer 1962): 171–185.

Nelson, John K. *A Blessed Company: Parishes, Parsons and Parishioners in Anglican Virginia, 1690–1776*. Chapel Hill: University of North Carolina Press, 2001.

Olivas, J. Richard. "'God Helps Those Who Help Themselves': Religious Explanations of Poverty in Colonial Massachusetts, 1630–1776." In *Down and Out in Early America*, edited by Billy G. Smith, 262–288. University Park: Pennsylvania State University Press, 2004.

Oliver, Robert. "A Crumbling Fortress: The Tennessee Lunatic Asylum, 1837–1865." *Tennessee Historical Quarterly* 54, no. 2 (Summer 1995): 124–139.

"On Patriotism." *Christian Monitor* 1, no. 23 (December 9, 1815): 181.

Ordinances of the City of Baltimore and Acts of Assembly of the State of Maryland, Relating to the Public Schools in the City of Baltimore. Baltimore: J. Lucas, 1852.

Oxley, Geoffrey W. *Poor Relief in England and Wales, 1601–1834*. London: David and Charles, 1974.

Patton, James. *The Biography of James Patton*. Asheville: n.p., 1850.

Pease Jane H., and William H. Pease. *The Web of Progress: Private Values and Public Styles in Boston and Charleston, 1828–1843*. Oxford: Oxford University Press, 1985.

Phillips, Christopher. *Freedom's Port: The African American Community of Baltimore, 1790–1860*. Urbana and Chicago: University of Illinois Press, 1997.

Pickett, Albert J. *Eight Days in New-Orleans in February, 1847*. Montgomery. Ala.: A. J. Pickett, 1847.

Pinckney, Henry Laurens. *An Address Delivered before the Methodist Benevolent Society, July 1835*. Charleston: E. J. Van Brunt, 1835.

Pippin, Kathryn A. "The Common School Movement in the South, 1840–1860." Ph.D. diss. University of North Carolina, 1977.

Porter, Benjamin Faneuil. *The Past and the Present: A Discourse Delivered before the Erosophic Society of the University of Alabama*. Tuscaloosa: M. D. J. Slade, 1845.

Pratt, John W. *An Address Delivered before the Society of the Alumni of the University of Alabama, July 5th 1850*. Tuscaloosa: M. D. J. Slade, 1850.

The Proceedings of the 66th Anniversary of the Orphan House of Charleston, South Carolina. Charleston: A. E. Miller, 1855.

Proceedings of the 108th Anniversary of the Union Society at Bethesda, April 23rd 1858. Savannah: John M. Cooper, 1858.

Proceedings of the 109th Anniversary of the Union Society at Bethesda, April 25, 1859. Savannah: E. J. Purse, 1859.

Pyburn, Nita Katharine. *The History of the Development of a Single System of Education in Florida*. Tallahassee: Florida State University, 1954.

Quist, John W. *Restless Visionaries: The Social Roots of Antebellum Reform in Alabama and Michigan.* Baton Rouge: Louisiana State University Press, 1997.

Ravenscroft, John S. *A Sermon Delivered on the Anniversary of the Female Benevolent Society, Raleigh, on Sunday the 25th July 1824.* Raleigh: J. Gales and Sons, 1824.

Reinders, Robert C. "New England Influences on the Formation of Public Schools in New Orleans." *Journal of Southern History* 30, no. 2 (May 1964): 181–195.

Reisner, Edward H. *The Evolution of the Common School.* New York: Macmillan, 1930.

Report of the Board of Commissioners of Free Schools to the Citizens of Charleston. Charleston: Walker and Evans, 1857.

Reports of the Board of Directors and Superintendent of the Asylum for the Insane of North-Carolina. Raleigh: Holden and Wilson, Printers to the State, 1857.

Report of Charles C. Jones, Jr., Mayor, of the City of Savannah for the Year ending September 30, 1861. Savannah: John M. Cooper, 1861.

Report of Edward C. Anderson, Mayor, of the City of Savannah for the Year ending 31st October 1856. Savannah: Geo. N. Nichols, 1856.

Report on the Free Colored Poor of the City of Charleston. Charleston: Burges and James, 1842.

Reports on the Free School System to the General Assembly of South Carolina. Columbia: A. H. Pemberton, State Printer, 1840.

Report of the General Superintendent of Common Schools for the Year 1859. Raleigh: Holden and Wilson, Printers to the State, 1860.

Report of the General Superintendent of Common Schools for the Year 1860. Raleigh: Holden and Wilson, Printers to the State, 1861.

Report of James P. Screven, Mayor, of the City of Savannah for the Year ending 31st October 1857. Savannah: E. J. Purse, 1857.

Report of the President of the Howard Association of Charleston. Charleston: Walker, Evans, 1858.

Report on Public Education by Mr. [David W.] Lewis of Hancock. Milledgeville, Ga.: Broughton, Nisbet and Barnes, 1860.

Report and Proceedings on the Subject of a House of Refuge. Baltimore: Benjamin Edes, 1830.

Report of the School Commissioners. Baltimore: James Lucas, 1855.

Report of the Superintendent of Education of the State of Alabama. Montgomery: Brittan and Blue, State Printers, 1855.

Report of Thomas M. Turner, Mayor, of the City of Savannah for the Year ending 31st October 1859. Savannah: John M. Cooper, 1859.

Report of the Trustees of the Alms-house for Baltimore City and County, 1827. Baltimore: n.p., 1827.

Report of the Trustees, Superintendent and Resident Physician of the Lunatic Asylum of the State of Georgia for the Years 1858 and 1859. Milledgeville, Ga.: Federal Union, 1859.

Revised Constitution and By-Laws of the Raleigh Female Benevolent Society Adopted July 23rd 1823. With Reports of the Society from Its Commencement. Raleigh: J. Gales and Son, 1823.

Revised Statutes of the State of North Carolina. Raleigh: Turner and Hughes, 1837.

Rocke, Emma L. "An Englishman's Impressions of Alabama in 1846." *South Atlantic Quarterly* 7, no. 3 (July 1908): 223–231.

Rogers, William Warren, Robert David Ward, Leah Rawls Atkins, and Wayne Flynt. *Alabama: The History of a Deep South State.* Tuscaloosa and London: University of Alabama Press, 1994.

Rosengarten, Theodore. *Tombee: Portrait of a Cotton Planter.* New York: William Morrow, 1986.

Rothman, David J. *The Discovery of the Asylum: Social Order and Disorder in the New Republic.* Boston and Toronto: Little, Brown, 1971.

Rotundo, E. Anthony. "Body and Soul: Changing Ideals of American Middle Class Manhood, 1770–1920." *Journal of Social History* 16, no. 4 (Summer 1983): 23–38.

Rules and By-Laws of the Savannah Poor-House and Hospital Society. Savannah: Philip D. Woolhopter, 1810.

Rules of the Charleston Carpenters Society. Charleston: Gabriel Bouetheau, 1805.

Rules of the Fellowship Society, Established at Charles-Town, South-Carolina April 4, 1762. Charles-Town: Charles Crouch, 1769.

Rules and Orders of the Baltimore Benevolent Society. Baltimore: Samuel Sower, 1796.

Rules and Regulations of the Brown Fellowship Society Established at Charleston, S.C. 1st November, 1790. Charleston: J. B. Nixon, 1844.

Rules and Regulations of the Female Benevolent Society of Columbia, January 20, 1824. Columbia: Christian Herald, 1834.

Rules and Regulations for the Government of the Lancasterian School . . . called the "Anderson Seminary." Richmond: Pseud, 1830.

Rules and Regulations for the Government of the Richmond Lancastrian School. Richmond: J. Warrock, 1834.

Rules and Regulations of the Richmond Female Humane Society. Richmond: n.p., c. 1807.

Rules of the South Carolina Society. Charleston: A. E. Miller, 1842.

Rules of the Winyaw Indigo Society with a Short History of the Society. Charleston: Walker, Evans and Cogswell, 1874.

Salley, A. S., Jr., ed. *Minutes of the Vestry of St. Helena's Parish, South Carolina, 1726–1812.* Columbia: State Press, 1919.

The Savannah Benevolent Association. Savannah: The Morning News Print, 1896.

Scott, Anne F. *Natural Allies: Women's Associations in American History.* Urbana: University of Illinois Press, 1981.

Second Annual Report of the Dorcas Benevolent Society of West Baltimore Station, March 1842. Baltimore: Richard J. Matchett, 1842.

The Second Annual Report of the Rector and Managers of the Church Home. Baltimore: Joseph Robinson, 1857.

"2nd Annual Report," *Southern Evangelical Intelligencer* 1, no. 27 (September 25, 1819): 215.

Second Annual Report of the Union Protestant Infirmary of the City of Baltimore. Baltimore: W. M. Innes, 1857.

Sellers, Charles. *The Market Revolution: Jacksonian America, 1815–1846*. Oxford: Oxford University Press, 1991.

Sermon and Reports at the Second Anniversary Celebration of the Church Home. Charleston: A. E. Miller, 1852.

Sermon and Reports at the Fourth Anniversary Celebration of the Church Home. Charleston: A. E. Miller, 1854.

Sermon and Reports at the Fifth Anniversary Celebration of the Church Home. Charleston: A. E. Miller, 1855.

Sermon and Reports at the Sixth Anniversary Celebration of the Church Home. Charleston: A. E. Miller, 1856.

Sermon and Reports at the Seventh Anniversary Celebration of the Church Home. Charleston: A. E. Miller, 1857.

Sermon and Reports at the Eighth Anniversary Celebration of the Church Home. Charleston: A. E. Miller, 1858.

Sermons on Various Subjects by the Late Henry Kollock D.D. Savannah: S. C. and I. Schenck, 1822.

Services and Addresses at the Opening of the Church Home April 15, 1851. Charleston: A. E. Miller, 1851.

Seventh Annual Report of the Trustees of the Georgia Academy for the Blind in Macon, Jan. 1858. Milledgeville, Ga.: Federal Union, 1858.

Sheller, Tina H. "The Origins of Public Education in Baltimore, 1825–1829." *History of Education Quarterly* 22, no. 1 (Spring 1982): 23–44.

Siler, William H. "The Anglican Parish Vestry in Colonial Virginia." *Journal of Southern History* 22, no. 3 (August 1956): 310–337

Sixth Annual Report of the Commissioners for the Georgia Asylum for the Deaf and Dumb at Cave Spring, Ga., July 1, 1855. Macon: Benjamin F. Griffin, 1855.

Slack, Paul. *The English Poor Law, 1531–1782*. Cambridge: Cambridge University Press, 1990.

"The Society of the Sisters of Charity." *Southern Evangelical Intelligencer* 1, no. 21 (August 14, 1819): 175.

Soltow, Lee, and Edward Stevens. *The Rise of Literacy and the Common School in the United States*. Chicago and London: University of Chicago Press, 1981.

Sondley, F. A. *A History of Buncombe County, North Carolina*. Asheville: Advocate Printing Co. 1930.

The South Carolina Society for the Advancement of Learning: Report on the State of Free Schools. Columbia: Telescope Office, 1835.

The Southern Reader or Child's Second Reading Book. Charleston: Wm R. Babcock and M'Carter, 1841.

Speech of Mr. Stiles of Chatham on the Subject of Common-School Education. Milledgeville: Broughton, Nisbet and Barnes, 1856.

Stacey, Christopher L. "The Political Culture of Slavery and Public Poor Relief in the Antebellum South." *Journal of Mississippi History* 63, no. 2 (July 2001): 129–145.

The State Records of North Carolina, v. 24, Laws 1777–1788. Wilmington, N.C.: Colonial Records Project, 1994.

Steffen, Charles G. "Changes in the Organisation of Artisan Production in Baltimore, 1790 to 1820." *The William and Mary Quarterly* 3rd Ser. 36, no. 1 (January 1979): 101–117.

Stiles, William H. *An Address before the Alpha Pi Delta Society of the Cherokee Baptist College, Delivered at the Commencement on the 14th July 1858.* Savannah: George P. Nichols, 1858.

Stokes, Melvyn, and Stephen Conway. *The Market Revolution in America: Social, Political and Religious Expressions.* Charlottesville: University of Virginia Press, 1996.

Sunley, Emil McKee. *The Kentucky Poor Law 1792–1936.* Chicago: University of Chicago Press, 1942.

"System of Common Schools." *Southern Quarterly Review* 6, no. 12 (October 1844): 453–482.

Tenth Report of the Directors of the Baltimore Manual Labor School for Indigent Boys. Baltimore: John W. Woods, 1855.

The Third Annual Report of the Orphans Home, Corner of Constance and Fourth Streets, Fourth District. New Orleans: Daily Delta Steam Press Print, 1856.

Third Annual Report of the Trustees of the Georgia Academy for the Blind in Macon, January 1855. Milledgeville, Ga.: State Printers, 1855.

31st Annual Report of the Board of Commissioners of Public Schools to the Mayor and City Council of Baltimore. Baltimore: Bull and Tuttle, 1860.

Thornwell, Dr. James Henley. *Letter to Governor Manning on Public Instruction in South Carolina.* Charleston: News and Courier Book Press, 1885 [orig. pub. 1853].

Townsend, Camilla. *Tales of Two Cities—Race and Economic Culture in Early Republican North and South America: Guayaquil, Ecuador, and Baltimore, Maryland.* Austin: University of Texas Press, 2000.

Trescott, Wm. H. "The States' Duties in regard to Popular Education." *Debow's Review* 20, no. 2 (February 1856): 143–156.

Tripp, Steven Elliott. *Yankee Town, Southern City: Race and Class Relations in Civil War Lynchburg.* New York: New York University Press, 1997.

Turnbull, L. Minerva. "Early Public Schools in Norfolk and Its Vicinity." *William and Mary Quarterly* 2nd ser. 12, no. 1 (January 1932): 4–9.

Twelfth Annual Report of the Board of Managers of the Charleston Port Society. Charleston: Observer Office, 1835.

12th Annual Report of the School Commissioners of Baltimore County. Baltimore: J.W.B., 1862.

Varon, Elizabeth R. *We Mean to Be Counted: White Women and Politics in Antebellum Virginia.* Chapel Hill: University of North Carolina Press, 1998.

Vinovskis, Maris A. "Trends in Massachusetts Education, 1826–1860." *History of Education Quarterly* 12, no. 4 (Winter 1972): 501–529.

Vogt, Daniel C. "Poor Relief in Frontier Mississippi, 1798–1832." *Journal of Mississippi History* 51, no. 2 (August 1989): 181–199.

Walters, Ronald G. *American Reformers, 1815–1860.* New York: Hill and Wang, 1997.

A Warning to the Citizens of Baltimore. Baltimore: n.p., 1821.

Waterhouse, Richard. "The Responsible Gentry of Colonial South Carolina: A Study in Local Government, 1670–1770." In *Town and County: Essays on the Structure of Local Government in the American colonies,* edited by Bruce C. Daniels, 166–174. Middletown, Conn.: Wesleyan University Press, 1978.

Watkinson, James D. "'Fit Objects for Charity': Community, Race, Faith and Welfare in Antebellum Lancaster County, Virginia, 1817–1860." *Journal of the Early Republic* 21, no. 1 (Spring 2001): 41–70.

———. "Reluctant Scholars: Apprentices and the Petersburg Virginia Benevolent Mechanics' Association School." *History of Education Quarterly* 36, no. 4 (Winter 1996): 429–448.

———. "Rogues, Vagabonds and Fit Objects: The Treatment of the Poor in Antebellum Virginia." *Virginia Cavalcade* 49, no. 1 (Winter 2000): 17–29.

Watson, Alan D. "Orphanage in Colonial North Carolina: Edgecombe County as a Case Study." *North Carolina Historical Review* 52, no. 2 (April 1975): 105–119.

———. "Public Poor Relief in Colonial North Carolina." *North Carolina Historical Review* 54, no. 4 (October 1977): 347–366.

Watson, Harry L. "Slavery and Development in a Dual Economy: The South and the Market Revolution." In *The Market Revolution in America: Social, Political and Religious Expressions,* edited by Melvyn Stokes and Stephen Conway, 43–62. Charlottesville: University of Virginia Press, 1996.

Weaver, Bill L. "Establishment and Organisation of the Alabama Insane Hospital, 1846–1861." *Alabama Review* 48, no. 3 (July 1995): 219–232.

Wells, Jonathan Daniel. *The Origins of the Southern Middle Class, 1800–1861.* Chapel Hill: University of North Carolina Press, 2004.

Weston, N. "The Evolution of Mental Health in Antebellum Louisiana." *Louisiana History* 40, no. 3 (Summer 1999): 305–326.

Wheeler, Mary Bray, and Genon Hickerson Neblett. *Chosen Exile: The Life and*

Times of Synthia Sexton Middleton Rutledge, American Cultural Pioneer. Gadsden, Ala.: Rutledge, 1980.

White, George. *Historical Collections of Georgia.* New York: Pudney and Russel, 1854.

Whitefield, George. *Journals.* Edinburgh: Banner of Truth Trust, 1960.

Whorton, James. *Crusaders for Fitness: The History of American Health Reformers.* Princeton: Princeton University Press, 1982.

Wiberley, Stephen Edward, Jr. "Four Cities: Public Poor Relief in Urban America, 1700–1775." Ph.D. diss. Yale University, 1975.

Wisner, Elizabeth. *Public Welfare Administration in Louisiana.* Chicago: University of Chicago Press, 1930.

Wulf, Karin. "Gender and the Political Economy of Poor Relief in Colonial Philadelphia." In *Down and Out in Early America*, edited by Billy G. Smith, 163–188. University Park: Pennsylvania State University Press, 2004.

Yates, William B. *An Historical Sketch of the Rise and Progress of Religious and Moral Improvements among Seamen, with a History of the Port Society of Charleston, South Carolina.* Charleston: A. J. Burke, 1851.

Index

Timothy James Lockley is senior lecturer in history at the University of Warwick. He is the author of *Lines in the Sand: Race and Class in Lowcountry Georgia* (2001) and is assistant editor of the Routledge journal *Slavery and Abolition.*